STUDIES ON THE
TEXT OF
EURIPIDES

STUDIES ON THE TEXT OF
EURIPIDES

SUPPLICES · ELECTRA
HERACLES · TROADES
IPHIGENIA IN TAURIS · ION

JAMES DIGGLE

*Fellow of Queens' College
Cambridge*

OXFORD
AT THE CLARENDON PRESS
1981

Oxford University Press, Walton Street, Oxford OX2 6DP

OXFORD LONDON GLASGOW
NEW YORK TORONTO MELBOURNE WELLINGTON
KUALA LUMPUR SINGAPORE HONG KONG TOKYO
DELHI BOMBAY CALCUTTA MADRAS KARACHI
NAIROBI DAR ES SALAAM CAPE TOWN

Published in the United States by
Oxford University Press, New York

British Library Cataloguing in Publication Data

Diggle, James
  Studies on the text of Euripides
    1. Euripides – Criticism and interpretation
    I. Title
  882'.01   PA 3978   79-40592
  ISBN 0-19-814019-3

Printed in Great Britain
at the University Press, Oxford
by Eric Buckley
Printer to the University

PREFACE

De tripode dictiones edere Apollinis est: nos homunculos, qui erroris non immunes sumus, rationes reddere decet

> G. Hermann (ed. Helenae, praef.)

IN this book I discuss the text or interpretation of a variety of passages from the six plays which I have edited in *Euripidis Fabulae*, tomus ii (Oxford Classical Texts, 1981). Wherever possible I have tried to use my discussion as a basis for pursuing topics (whether linguistic or stylistic or metrical) which have some general interest; and as a result I hope that the book will be of some value to a wider range of readers than future commentators on those six plays.

The passages discussed are arranged play by play according to line-number. In addition, if I have already discussed a passage from these plays in a published article, I have incorporated a reference to that discussion at the appropriate place, sometimes adding new material. And if I have discussed or alluded to a passage from these plays elsewhere in this book, I have similarly incorporated a cross-reference at the appropriate place.

I am grateful to the Delegates of the Oxford University Press for undertaking the publication of a book which, in these times, is unfashionable in scope and content. Mr G. W. Bond kindly read the chapter on *Heracles*. I should have written at much greater length about the problems of that play had I not found myself so largely in agreement with the views expressed by Mr Bond in his forthcoming commentary.

In the Preface to my Oxford Text I have given some indication of what I owe to the late Sir Denys Page. Although he and I discussed together many of the passages with which I deal in this book, his final illness prevented him from seeing the book in its present form, except for the chapter on *Troades*. If he had seen the rest, it would have been a better book. I dedicate it to his memory, in the hope that it will be found to be a not unworthy tribute to a scholar to whom I cannot adequately express in words the extent of my indebtedness and devotion.

J. D.

Queens' College
Cambridge
December 1978

CONTENTS

EDITIONS*

1. *Complete editions of Euripides*

M. Musurus (ed. Aldina), Venice 1503

G. Canter, Antwerp 1571

J. Barnes, Cambridge 1694

S. Musgrave, Oxford 1778

C. D. Beck, Leipzig 1778–88

A. Matthiae, Leipzig 1813–36

L. Dindorf, Leipzig 1825

F. H. Bothe, Leipzig 1825–6

W. Dindorf, Oxford 1832–40

T. Fix, Paris 1844

J. Hartung, Leipzig 1848–53

A. Nauck, Leipzig 1854^1, 1857^2, 1871^3

A. Kirchhoff, Berlin 1855^1, 1867^2

F. A. Paley, London 1857–60^1, 1872–80^2

R. Prinz and N. Wecklein, Leipzig 1878–1902

G. Murray, Oxford 1902–13 (i 1902, ii 1904^1, 1908^2, 1913^3, iii 1909^1, 1913^2)

2. *Individual plays discussed in this volume*

SUPPLICES

J. Markland, London 1763^1, 1775^2

G. Hermann, Leipzig 1811

U. von Wilamowitz-Moellendorff, in *Analecta Euripidea*, Berlin 1875

F. A. Paley, Cambridge 1888

N. Wecklein, Leipzig 1912

H. Grégoire (Budé ed.), Paris 1923

T. Nicklin, Oxford 1936

G. Italie, Groningen 1951

G. Ammendola (revised by V. Agostino), Turin 1956

C. Collard, Groningen 1975

* This bibliography includes only editions which are referred to in this volume.

ELECTRA

P. Victorius, Rome 1545
A. Seidler, Leipzig 1813
P. Camper, Leiden 1831
C. A. Walberg, Leipzig 1869
C. H. Keene, London 1893
H. Weil, Paris 1903[3]
N. Wecklein, Leipzig 1906
L. Parmentier (Budé ed.), Paris 1925
J. D. Denniston, Oxford 1939

HERACLES

G. Hermann, Leipzig 1810
A. J. E. Pflugk and N. Wecklein, Leipzig 1877
A. Gray and J. T. Hutchinson, Cambridge 1886[2]
U. von Wilamowitz-Moellendorff, Berlin 1895[2]
L. Parmentier (Budé ed.), Paris 1923
G. W. Bond, Oxford (forthcoming)

TROADES

G. Burges, Cambridge 1807
A. Seidler, Leipzig 1812
A. Kirchhoff, Berlin 1852
R. Y. Tyrrell, London 1897[2]
L. Parmentier (Budé ed.), Paris 1925
G. Schiassi, Florence 1953
W. Biehl, Leipzig 1970
K. H. Lee, London 1976

IPHIGENIA IN TAURIS

J. Markland, London 1771
A. Seidler, Leipzig 1813
G. Hermann, Leipzig 1833
J. H. Monk, Cambridge 1845
C. Badham, London 1851
C. S. Jerram, Oxford 1885
E. B. England, London 1886
F. G. Schöne, H. Köchly, E. Bruhn, Berlin 1894

H. Weil, Paris 1903[3]
N. Wecklein, Leipzig 1904
M. Platnauer, Oxford 1939
H. Strohm, Munich 1949

ION

G. Wakefield, London 1794
F. Hülsemann, Leipzig 1801
G. Hermann, Leipzig 1827
C. Badham, London 1851; 1853; 1861
H. van Herwerden, Utrecht 1875
K. Kuiper, Leiden 1885
A. W. Verrall, Cambridge 1890
M. A. Bayfield, London 1891[2]
C. S. Jerram, Oxford 1896
N. Wecklein, Leipzig 1912
H. Grégoire (Budé ed.), Paris 1923
U. von Wilamowitz-Moellendorff, Berlin 1926
A. S. Owen, Oxford 1939
G. Italie, Leiden 1948

3. *Other plays of Euripides*

Alcestis, ed. A. M. Dale, Oxford 1954
Medea, ed. D. L. Page, Oxford 1938
Hippolytus, ed. W. S. Barrett, Oxford 1965
Andromache, ed. P. T. Stevens, Oxford 1971
Helen, ed. A. C. Pearson, Cambridge 1903
        ed. A. M. Dale, Oxford 1967
        ed. R. Kannicht, Heidelberg 1969
Phoenissae, ed. A. C. Pearson, Cambridge 1909
Hypsipyle, ed. G. W. Bond, Oxford 1963
Phaethon, ed. J. Diggle, Cambridge 1970

ABBREVIATIONS AND REFERENCES

Austin   *Noua fragmenta Euripidea in papyris reperta*, ed. C. Austin (Berlin 1968)

Breitenbach   W. Breitenbach, *Untersuchungen zur Sprache der euripideischen Lyrik* (Stuttgart 1934)

Bruhn, *Anhang*   Sophokles, erklärt von F. W. Schneidewin und A. Nauck, achter Band, Anhang, zusammengestellt von E. Bruhn (Berlin 1899)

Dale, *Lyric Metres*   A. M. Dale, *The Lyric Metres of Greek Drama*, 2nd ed. (Cambridge 1968)

Dawe, *Studies*   R. D. Dawe, *Studies on the Text of Sophocles* (Leiden, vols. i–ii 1973, vol. iii 1978)

Denniston, *GP*   J. D. Denniston, *The Greek Particles*, 2nd ed. (Oxford 1954)

Dionysiaca   *Dionysiaca: Nine Studies in Greek Poetry by Former Pupils Presented to Sir Denys Page on his Seventieth Birthday*, ed. R. D. Dawe, J. Diggle, P. E. Easterling (Cambridge, The Editors, 1978)

Jackson, *Marg. scaen.*   J. Jackson, *Marginalia scaenica* (Oxford 1955)

GLP   *Greek Literary Papyri, i: Poetry*, ed. D. L. Page (Loeb Class. Libr., London etc. 1942) later repr. as *Select Papyri, iii*

KB   R. Kühner–F. Blass, *Ausführliche Grammatik der griechischen Sprache*, erster Teil: Elementar- und Formenlehre (Hanover and Leipzig 1890–92)

KG   R. Kühner–B. Gerth, *Ausführliche Grammatik der griechischen Sprache*, zweiter Teil: Satzlehre (Hanover and Leipzig 1898–1904)

LSJ   H. G. Liddell and R. Scott, *A Greek–English Lexicon*, 9th ed., revised by Sir H. Stuart Jones (Oxford 1940)

PMG   *Poetae melici Graeci*, ed. D. L. Page (Oxford 1962)

Schwyzer   E. Schwyzer, *Griechische Grammatik* (Munich 1939–53)

Wilamowitz, *Anal. Eur.*   U. von Wilamowitz-Moellendorff, *Analecta Euripidea* (Berlin 1875)

Wilamowitz, *Verskunst*   U. von Wilamowitz-Moellendorff, *Griechische Verskunst* (Berlin 1921)

Zuntz, *Inquiry*   G. Zuntz, *An Inquiry into the Transmission of the Plays of Euripides* (Cambridge 1965)

I. SUPPLICES

24–8 ὅς μ' ἐξοτρύνει παῖδ' ἐμὸν πεῖσαι λιταῖc
νεκρῶν κομιcτὴν ἢ λόγοιcιν ἢ δορὸc   25
ῥώμηι γενέcθαι καὶ τάφου μεταίτιον,
μόνον τόδ' ἔργον προcτιθεὶc ἐμῶι τέκνωι
πόλει τ' Ἀθηνῶν.

Adrastus (says Aethra) urges her to persuade her son to recover and
bury the corpses. 'He is' (she adds) 'imposing *only* this task upon my
son and the city of Athens.' μόνον is explained by Matthiae in this
way: '*nihil nisi hoc operis iniungens filio meo*, ut occisos sepeliendos
curet, non ut ea etiam peragat, quae ipse Adrastus efficere non
potuerat, urbem expugnet et exsules reducat uel cladem Argiuis
illatam ulciscatur.' The antithesis which Matthiae alleges cannot be
inferred from the bare adjective μόνον, for 'there is nothing in the
prologue to explain such a restriction' (Collard). And what casuistry
this would be, to varnish with a deprecating *nihil nisi hoc operis* a task
which, it is already admitted, may need to be performed by force
of arms.

Reiske's μόνωι is no better. Those who accept it (Markland was
the first, Collard is the latest to do so) refer to the similar sentiment
at 188–9 πόλιc δὲ cὴ / μόνη δύναιτ' ἂν τόνδ' ὑποcτῆναι πόνον. What is
there expressed in eight words cannot be expressed here in the one
word μόνωι: to translate 'imposing this task upon you *because you
alone are capable of performing it*' would be to impose upon μόνωι
a task which, alone, it cannot perform.

Vitelli's καινὸν (*RFIC* 8 [1880] 475) has nothing to commend it.
J. M. Stahl's κοινόν[1] is exactly right: compare *Tr.* 53–4 φέρω δὲ coì /
κοινοὺc ἐμαυτῆι τ' ἐc μέcον λόγουc, ἄναξ, A. *Ag.* 522–3. For the confusion of κ and μ see *Su.* 421, *Herc.* 855, A. *Su.* 785 (ἐκ- and ἐμ- are
confused at *Alc.* 1001, 1125, A. *Pe.* 518, and perhaps E. *IT* 98),
Jackson, *Marg. scaen.* 120, and *Dionysiaca* 174 n. 4. It is no valid
objection to κοινὸν that the word appeared at the beginning of line 20.
For such repetitions see *Phaethon* 56 n., *Illinois Class. Stud.* 2 (1977)

---

[1] I have not traced where it was published.

118 n. 14, and to the references given there add Collard on *Su.* 16b–17.

44–7 See *GRBS* 14 (1973) 241–4.

58–9   ... μετάδος δ', ὅσον ἐπαλγῶ
      μελέα ⟨'γὼ⟩ φθιμένων οὓς ἔτεκον.

58 ὅcον] ὅccον Tr², oἷον Stinton

Stinton's arguments (*JHS* 97 [1977] 145) are not quite strong enough to show that his conjecture is preferable to that of Triclinius. These arguments are: (i) 'the epic form in -cc- is not found in Euripides', and (ii) oἷoc is 'rather commoner than ὅcoc in the causal sense'. Only the former argument carries any weight. But, as Stinton observes, Aeschylus and Sophocles use τόccoc; and we may add that Euripides uses the epic -cc- in dative plurals (see p. 97 and *PCPS* n.s. 20 [1974] 22 n. 2)[1] and in aorist endings (see p. 49). As Stinton says in another connection (discussing the non-tragic ζωός, on p. 146), 'there is no reason why Euripides should not for once have used it here'. The second argument is, in itself, true. I count nine instances of causal oἷoc in Euripides (*Med.* 165 [Kaibel], *Hi.* 879, *Herc.* 817, *IT* 150, *Ion* 799, *Hel.* 664, *IA* 299, *Rh.* 746, 897), three of causal ὅcoc (*Andr.* 994 [Lobeck], *Hel.* 74, fr. 449. 2). But the inquiry is incomplete: one question, whether in respect of sense oἷον has any advantage over ὅccον, has been left unasked.

oἷoc, both causal and exclamatory, is indeed used in contexts like ours: Stinton quotes *Hi.* 845 oἷον (exclamatory) εἶδον ἄλγος, and I add *Ion* 799 oἷον oἷον (causal) ἄλγος ἔπαθον. But in both instances oἷον is an adjective, not an adverb. Adverbial oἷον is indeed found: it introduces both exclamations (*Ion* 1471 oἷον oἷον ἀνελέγχομαι) and indirect questions (*Hi.* 557 cυνείποιτ' ἂν ἁ Κύπρις oἷον [Monk: oἷον ἁ κ- codd.] ἕρπει, *El.* 1206–7 κατεῖδες oἷον ... ἔβαλεν ἔδειξε μαστόν ... ;). Adverbial oἷον is never found in the causal use. But that is less significant than the lack of a parallel for adverbial oἷον (whether causal, exclamatory, or introducing an indirect question) with a verb of the same nature as ἐπαλγῶ. If we examine the uses of ὅcoc, we find a different picture. In the three instances of its causal use listed above it is used, like oἷoc, only as an adjective. Like oἷον it is used adverbially to introduce exclamations and indirect questions;

[1] Add fr. 791. 3, A. *Pe.* 1022, S. fr. 371. 4 P.

but, unlike οἷον, it is used with verbs which are comparable with
ἐπαλγῶ: *Andr.* 822 ὅσον στένει (ind. qu.), *Ph.* 1425 ὅσον στένω (exclam.).

60–2   παράπεισον δὲ σόν, ὤ, †λισσόμ'†, ἐλθεῖν τέκνον Ἰσμη-
νὸν ἐμάν τ' ἐς χέρα θεῖναι νεκύων
θαλερῶν σώματα †λάινον τάφον†.

60 ὤ Nauck: ὅ ⟨L⟩ P   λισσόμ' Lᵖᶜ uel Tr: λισόμ' L ut uid.   62 θαλερῶν
p: -ερὰ L

In 60 p's λισσόμεθ', accepted by all, must yield its place in the text to
λίσσομαι (Stinton *apud* Collard). Collard rejects this proposal with
the argument that 'the loss of αι is harder to explain before ελθ'.
On the contrary, it is readily explained by the habitual failure of
scribes to recognize correption and by their consequent substitution
of elision or crasis. See *Alc.* 90 στατίζεται Hermann: στατίζετ' codd.;
Alc. 120 ἔχω ἐπὶ BVP: ἔχω 'πὶ L; *Hi.* 770 ἅψεται et ἅψετ' codd.;
Hi. 1109 ἵσταται et ἵστατ' codd.; *Hec.* 69 αἴρομαι (αἴρομ' GSV) ἔννυχος;
Su. 278 ἄντομαι Tr²: ἄντομ' ⟨L⟩P; *El.* 486 ὄψομαι Erfurdt: ὄψομ' L;
IT 176 καὶ ἐμᾶς Porson: κἐμᾶς L; *A. Pe.* 60 οἴχεται (οἴχετ' HOY)
ἀνδρῶν; S. *Ai.* 197 ὁρμᾶται T (i.e. Triclinius): ὁρμᾶτ' cett.

In 62 Hermann proposed σώματ' ἀλαίνοντα τάφου, 'which I grieve
to find defaced in the Oxford edition' (by Murray's ἀλαίνοντ' ἄταφα),
says G. Zuntz, *The Political Plays of Euripides* (1955) 106 n. 2, a view
which he has imposed on Collard. Of the alleged analogies for a separative genitive after ἀλαίνω which editors are accustomed to quote
only one stands up to scrutiny: Pi. *Ol.* 1. 58 εὐφροσύνας ἀλᾶται. They
all cite *Tr.* 640 ψυχὴν ἀλᾶται τῆς πάροιθ' εὐπραξίας, but here the
genitive is of a different nature and is rightly explained by R. S.
Bluck, *CQ* n.s. 11 (1961) 125–6. Collard (whose citation of *El.* 201–2
is an unfortunate slip) cites *Hel.* 523 ἀλατείαι βιότου, which does not
mean 'through want of livelihood' (although Kannicht so interprets
it) but 'with a life spent in wandering' (so Dale). Since ἄταφα is
supported by *Tr.* 1084–5 σὺ μὲν φθίμενος ἀλαίνεις / ἄθαπτος, it should
be preferred to the doubtful genitive.

71–4   ἀγὼν ὅδ' ἄλλος ἔρχεται γόων γόοις[1]
διάδοχος, ἀχοῦσι προσπόλων χέρες.
ἴτ', ὦ ξυνωιδοὶ †κακοί†,
ἴτ', ὦ ξυναλγηδόνες . . .

[1] γόων γόοις Valckenaer: γόων γόων L: γόοις γόων Fritzsche: cf. *Hec.* 588.

~ 79–82   ἄπληστος ἅδε μ' ἐξάγει χάρις γόων
           πολύπονος, ὡς ἐξ ἀλιβάτου πέτρας   80
           ὑγρὰ ῥέουσα σταγὼν
           ἄπαυστος αἰεὶ †γόων†.

72 is a syncopated iambic trimeter; 80 is an iambic metron followed by a telesillean, i.e. alcaic hendecasyllable. The latter colon is found at S. *Phil.* 716 ~ 728, but there the metrical context suits it; here it can have no place, and so Heath's ἀχοῦϲιν προπόλων, which restores the same rhythm in 72, cannot be right. Correction must attempt to restore iambic rhythm in 80. Hermann proposed ἀλιβρόχου for ἀλιβάτου; Wilamowitz proposed[1] ἀλιβλήτου, which postulates a more plausible corruption. But Wilamowitz had earlier formulated against Hermann's conjecture an objection which, if valid, is no less valid against his own. He argued that ἀλιβρόχου introduces an inappropriate image: 'cum inexhausto lacrimarum fluctu Graeci non solent conponere scopulum mari certis interuallis exaestuante perfusum (nec nimis apte hoc fieret), sed riuulos e rupibus praecipitibus stillantes' (*Anal. Eur.* 83). He cites *Il.* 16. 3–4 δάκρυα θερμὰ χέων, ὥς τε κρήνη μελάνυδρος, / ἥ τε κατ' αἰγίλιπος πέτρης δνοφερὸν χέει ὕδωρ (cf. 9. 14–15). He might have added *Andr.* 116 τάκομαι ὡς πετρίνα πιδακόεϲϲα λιβάϲ, 532–4 λείβομαι δάκρυϲιν κόραϲ, / ϲτάζω λιϲϲάδοϲ ὡς πέτραϲ / λιβὰϲ ἀνήλιοϲ. Further, one would imagine that Euripides is imitating Hes. *Th.* 785–7 ὕδωρ / ψυχρόν, ὅ τ' ἐκ πέτρης καταλείβεται ἠλιβάτοιο / ὑψηλῆς and that here was the source of his ἀλιβάτου. Other instances of this picture of the stream cascading from a high rock are *Od.* 17. 209–10, Theoc. 1. 7–8, Cat. 68. 57–8, Q. Smyrn. 10. 415–23.

   I confess bafflement. I should like to agree with Wilamowitz that what we want here is the familiar image of the rock dripping, like Niobe, all tears. But metre appears to direct us firmly towards the sea-buffeted cliff.

   In place of κακοί in 73 everyone used to accept κακοῖϲ (apogr. Par.). Then Wilamowitz proposed κτύποι (*Anal. Eur.* 82), and this was accepted by Wecklein (1898 but not 1912) and by Murray. Nicklin proposed κόποι, and this has been accepted by Collard. Neither κτύποι nor κόποι can be right. Both words, in a context of this kind,

---

[1] First in his verse translation (*Griechische Tragödien, iii: Euripides, Der Mütter Bittgang* [1899]). The textual notes were not added until the fourth edition (1904), but most of them are presupposed by the 1899 version. He repeated the conjecture in *Hermes* 54 (1919) 65 = *Kl. Schr.* 4 (1962) 303.

describe a blow to the breast (87 στέρνων κτύπον, 604-5 στερνοτυπεῖς ...
κτύποι, *Tr.* 794 στέρνων τε κόπους [Seidler: κτύπους VP]) or to the
head (*Ph.* 1351 ἐπὶ κάρα . . . λευκοπήχεις κτύπους χεροῖν, *Or.* 963
κτύπον . . . κρατός). In the present context they must describe the
sound of such a blow. 'Go, harmonious sounds of blows (to breast or
head), go, fellow griefs, . . . and make the cheek bloody.'¹ Blows to
the breast or the head do not draw blood on the cheek; nor is it
conceivable that κτύπος or κόπος could be referred to any activity
directed against the cheek, for the cheek is not beaten but scratched;
and the scratching of the cheek makes no noise that can be described
as κτύπος or κόπος. Furthermore, in the exhortation 'go, fellow
griefs, . . . make the cheek bloody', ξυναλγηδόνες must be interpreted
as abstract noun used for the personal agent (for ξυναλγοῦσαι, as
Markland says), as, for example, 173 πρεσβεύματα, 802-3 ὦ παῖδες,
ὦ πικρὸν φίλων | προσηγόρημα ματέρων, *Ba.* 803 δουλείαις ἐμαῖς,
S. *Ant.* 320 λάλημα, 533 δύ' ἄτα κἀπαναστάσεις θρόνων, 756 δούλευμα,
OC 863 ὦ φθέγμ' ἀναιδές. On these and other Sophoclean examples
see A. A. Long, *Language and Thought in Sophocles* (1968) 113-25;
also Bruhn, *Anhang* § 236, Breitenbach 178-9, and p. 90 below.
(I do not know why Collard finds 'the poetry impaired' if ξυναλγηδόνες is treated as a personification rather than as a genuine abstract.
In the instances which he cites of 'appeals to "abstracts"', the
abstract is not requested to perform an action in the imperative
mood.) But, although ξυναλγηδόνες must be treated as a personification, no such plea can be made for ὦ ξυνωιδοὶ κτύποι (κόποι):
a person in mourning may be described as a 'fellow grief' but not as
a 'harmonious blow'. We are driven back (as was Wilamowitz in his
verse translation) to κακοῖς, with which we must understand ἐμοῖς:
cf. *Ph.* 1518 ἐμοῖς ἄχεσι συνωιδός, *Or.* 132-3 τοῖς ἐμοῖς θρηνήμασι . . .
ξυνωιδοί.

78   τὰ γὰρ φθιτῶν τοῖς ὁρῶσι κόσμος.

The old translation 'hic enim honor mortuis tribuitur a uiuis',²
Wilamowitz's 'Zu der Toten Ehre ist's der Lebendigen Schmuck', and
Grégoire's 'tel est aux trépassés l'hommage des vivants' interpret
τοῖς ὁρῶσι as if it were παρὰ τῶν ὁρώντων. Italie actually writes:
'De dativ. is te verklaren door de passieve strekking van de zin:

---

¹ On the text of 76-7 see *GRBS* 14 (1973) 247 n. 19.
² For the identity of the translators see *GRBS* 14 (1973) 266 n. 66.

οὕτως οἱ φθιτοὶ τοῖς ὁρῶσι (= ὑπὸ τῶν ὁρώντων) κοσμοῦνται, cf. Hom.
θ 479 πᾶσι γὰρ ἀνθρώποισιν . . . ἀοιδοὶ τιμῆς ἔμμοροί εἰσι.' If that is a
parallel, then ὅδε πᾶσι φίλος καὶ κόσμιος (τίμιος Od. 10. 38) ἐςτιν
would mean 'he is liked and honoured by all'. Heath's 'honores enim
mortuorum sunt uiuentium decus', Fix's '(praestita) namque iusta
mortuis uiuentibus (sunt) decus',[1] Paley's 'the honours of the dead
are a credit to the living', and the similar translations of Nicklin,
Ammendola, and Collard join τὰ φθιτῶν in the sense 'honours paid to
the dead', which is scarcely possible. Collard quotes *Hel.* 1421 τὰ τῶν
θανόντων οὐδὲν ἀλλ' ἄλλως πόνος, which is much more general in sense
('das, was mit den Toten zu tun hat', Kannicht; Pearson speaks of
'the vagueness of the subject τὰ τῶν θανόντων, covering both "the lot
of the dead" and "our dealings with the dead" '). Wecklein, in both
his editions, printed φθιτοὺς: 'denn solches ziemt sich beim Anblick
von Toten'.[2] But the dead are not 'beim Anblick', 'in sight'. The
meaning is probably 'for that is the proper honour for the dead in the
eyes of the living'. For φθιτῶν κόσμος see *Tr.* 1147 ὅταν cὺ κοσμήςηις
νέκυν, *Or.* 611 κοσμήςων τάφον, and the similar use of ἄγαλμα at
Herc. 357–8 γενναίων δ' ἀρεταὶ πόνων / τοῖς θανοῦσιν ἄγαλμα. For τοῖς
ὁρῶσι see KG 1. 421b ('nach dem Urteile, in den Augen jemandes').
I owe this explanation of the dative to Sir Denys Page. The dative
is similarly used in Latin: Ov. *Met.* 8. 130 *scelus hoc patriaeque patrique*
('a crime in the eyes of'); cf. Kühner–Stegmann 2.322 Anmerk. 9.
For the demonstrative τά see *Hec.* 626, *El.* 940, *Herc.* 227 (Elmsley),
Tr. 218 (where I write τὰ δὲ for τάδε since an adversative connection
is needed). Note also the Homeric τὸ γὰρ γέρας ἐςτὶ θανόντων (*Il.*
16. 457, 675, *Od.* 24. 296).

84–5 For the interpretation of ἐπίπονόν τι κατὰ γυναῖκας / ἐς γόους
πάθος πέφυκεν see *Dionysiaca* 175 n. 11.

154   ταυτὶ δικάζων ἦλθον· εἶτ' ἀπωλόμην.

It ought not to be necessary to remind editors that forms like ταυτί
are foreign to tragedy (cf. Porson on *Med.* 157 [154], KB 1. 620).
But since a recent editor has printed οὑτωςί at *Hec.* 69, a review of
the evidence will not be amiss. Such forms are attested at *Andr.* 688
ταυτὶ ut uid. M² (ταῦτ' εἶ M, ταῦτ' εὖ cett.), *Hec.* 69 οὑτωςὶ Triclinius

---

[1] Approved by Herwerden, *Mnem.* 27 (1899) 237.
[2] First proposed in *SBAM* 1897, 477.

(οὕτω cett.), *Su.* 306 νυνὶ δὲ L (νῦν δ᾽ ἴϲθι Bothe), *Herc.* 665 τωδὶ
Triclinius (τῶδε L: τῶιδ᾽ ἂν Hermann, τῶιδ᾽ ἦν Porson), *Ion* 691
τοδί ποτ᾽ εὐ- Triclinius (τόδε τ᾽ εὐ- L: τάδε θεοῦ Nauck; cf. Zuntz,
Inquiry 196), fr. 572. 1 τουτί at the end of an iambic trimeter, S. fr.
207. 4 P (I. fr. 2. 4 Carden) τουτί *u.l.* for τοῦτο. In satyric drama
τουτί is admitted at *Cycl.* 169, S. *Ichn.* 114.

The correction generally accepted is ταῦτ᾽ ἐκδικάζων, proposed
independently by Hermann, Lenting, and Matthiae. Murray proposed ταύτηι δικάζων, which had been anticipated by Blomfield
in his glossary on A. *PV* 197. Collard translates ταύτηι as 'in this
manner' and dismisses it as 'inappropriate'. When correctly interpreted it will be seen to be highly appropriate, and since it is an
easier corruption it must be preferred. The meaning is 'it was on this
side (that of Polyneices) that I came δικάζων'. The expression ταύτηι
δικάζων is much the same as ταύτηι γνώμην τιθέμενοc. At S. *Ph.* 1448
I should read κἀγὼ γνώμην (Bˢ¹ et Lambinus: -η(ι) cett.) ταύτηι
(ταὐτῆι Dobree, ταύτην B et Elmsley) τίθεμαι, as do R. D. Dawe
(Teubner ed. 1979) and Jebb, who compares Lys. 24. 23 μηδαμῶς, ὦ
βουλή, ταύτηι θῆcθε τὴν ψῆφον (τῇ ψήφῳ codd.), Isae. 8. 46 ᾗ δίκαιόν
ἐcτι, ταύτηι τὴν ψῆφον τίθεcθε. Similar are Hdt. 1. 120. 4 ταύτηι πλεῖcτοc
γνώμην εἰμί (cf. 7. 220. 2, 9. 120. 4), 7. 143. 3 ταύτηι Θεμιcτοκλέοc
ἀποφαινομένου (sc. γνώμην), Plat. *Theaet.* 202 c τίθεcαι ταύτηι, *Leg.*
662 ε ταύτηι . . . ὁ τιθέμενοc, whence at *Leg.* 674 A οὐκ ἂν τιθείμην
ταύτην τὴν ψῆφον I suggest ταύτηι. There is also a good case for
introducing this locution at Ar. *Eccl.* 658 κἀγὼ ταύτην (ταύτηι Toup)
γνώμην τίθεμαι, Theogn. 717 γνώμην ταύτην (ταύτηι Bergk) κατα-
θέcθαι. In Euripides the nearest parallel is *Andr.* 610 οὔτι ταύτηι cὸν
φρόνημ᾽ ἐπούριcαc. For the corruption of η to ι see *Su.* 296 ἔπη κρύπτειν
Hermann: ἐπικρύπτειν L; 1035 πένθημ᾽ ὁμαιμόνων Kirchhoff: πέν-
θιμον δαιμόνων L; also *Tr.* 215, 271, 1155, *Ion* 875.

201–4   αἰνῶ δ᾽ ὃc ἡμῖν βίοτον ἐκ πεφυρμένου
          καὶ θηριώδουc θεῶν διεcταθμήcατο,
          πρῶτον μὲν ἐνθεὶc cύνεcιν, εἶτα δ᾽ ἄγγελον
          γλῶccαν λόγων δούc, ὥcτε γιγνώcκειν ὄπα.

God is praised for 'first giving us intelligence, then a tongue
with which to communicate words, so that we might understand
speech'. The phrase ὥcτε γιγνώcκειν ὄπα is rightly explained by
Collard as a comment on both of the preceding clauses: the faculty

of understanding human speech is acquired only when the faculties
both of understanding and of speaking have already been acquired.
The text is readily comprehensible. And yet Jacobs's and Wakefield's
ὡc γεγωνίcκειν ὄπα ('giving us a tongue, so that we might make the
sound of speech') conveys a sense which seems so much more straightforward that it will continue to attract editors (Nauck, Wilamowitz,
and Wecklein put it in the text, and most editors at least record it)
until a decisive argument is adduced against it.

Collard speaks of 'the rarity of ὡc = ὥcτε in E.'. I should put
the matter less cautiously. There is an overwhelming probability
that not a single genuine instance exists in Euripides of a consecutive
infinitive governed by ὡc instead of ὥcτε. One instance is offered
by the manuscripts at *Alc.* 358–9 ὡc τὴν κόρην Δήμητρος ἢ κείνης
πόcιν . . . λαβεῖν. Three instances are offered by L in plays which
depend on that manuscript alone: *Cycl.* 647–8 ὡc αὐτόματον τὸν
δαλὸν . . . ὑφάπτειν, *El.* 667 ὡc ταῦτά γ᾽ ἐκ coῦ cτόματος εἰρῆcθαι
δοκεῖν, *IT* 300 ὡc αἱματηρὸν πέλαγος ἐξανθεῖν ἁλός. I have found
a further four instances attested by a part of the manuscripts: *Med.*
308 (ὡc for ὥcτ᾽ A), *Hi.* 823 (where ὡc is unmetrical), *Ph.* 506
(ὡc for ὥcτ᾽ A), *Rh.* 666 (ὡc LP: ὥcτ᾽ cett.). These four last passages,
where nobody prints ὡc, may be left out of account.

Consider the four passages in which ὡc is the only attested reading.
Editors disbelieve the manuscripts at *Alc.* 358 and print Reiske's
ὥcτ᾽ ἢ for ὡc τὴν, and they disbelieve L at *El.* 667 and print Elmsley's
ὥcτ᾽ αὐτά γ᾽, in both places to the improvement of the style. And yet,
while they are content to remove two instances by the simple expedient of redividing the transmitted letters, they hesitate to remove
the other two instances by the scarcely radical expedient of adding
a single letter: *Cycl.* 647 ὡc⟨τ᾽⟩ αὐτόματον (Blaydes), *IT* 300 ὡc⟨θ᾽⟩
αἱματηρὸν (Markland, comparing 935 ὥcθ᾽ αἱματηρά). Such an
expedient cannot be avoided at fr. 497. 6 ὡc ἐξίτηλος ἀρετὴ καθίcταται,
where the sense demands Elmsley's ὥcτ᾽ (*Mus. crit.* 2 [1826] 302).
And the reverse corruption has happened at *Med.* 1156 (ὡc LP: ὡc
τ᾽ A, ὥcτ᾽ VB, impossibly), *Hi.* 407 (ὥcτ᾽ pars codd., improbably),
Herc. 146 (ὡc Matthiae: ὥcθ᾽ L), S. *OC* 45 (ὡc Elmsley: ὥcτ᾽ codd.).

Now, in both places where editors accept ὡc, the following word
begins with a vowel, so allowing the correction to ὥcτ(ε). There
was therefore no metrical advantage to Euripides in using ὡc. There
was metrical advantage available if the following word began with
a consonant; and it is in these circumstances (and only these) that

Aeschylus and Sophocles use ὡς for ὡστε.[1] But Euripides declined to use that advantage. Murray, indeed, prints ὡς τῶι (Hermann: ὡστε L) ξυνάπτειν καὶ cυναποκαμεῖν μέλη at *IT* 1371, but the truth is Hermann's earlier conjecture ξυναλγεῖν.[2] And consider finally the number of alleged instances of ὡς = ὡστε in relation to the total number of instances of ὡστε and infinitive in Euripides. Allen and Italie do not give a complete list, and so I must rely on my own observation. I have counted 103 instances of ὡστε and infinitive; in 41 of these instances the word is elided (ὡστ' or ὡσθ'). And so if we trust the manuscripts and suppose that Euripides did not debar himself from using ὡς = ὡστε, a paradoxical conclusion emerges: that he used ὡστε in 41 places where metre would admit ὡς, and ὡς in a small number of places where metre would admit ὡστε, and yet never once used ὡς where metre would *not* admit ὡστε. In short, if we trust the manuscripts, we must accept that he behaved so unaccountably that he abandoned his own normal practice when no metrical need existed and yet failed to do so when a metrical need did exist.[3]

248–9   χαίρων †ἴθι· μὴ γάρ† βεβούλευcαι καλῶς
†αὐτὸc πιέζειν τὴν τύχην ἡμᾶc λίαν†.

In 248 editors print χαίρων ἴθ'· εἰ γὰρ μὴ κτλ. But they ascribe the conjecture to Matthiae, who in fact conjectured εἰ μὴ γὰρ. The conjecture εἰ γὰρ μὴ is a conflation by later editors of Matthiae's conjecture and Hermann's εἰ δὲ μὴ. What objection is there to εἰ μὴ γὰρ? Since editors do not say, I must do so. The position of γὰρ immediately after the penthemimeral caesura is not objectionable: Descroix, *Le trimètre ïambique* (1931) 286, cites nineteen Euripidean examples,[4] and *Hcld.* 729 makes twenty. And Euripides writes εἰ μὴ γὰρ seven times (*Hi.* 657, *Su.* 200, *IT* 1412, *Ion* 669, *Ph.* 946, *Ba.* 333, fr. 847), εἰ γὰρ μὴ only once. But in none of those seven instances does metre permit εἰ γὰρ μὴ, while in the one place where

---

[1] There are thirteen instances in Aeschylus (at *Su.* 622 ὡς not ὡς should be read), four in Sophocles.

[2] It was also proposed by R. Rauchenstein, *Disputatio de locis aliquot Eur. Iph. Taur.* (1860) xvii.

[3] I have not seen M. Fellmann, *De ὡς, ὡστε particulis consecutiuis earumque apud tragicos Graecorum poetas usu et ui* (1883). But I have consulted Th. Barthold, *Specimen lexici Euripidei, quo explicatur usus particulae ὡς* (1869).

[4] The references to the fragments should read fr. 49. 1, 252. 1, 285. 5, 502. 3, 978. 3.

metre left Euripides a choice between the two word-orders he chose
the more natural order: *IA* 907 εἰ γὰρ μὴ γάμοισιν ἐζύγης. One cannot,
indeed, embrace as indubitably Euripidean anything which appears
in *IA*. But this line occurs in a passage whose Euripidean author-
ship I see no good reason to doubt. If, as I am assuming, Euripides
wrote εἰ γὰρ μὴ in *IA* 907, it will be reasonable to assume that
he also wrote εἰ γὰρ μὴ in *Su*. 248, where metre again gives a free
choice.

Line 249 remains uncured. But we may dismiss one popular conjecture (it is printed by Wecklein, Murray, and Grégoire), Nauck's
αὐτὸς πιέζειν τὴν τύχην, ἡμᾶς δ' ἐᾶν. The conjecture rests, as Collard
says, 'upon (1) two imperative infinitives and (2) a sense of πιέζειν
for which there is no certain analogy'. Item (2) has been thoroughly
dealt with by Collard, but his treatment of item (1) is less satisfactory and I wish to treat the evidence for imperatival infinitives in
Euripides afresh.

Of the three 'certain instances' which Collard cites two only are
certain: *Tr*. 422, *Or*. 624 (but note the preceding λέγω in 622).
The third is *Hcld*. 313, where I should accept (as Murray does)
Kirchhoff's μέμνηςθέ μοι for μεμνημένοι in 314, which removes from
the infinitive its imperatival function. He rightly rejects *Ion* 1396
(cίγα for cιγᾶν Dindorf; cf. H. D. Broadhead, *CQ* 44 [1950] 121–2)
and *Hel*. 1663 (πλεῖ for πλεῖν Cobet, *Nov. lect.* 204; see Kannicht ad
loc.), but there is no compelling need to change διωκαθεῖν to διωκα-
θῆις (Cobet) at fr. 362. 25 (*Erectheus*, fr. 53. 25 Austin). At *Ion* 98–101
L has cτόμα τ' εὔφημον φρουρεῖτ' ἀγαθὸν / φήμας τ' ἀγαθὰς / τοῖς
ἐθέλουςιν μαντεύεςθαι / γλώςςης ἰδίας ἀποφαίνειν, where, if the text is
sound, ἀποφαίνειν is imperatival. But cτόμα εὔφημον ἀγαθόν is insipid
style, which is not, however, to be rectified by writing φρουρεῖν
ἀγαθὸν (sc. ἐcτί) with L. Dindorf, since 'mirum ni ἀγαθὸν et ἀγαθὰς
99 sibi inuicem respondent, neque mandato conuenit periphrasis
per ἀγαθόν' (Badham), an objection which may be applied to the
different solution advocated by Collard. Write εὔφημοι (Camper)
and delete the τε after φήμας (Hermann), so that ἀποφαίνειν becomes
epexegetic infinitive. At *Hcld*. 751 Collard seems reluctant to accept
Wilamowitz's ἐνέγκαι for ἐνέγκατ',[1] but the transmitted reading cannot

---

[1] *Hermes* 14 (1879) 181 = *Kl. Schr*. 4 (1962) 17. He later proposed ἐνεγκεῖν
(*Verskunst* 451 n. 2). It is true that ἐνέγκαι is not found before the fourth century;
but ἤνεγκα and ἐνέγκαιμι are not avoided in tragedy, and of the five places where
ἐνεγκεῖν is used (*IT* 584, *Ion* 424, A. *Su*. 766, S. *Ph*. 873, *OC* 1599) ἐνέγκαι would
be allowed by the metre in only one (S. *OC* 1599).

be right, since it entails elision at catalectic period-end (as does Hermann's ἐνέγκαιτ').[1] At fr. 532 τοὺς ζῶντας εὖ δρᾶν· κατθανὼν δὲ πᾶς ἀνήρ κτλ. 'the quotation is probably incomplete' (Collard). That is unverifiable speculation; but it is easy to write δρᾶ. I should add a further probable instance: at Tr. 594 the manuscripts have κόμισαι (uel sim.) and the solution must be either Burges's κομίσαι (infinitive for imperative) or Seidler's κοίμισαι (middle imperative). The latter is less likely, since the middle of κοιμίζω is not attested. Yet a further possible instance is fr. 93. 1 and 3; but this quotation does look as if it may be incomplete.

To sum up: certain instances of imperatival infinitive are Tr. 422, Or. 624, probable or possible instances are Hcld. 751, Tr. 594, fr. 93. 1 and 3, fr. 362. 25. For a general treatment of imperatival infinitives see also Schwyzer 2. 380–2. We cannot therefore reject Nauck's conjecture in Su. 249 because of its imperatival infinitives (although Euripides' failure to write the obvious πίεζε . . . ἔα would be inexplicable); rather it is against the use of πιέζειν that the objection must be laid.

The only plausible conjecture available is Hermann's αὐτόc, πιέζειν cὴν τύχην ἡμᾶc τί δεῖ; This gives πιέζειν its proper sense: cf. Alc. 893–4 cυμφορὰ δ' ἑτέρουc ἑτέρα πιέζει. The sentiment is comparable with 226–8 κοινὰc γὰρ ὁ θεὸc τὰc τύχαc ἡγούμενοc / τοῖc τοῦ νοcοῦντοc πήμαcιν διώλεcεν / τὸν οὐ νοcοῦντα (Lambinus: τὸν cυννοc- L) κοὐδὲν ἠδικηκότα, and more particularly with 591–2 (προcτάccω) κἀμοὶ μὴ ἀναμείγνυcθαι τύχαc / τὰc cάc. The enjambment of αὐτόc is effective: cf. A. ScT 673, also E. Su. 592 and Collard on 16. And for the contrasting of αὐτόc and ἡμᾶc see Herc. 213–14 εἰ δ' οὖν ἔχειν γῆc cκῆπτρα τῆcδ' αὐτὸc θέλειc, / ἔαcον ἡμᾶc κτλ. For τί δεῖ at the end of the line see Med. 565, Hec. 960, IA 1144, S. Ph. 11. But the change of τί δεῖ to λίαν is not easily explained.

309   τάφου τε μοίραc καὶ κτεριcμάτων λαχεῖν.

Herwerden's μοῖραν (RPhil 2 [1878] 37) should be accepted. See h. Herm. 428 λάχε μοῖραν ἕκαcτοc, Hclit. B 25 DK μέζοναc μοίραc λαγχάνουcι, Hdt. 5. 57 ἀπολαχόντες τὴν Ταναγρικὴν μοῖραν, A. ScT 947–8 ἔχουcι μοῖραν λαχόντεc . . . διοδότων ἀχθέων (Wecklein: ἀχέων codd.), Bacchyl. 4. 19–20 παντοδαπῶν λαγχάνειν ἄπο μοῖραν ἐcθλῶν.

---

[1] See T. C. W. Stinton, BICS 22 (1975) 95; also L. P. E. Parker, 'Catalexis', CQ n.s. 26 (1976) 14–28.

321-3   ὁρᾶις ἄβουλος ὡς κεκερτομημένη
          τοῖς κερτομοῦσι †γοργόν᾽ ὡς† ἀναβλέπει
          cὴ πατρίς;

'L's text is essentially correct, only the accentuation being wrong', says Collard, who prints ἄβουλος ὡc and γοργὸν ὡc, taking the second ὡc as the conjunction and the first as dependent on κεκερτομημένη. The second ὡc, placed so late in the sentence and preceded by another ὡc playing a different role (and the first ὡc does not want an accent, even with Collard's interpretation), cannot possibly be the conjunction. Collard's argument against taking the first ὡc as the conjunction is that 'a bare predic. adj. ἄβουλος cannot stand with κεκερτομημένη' : this is answered by S. *OT* 412 τυφλόν μ᾽ ὠνείδισας. And for the omission of the participle (οὖσα) with the predicate compare *Andr.* 70 πέπυσται τὸν ἐμὸν ἔκθετον γόνον; *Herc.* 516 ὃν γῆς νέρθεν εἰσηκούομεν; see also KG 2. 66–7 and Jebb on S. *OC* 586. It is therefore possible to take the first line to mean 'Do you see how (ὡc) your country when mocked (as being) ill-advised . . . ?' But there is another possibility: to take ὡc not as the conjunction but as dependent on κεκερτομημένη, with a slight dislocation of the normal order comparable with *Alc.* 1131 προσείπω ζῶcαν ὡc δάμαρτ᾽ ἐμήν; *IT* 383 μυσαρὸν ὡc ἡγουμένη, 1041 coῦ θιγόντος ὡc. In this case we must punctuate with a question-mark after ὁρᾶις, as the old editors did. The poets often start a sentence with a provocative ὁρᾶις; 'pointing (often reproachfully) at a proof or illustration of something that the speaker has been saying or thinking' (P. T. Stevens on *Andr.* 87 and *Colloquial Expressions in Euripides* [1976] 36–7, to whose examples add Ar. *Equ.* 92, *Vesp.* 45, Men. *Sik.* 277). But perhaps the sentence runs more smoothly if we keep the question-mark after πατρίς and take ὡc as the conjunction, slightly postponed as at *IT* 1298 ὁρᾶτ᾽ ἄπιστον ὡc γυναικεῖον γένος, *Hcld.* 734, *El.* 239, *Or.* 1054–5.

In 322 Wecklein's γοργὸν ὄμμ᾽, which Collard calls 'insidious', may be considered certain (as it was by Wilamowitz on *Herc.* 563). See *Ph.* 146 ὄμμασι γοργός, A. *ScT* 537 γοργὸν δ᾽ ὄμμ᾽ ἔχων, and similar collocations at *Il.* 8. 349 Γοργοῦς ὄμματ᾽ ἔχων, *Herc.* 990 ἀγριωπὸν ὄμμα Γοργόνος, A. *PV* 356 ἐξ ὀμμάτων δ᾽ ἤστραπτε γοργωπὸν cέλας. For the internal accusative see *Med.* 187–8 τοκάδος δέργμα λεαίνης | ἀποταυροῦται, *Herc.* 563 φῶς ἀναβλέψεσθε, *Ion* 1262–3 πυρὸς | δράκοντ᾽ ἀναβλέποντα φοινίαν φλόγα, A. *Pe.* 81 κυάνεον δ᾽ ὄμμασι λεύσσων φονίου δέργμα δράκοντος, and possibly A. *PV* 902–3 μηδὲ κρεισσόνων θεῶν

ἔρως ἄφυκτον ὄμμα προςδράκοι με, although Page alters the text to
eliminate the internal accusative (on the text see T. C. W. Stinton,
JHS 96 [1976] 123–4, H. Friis Johansen, *Gnomon* 48 [1976] 335;
over the interpretation of ὄμμα I side with H. Lloyd-Jones, *CR*
n.s. 26 [1976] 8). When Collard objects to the use of ὄμμα as internal
accusative on the ground that ὄμμα is not used in the abstract sense
'glance', unless the transmitted text of A. *PV* 903 is sound, the answer
is provided by *Herc.* 221 ὄμμ' ἐλεύθερον βλέπειν (on this line see
p. 48); see also Barrett on *Hi.* 246. The corruption is explicable:
γοργὸν ὄμμ' was reduced by lipography to γοργὸν and ὡς was inserted to mend the metre. Much the same has probably happened
at *Tr.* 747, where the manuscripts have οὐχ' ὡς cφάγιον (οὐχὶ cφάγιον
Chr. Pat. 77) and Nauck restored οὐ cφάγιον ⟨υἱὸν⟩.[1]
The only alternative worth even a moment's thought is Marchant's
γόργ' ὁρῶς' (*CR* 8 [1894] 7); cf. Hyps. fr. 18. 3 γ]οργωπὰ λεύccω[ν.
But the participle is redundant.

347–8 See *GRBS* 14 (1973) 244–5. Collard has misrepresented my
argument. He writes that 'there is no question here of ἤδη being used
of a future event of *uncertain* time'. I wrote that 'it is not clear that it
[ἤδη] may legitimately be used in the apodosis of a conditional
sentence to refer to an event which, so far from being immediate,
is contingent upon a future event of uncertain time'. In case anyone
should wish to modify my conjecture and read εἰ δὲ μή, βία (for
βίαι) δορὸς / ἤδη τότ' ἔcται, I call attention to *Cycl.* 258 κοὐδὲν ἦν
τούτων βίαι.

371 See *GRBS* 14 (1973) 245–7. 'Mention of the Cho.'s grief . . .
is here incongruous' (Collard). It was mentioned two lines earlier
(369 ἐμῶν κακῶν).

478 See *GRBS* 14 (1973) 247–50. In n. 26 ('Sophocles twice has
βράχιcτος ') I should have said 'thrice': add fr. 169 P; and Pearson
ad loc. is to be included in the list of those who have interpreted
Su. 478 correctly (Collard adds Lenting on *Andr.* 1159).

508–9   cφαλερὸν ἡγεμὼν θραcὺς
              νεώς τε ναύτης· ἥcυχος καιρῶι, cοφός.

---

[1] The reservations of G. Björck, *Das alpha impurum und die tragische Kunstsprache*
(1950) 247, about the suitability of the word υἱός are unjustified.

The punctuation offered by L and adopted by Wilamowitz and Murray is rejected with good reason by Collard. The punctuation given above is Markland's, and Collard has changed it for the worse and has further introduced a conjecture which is probably not wanted. He prints cφαλερὸν ἡγεμὼν θρασὺc / νέος τε ναύτης· ἥcυχος, καιρῶι cοφός, where νέος is Orelli's conjecture ('locum reperire non poteram' Collard; see his edition of Isocr. *Antidosis* [1814] 385). Collard translates 'A rash general or young sailor is prone to error, but a steady one is wise in a crisis'. First, ἥcυχος does not mean 'steady'. Second, ἡcυχία is not always the wise man's course.[1] Third, if we look back to the beginning of this homily, we find in 506 that the speaker is defining the wise man ('wise men should love their children and . . .'); he must end on the same note, with a definition of the wise man, not with a definition of the man who is wise in certain circumstances. Fourth, the conjecture νέος introduces a notion which we do not want. 'A rash general and a young sailor are fallible.' Of course young sailors are fallible, but their fallibility is the result of inexperience (Orelli's translation tellingly gives 'inexperienced' as a gloss on 'young': 'ein junger, unerfahrner Schiffer'). Youth has nothing to do with this warning against the dangers of overreaching oneself, in whose illustration the rash general is cited. It is not an altogether satisfactory answer to say, as Collard does, that νέος 'will carry its usual overtone of rashness' (for this see Dodds on *Ba.* 973-6), since that overtone does not alter the basic meaning of the adjective, which still must connote youthfulness, and any notion of youthfulness will still be out of place. The expression νεώς . . . ναύτης, it must be admitted, is oddly pleonastic; but not much more so than *IA* 266-7 ναυβάτας ναῶν, S. *Ph.* 540 νεὼς . . . ναυβάτης.

566 See *PCPS* n.s. 15 (1969) 47-8. To the passages cited add A. *Eum.* 586 ἔπος δ᾽ ἀμείβου πρὸς ἔπος ἐν μέρει τιθείς.

573-5 Θη. πολλοὺς ἔτλην δὴ χἀτέρους ἄλλους πόνους.
Κη. ἦ πᾶcιν οὖν ⟨c᾽⟩ ἔφυcεν ἐξαρκεῖν πατήρ;
Θη. ὅcοι γ᾽ ὑβρicταί· χρηcτὰ δ᾽ οὐ κολάζομεν.

'Sed an Graece dicitur ἑτέρους ἄλλους? credam cum exemplum indubitabile uidero' said Markland. A collection of indubitable

---

[1] For discussion of contemporary attitudes to ἡcυχία see Dodds on *Ba.* 389-92, Bond on *Herc.* 166 and 266. Here the notion ἥcυχος καιρῶι is picked up by προμηθία in 510.

examples was furnished by Porson, *Tracts and Miscellaneous Criticism*,
ed. T. Kidd (1815) 200. They are quoted by Collard, and from
Dindorf's note on *Or.* 345 may be added two instances in Galen.
That the combination is not simply pleonastic has long been realized.
Collard quotes Hermann: 'ἄλλους dicit simpliciter alios, ἑτέρους
diuersos.' Similarly Cobet, *Misc. crit.* 75, writes that 'hoc dicit
Theseus *multos se alios et diuersi generis labores exantlasse*'. In itself, then,
the expression χἀτέρους ἄλλους is without linguistic fault. But editors
have failed to recognize that the herald's reply, 'Did your father
beget you, then, to be a match *for everyone*?', will follow rather more
naturally if 573 contains a dative: 'I have endured many other
labours *for others*.' This has been recognized only by Blomfield (on
A. *Pe.* 249 [ed. 1814]) and Lenting (*Noua acta lit. soc. Rheno-Traiect.*
1 [1821] 57), who both proposed χἀτέρους ἄλλοις. In support of the
collocation πολλοὺς . . . χἀτέρους may be quoted fr. 1077. 1 πέπονθας
οἷα χἄτεροι πολλοὶ βροτῶν, and even *Hcld.* 144 πολλῶν δὲ κἄλλων
(where Elmsley, quoting *Su.* 573, remarks 'notae sunt locutiones
πολλοὶ καὶ ἄλλοι, πολλὰ καὶ δεινά, πολλὰ καὶ κακά', which is more than
misleading, since in that line, as in *Su.* 573, καί is the intensifying
particle, not the copula).

But perhaps it is more stylish to write χἀτέροις ἄλλους. With χἀτέροις
compare *Hi.* 728 ἀτὰρ κακόν γε χἀτέρωι γενήσομαι, *Tr.* 619 νοσεῖς δὲ
χἄτερα, *IT* 672 ἀτὰρ διῆλθον (Porson: διῆλθε L) χἄτερον λόγον τινά;
with πολλοὺς . . . ἄλλους compare πολλῶν μετ' ἄλλων *Hi.* 835, *Andr.*
1152, and μυρίων . . . ἄλλων πόνων *Herc.* 1275.

584-7   ὁρμᾶσθαι χρεὼν
πάντ' ἄνδρ' ὁπλίτην ἁρμάτων τ' ἐπεμβάτην
μοναμπύκων τε φάλαρα κινεῖσθαι στόμα
ἀφρῶι καταστάζοντα Καδμείων χθόνα.

I have no plausible solution to the problem of 586-7. But since
recent editors are unaware that a problem exists, I can at least define
what that problem is.

'Forward must go every hoplite and charioteer, and the single-
horses' cheek-pieces, making the mouth drip with foam ['dripping at
the mouth with foam' Collard], must be set in motion to the Cadmean
land.' Since cheek-pieces neither make the mouth drip with foam nor
drip at the mouth with foam, there is only one way to make sense of
586. That is to suppose, as Markland did, that μοναμπύκων φάλαρα

is a roundabout way of saying 'single-horses with cheek-pieces', in the hope that responsibility for making the mouth drip with foam can be transferred from the cheek-pieces to the horses: 'μοναμπύκων φάλαρα sunt μονάμπυκας φαλάροις κατεσκευασμένους, equos instructos φαλάροις.' If Antigone, looking down from the rooftop at the Argive encampment, had told her paidagogos that she could see the cheek-pieces of the enemy horses, well and good: we should not infer that, because she mentioned only the φάλαρα, she had failed to notice the horses. To mention a distinctive part instead of the whole is right and fitting when the part is, from the speaker's viewpoint, a true representative of the whole, performing a function of the same nature as the whole would have performed. But if Antigone had said that she had seen the horses' cheek-pieces foaming at the mouth, she would have been sent to her room as a giddy girl.[1]

It is possible that something is radically amiss here, and that the text harbours some substantial corruption or dislocation or even gloss.[2] The word upon which suspicion falls most heavily is ϲτόμα, which it is impossible to bring into the syntax of the sentence. 'ϲτόμα suspectum', declared Nauck; 'haud iniuria', added Kirchhoff; and Wilamowitz (*Anal. Eur.* 104) agreed, but comprehended within his obeli the whole phrase ϲτόμα ἀφρῶι καταϲτάζοντα. (In his verse translation he gives 'die Reiter auch, die ihre Rosse kaum / mit schäumendem Gebiß zurücke halten': pretty, but what would it be in Greek?) Omit ϲτόμα and sense of a sort is left: 'the single-horses' cheek-pieces, dripping with foam, must be set in motion to the Cadmean land.' This sense is maintained in Herwerden's κινεῖϲθαι πολὺν / ἀφρὸν καταϲτάζοντα.[3] Setting cheek-pieces in motion is still a quaint idea, but it is better than having them foam at the mouth. But the roles are not yet quite rightly distributed, for we want the horses to move and the cheek-pieces to drip.[4] This they do in a conjecture of

---

[1] Markland is followed by Paley, Wecklein, Nicklin, Ammendola, and Italie. Markland did at least speak straightforwardly. Watch the contortions of Grégoire: 'et sane μοναμπύκων φάλαρα καταϲτάζοντα ἀφρῶι ϲτόμα parum accurate dictum, sed idem ualet ac μονάμπυκες καταϲτάζοντες ἀφρῶι (κατὰ) τὸ ϲτόμα τὰ φάλαρα.' He translates 'Allons ... que les couriers secouent d'écumantes gourmettes et volent ... au pays de Cadmus', wisely ignoring both text and paraphrase.

[2] For example, φάλαρα glossing -αμπύκων, as at S. *OC* 1069 ἀμπυκτήρια [φάλαρα] (del. Bothe cl. Hesych. ἀμπυκτήρια· τὰ φάλαρα). And it is just conceivable that ϲτόμα may have begun life as a gloss ϲτόμια.

[3] For the construction compare *Herc.* 934 ἀφρὸν κατέϲταζ' εὔτριχος (Wilamowitz: -τρίχου L) γενειάδος.

[4] I have no Greek illustration of dripping cheek-pieces. But in Roman poetry the bridle or reins, which occupy much the same region as the cheek-pieces, are

Marchant (*CR* 8 [1894] 7), who replaces στόμα with στίχας, explaining
the construction as 'στίχας τε μοναμπύκων κινεῖσθαι φάλαρα (accus. of
respect) ἀφρῶι καταστάζοντα'. But φάλαρα cannot be explained away
so casually. He would have done better to replace στόμα with στόλον[1]
(for the corruption compare 1221 ἑπτάστομον Heath: -στολον L) and
to take the word-order to be μοναμπύκων τε κινεῖσθαι στόλον, φάλαρα
ἀφρῶι καταστάζοντα (masc.), Καδμείων χθόνα, which involves a rather
violent, though not unparalleled, hyperbaton.[2]

598–609   See *GRBS* 14 (1973) 250–2.

638–9   λόγου δέ σε
            μακροῦ ἀποπαύσω.

In favour of Herwerden's ἀπολύσω see *GRBS* 14 (1973) 243 n. 11
(where, in support of my argument, it would have been appropriate
to quote S. *El.* 798 εἰ τήνδ᾽ ἔπαυσας τῆς πολυγλώσσου βοῆς). Note also
Rh. 281 λόγου δὲ δὶς τόσου μ᾽ ἐκούφισας, S. *Tr.* 180–1 πρῶτος ἀγγέλων /
ὄκνου σε λύσω. For the corruption see *Hel.* 1153–4 πόνους ἀμαθῶς
(Tyrwhitt: ἀπαθῶς L) θνατῶν καταπαυόμενοι,[3] where Herwerden
again suggests καταλυόμενοι, which must be right: compare the prose
expressions καταλύεσθαι πόλεμον, ἔχθρας, and S. *El.* 1246–50 κατα-
λύσιμον . . . κακόν.

650–67   See *GRBS* 14 (1973) 252–63. Two addenda. (i) I argued
(p. 254) that Cecropia 'was felt to be limited to Athens, as centred
on the Acropolis', but added the caution that 'I do not say that
Cecropia was felt to be synonymous with the Acropolis'. I need not
have been so cautious: see Σ Ap. Rhod. 1. 214 (p. 27 Wendell) ἡ
ἀκρόπολις τῆς Ἀττικῆς Κεκροπία ἐκαλεῖτο τὸ πρότερον. On the use of
the name Κεκροπίδαι for Athenians see Wilamowitz, *Aristoteles und
Athen* (1893) 2. 180–5. See also p. 110 below. (ii) To the illustrations

---

often so described: V. *Aen.* 4. 135 *frena . . . spumantia*, 5. 817–18, Ov. *Am.* 2. 9. 29–
30, *Met.* 15. 519 *frena . . . spumis albentibus oblita*.

[1] στόλος is more commonly applied to a detachment of ships. But it is applied
to a detachment of horses and chariots at A. *Su.* 187. *Or.* 989 τεθριπποβάμονι
στόλωι ('four-horse equipage') is not quite the same.

[2] See T. C. W. Stinton, *PCPS* n.s. 21 (1975) 82–8. The example cited from Ar.
Eccl. 1049–50 (p. 87) can be removed by an easy emendation of Bothe's: see
Jackson, *Marg. scaen.* 230.

[3] I quote these words in the order restored by Headlam (*CR* 16 [1902] 251).
His restoration is accepted by Murray (who claims it for himself) and Kannicht.

of the formula λεύccων δὲ ταῦτα κοὐ κλύων (684) quoted on p. 262 n. 60 add *Med.* 652, *Tr.* 481–2, *Hel.* 117, Hes. fr. 199. 3 MW, Plaut. *Bacch.* 469. And for '*PV* 266' read '*Pe.* 266'.

699   See *GRBS* 14 (1973) 263–5.

811   προcάγετε ⟨   ⟩ δυcπότμων.

Editors mend the metre by adding ⟨τῶν⟩ with Hermann. In *GRBS* 14 (1973) 265 I proposed προcάγετ' ⟨ἄγετε⟩, comparing such passages as *Med.* 1252 κατίδετ' ἴδετε (κατίδετε AVBP) and *Or.* 1465 ἀνίαχεν ἴαχεν (ἀνίαχεν P). To the literature cited in n. 64 'on the habit of following a compound verb with a simple verb in which the force of the compound is maintained' add W. Clausen, *AJP* 76 (1955) 49–51, G. Luck, *HSCP* 65 (1961) 249, R. Renehan, *Studies in Greek Texts* (1976) 11–27 and *CP* 72 (1977) 243–8. To this conjecture Collard has objected, on the authority of Dale, *Lyric Metres* 73, that 'then resolution precedes syncopation . . . a licence not found in iambotrochaic'. This objection cannot be upheld.

Resolution precedes syncopation in tragic iambics in the following passages: (i) A. *ScT* 565 μέγᾰλᾰ μέγᾱ|λῆγὄρῶν | κλῠοῦcᾱι ~ 628 δὄρῐπὄνᾰ κᾱκ' | ἐκτρέπὄν|τἒc ⟨ἐc⟩ γᾶc. (ii) E. *Hi.* 1145 ἐτἒκἒc ᾰνὄ| νᾱτᾰ φεῦ. An alternative colometry would give μᾱτἒρ ἐτἒκἒc ᾰ|νὄνᾱτᾰ φεῦ, but this entails two split resolutions: see L. P. E. Parker, *CQ* n.s. 18 (1968) 255. (iii) *Andr.* 1219 ᾰμπτᾰμένᾰ | φροῦδᾰ πᾱν|τᾰ κεῖτᾱι (~ 1204–5 ὦ φῐλὄc | δὄμὄν ἐλῐπἒc | ἐρῆμὄν). (iv) *Hec.* 1092 ὦ ῐτἒ μὄλἒτἒ | πρὄc θἒῶν. S. G. Daitz (Teubner ed. 1973) prints ἰὼ ἴτε κτλ. from one manuscript and analyses as dochmiac and cretic. But ὦ ἴτε is the regular formula: see *Ba.* 152, *Phaethon* 112 n., Call. *H.* 5. 13, Antagoras, *AP* 9. 147. 1 (= 164 Gow–Page). (v) *Ion* 689 ἐφ' ὄ⟨τῐ⟩ πὄτἒ | βᾱcἒτᾱι ~ 707 κᾱλλῐφλὄγᾰ | πἒλᾶνὄν ἐπῐ. Fix supplied ⟨τι⟩. An alternative remedy is Badham's ἔφ' ὅ πὄτ' ἐ⟨κ⟩|βᾱcἒτᾱι. But ὅ⟨τι⟩ ποτὲ is commended by *El.* 1161, *Hel.* 186, *Ph.* 1299, *Ba.* 894, *Rh.* 135. And ⟨τι⟩ is commonly lost before π.[1] (vi) *Ion* 1449 πὄθἒν ἐλᾰβὄ|μἒν χᾰρᾶν (Murray's colometry is astray).

---

[1] See *Med.* 1256 -τι πίτνειν AVB: πίτνειν LP; *Ion* 719 μή ⟨τι⟩ ποτ' (Hermann cl. A. *Su.* 392); 1035 μή ⟨τι⟩ πᾶcι (Wakefield; cf. *Alc.* 210, S. *Tr.* 383); *Hel.* 358 ἐνίζον⟨τι⟩ Πριαμίδαι (Badham: -έβιζον πρ- L); A. *ScT* 1066 ⟨τι⟩ πόλιc (Elmsleii

These are the instances which I regard as either certain or very probable. There are several other instances which have a claim on our consideration, although in some of them the text is doubtful and in others an alternative colometry is possible. (vii) S. *El.* 1265 ἐφρᾰσᾰ͡ς ὔ|περτέρᾱν (∼ 1245 ὄττότοῖ | ⟨ὄττότοῖ⟩). So H. A. Pohlsander, *Metrical Studies in the Lyrics of Sophocles* (1964) 61, and R. D. Dawe (Teubner ed. 1975, p. 190). Others take this as an instance of a colon × ∾ ◡ – × – which occurs elsewhere in Sophocles: see Dale, *Lyric Metres* 102–3, L. P. E. Parker, *CQ* n.s. 18 (1968) 258–9, T. C. W. Stinton, *JHS* 97 (1977) 130. (viii) S. *Tr.* 654 ἐξέλῡ|σε͡ν ἐπῐπόνὄν | ᾱμέρᾱν ∼ 662 cῡντᾰκεῖς | θῆρὸς ὑπὸ | πᾰρφᾰσεῖ: Pearson's text, but the reading is quite uncertain. (ix) S. *Tr.* 846 ἤ πὄυ ὀλὄ|ᾱ ϲτένεῖ ∼ 857 ᾱ τότε͡ θὄ|ᾱν νῡμφᾱν: so Pohlsander p. 141 (there is a misprint in his notation), but for an alternative interpretation see Dale, Parker, and Stinton, cited above. (x) E. *Hcld.* 81–2 ξῡνὄικόν ἠλ|θέϲ λᾱὄν ἤ || πέρᾱθέν ᾱλῐ|ὦι πλᾰτᾱι ∼ 102–3 κᾱι μῆ βῐᾱι|ὦι χὲιρὶ δᾱι||μὄνῶν ᾱπὄλῐ|πεῖν ϲφ' ἔδῆ[1] (alternatively πέρᾱθέν ᾱ|λῐὦι πλᾰτᾱι ∼ -μὄνῶν ᾱπὄ|λῐπεῖν ϲφ' ἔδῆ: see on *Tr.* 319 ∼ 333 [no. xiii below]). So Denniston in *Greek Poetry and Life* 131. As an argument against this analysis it may be observed that word-end after long anceps in the second metron of an iambic dimeter is rare: see L. P. E. Parker, *CQ* n.s. 16 (1966) 14–16. N. C. Conomis, *Hermes* 92 (1964) 30 n. 5, analyses as ◡ – ◡ – | – – | ◡ – ◡ – || ◡ ∾ – ◡ –: for the doubly syncopated second metron see S. *OT* 1339 ∼ 1359. I am not attracted by the analysis of Stinton, *BICS* 22 (1975) 105 n. 1. (xi) *Hi.* 594 τᾰ κρῡπτᾰ γᾱρ | πέφῆνέ δῐᾱ͡ | δ' ὀλλῡcᾱι: 'not ... prima facie corrupt' Barrett, who, however, restores dochmiacs by a heavy change. (xii) *El.* 481 cᾰ λέχέᾰ κᾰκὄ|φρὄν κὄρᾱ:[2] we might interpret as cᾱ λέχέᾰ κᾰ|κὄφρὄν κὄρᾱ, with less natural word-division. (xiii) *Tr.* 319 έγῶ δ' έπῐ γᾰ|μὄιϲ έμὄιϲ ∼ 335 βὄᾱϲόν ῡμέ| νᾱιὄν ῶ (for the text of 335 see pp. 61–2). We might interpret as έγῶ δ' έπῐ͡ | γᾰμὄιϲ έμὄιϲ ∼ βὄᾱϲόν ὔ|μένᾱιὄν ῶ: the sequence ◡ – ∾ | ◡ – ◡ – is uncommon but is established by the metrical context for *Tr.* amicus); Men. *Dysk.* 772 ⟨τι⟩ πρᾶγμ' (ed. pr.); fr. 586K ⟨τι⟩ περιπλάττωϲι (Salmasius).

---

[1] 102 χειρὶ ed. Hervag.² : χερὶ L; 103 ἀπολιπεῖν Seidler : -λείπειν L; ϲφ' Musgrave: c' L.

[2] cᾰ λέχεα Seidler, κακόφρον Radermacher, κόρα Dindorf: -c ἀλέχεα κακόφρων κούρα L. The metre is not seriously in doubt.

564 κᾰρᾱτόμ͜ος | ἐρῆμῐᾱ. Stinton (*BICS* 22 [1975] 92) argues that in our passage too the metrical context favours the analysis ∪ - ∾ | ∪ - ∪ -. But the context is far from decisive, and the incidence of word-division is no help either. (xiv) *Tr.* 1087 ἱππό͡βο͡τον | Ἄργος ἵνᾰ | ⟨τέ⟩ τεῖχη ~ 1105 Ἰλῐόθͤν | ὅτͤ μͤ πόλῠ|δᾱκρῡ⟨τό⟩ν. This appears to be much the best way of restoring sense and metre to these lines (1087 ⟨τε⟩ τείχη Seidler: τείχεα VP; 1105 πολυδάκρυ⟨το⟩ν Seidler). For the metre see *Andr.* 1219~1204–5 (no. iii above). (xv) *IT* 832 κᾱτᾰ δͤ δᾱκρῡ | κᾱτᾰ δͤ γοῦς | ᾱμᾱ χᾱρᾱ. We can accept Dindorf's δάκρυα and analyse as dochmiacs. It is less likely that we should analyse the transmitted text as dochmiacs by scanning δᾱκρυ, since lengthening before mute and liquid in dochmiacs is uncommon: see N. C. Conomis, *Hermes* 92 (1964) 39. Even with δάκρυα we can analyse as iambics, with one instance, instead of two, of resolution preceding syncopation. It should be noted that the line, if interpreted as dochmiac, cannot be given to Orestes, who has only iambics in this duet. But the line was rightly assigned to Iphigenia by R. Lohmann, *Noua studia Euripidea* (1905) 423, and independently by P. Maas, *Hermes* 61 (1926) 240 (= *Kl. Schr.* [1973] 49; see also his *Greek Metre* § 76). I should also give 833 to Iphigenia. (xvi) *Ion* 1472 πῶς εῑπᾱς; ᾱλ|λόθͤν γͤγό͡νᾱς | ᾱλλόθͤν. Alternatively -όθεν γͤγό͡|νᾱς ᾱλλόθͤν or ⟨σὺ⟩ γέγ- Dindorf, ⟨γε⟩ γέγ- Nauck, γέγονας ἄρ' Heath. (xvii) *Hel.* 335 ἱῶ μͤλͤο͡ς | ᾱμͤρᾱ: alternatively ἱῶ μͤλͤ|ο͡ς ᾱμͤρᾱ (see on *Tr.* 319 ~ 335 [no. xiii above]). (xviii) *Or.* 329–30 τρῐπο͡δδος ᾱπο͡ φᾱ|τῐν ᾱν ὁ Φο͡ι|βο͡ς ͡ελᾱκͤν ͡ελᾱ||κͤ δͤξᾱμͤνο͡ς | ᾱνᾱ δᾱπͤδον ~ 345–6 τῐνᾱ γᾱρ ͤτῐ πᾱ|ρο͡ς ͞οικον ᾱλ|λον ͡ετͤρον ῆ || τον ᾱπο͡ θͤο͡γό|νͦ̄ων γᾱμͦ̄ων. Text and colometry are disputed, and this is no place for a full discussion. The colometry given here was suggested to me by Sir Charles Willink. (xix) *Rh.* 33 ζͤυγνῠτͤ κͤ| ρόδͤτᾰ τό|ξᾰ νͤυρᾱͅς ~ 51 μῆͤποτͤ τῐν' | ͤς ͤμͤ μͤμ|ψῐν εͤιπῇς (Lindemann: μῆͤποτͤ τῐ|νᾱ μͤμψῐν ͤις | ͤμ' εͤιπῇς codd.). Murray accepts Bothe's μῆͤποτ' ͤς ͤ|μͤ τῐνᾱ μͤμ|ψῐν εͤιπῇς, which has slightly less agreeable word-divisions. But it is possible (though I think it less likely) that the fault of responsion lies in the strophe and not in the antistrophe: see W. Ritchie, *The Authenticity of the Rhesus of Euripides* (1964) 298.

And there is a good case for restoring another instance of this

phenomenon in *Supplices*. At 920–2 Murray's colometry gives πόνουϲ
ἐνεγκοῦϲ' ἐν ὠδῖϲι· καὶ | νῦν Ἅιδαϲ τὸν ἐμὸν | ἔχει μόχθον ἀθλίαϲ, in which
no metrical sense can be made of the second line. Collard prints . . .
ω̄|δῖ̆c̆ῑ̆· || καῑ νῦν Ᾱῑ|δᾱc, in which the spondee followed by the molossus
does not appeal. Wilamowitz (*Verskunst* 156) proposed πόνουϲ ἐνεγ-
κοῦϲ' ἐν ὠδῖϲιν· | καὶ νῦν τὸν ἐμὸν Ᾱῑδᾱc κτλ., which gives – – ◡ ◡̮ | – ◡ –
in the second line. For the cretic scansion of Ᾱῑδᾱc see *El.* 122 (no
faith can be placed in the text of *El.* 143, and *Herc.* 117 must be
emended,[1] and fr. 936 if sound is not necessarily tragic), S. *OC* 1690
Ᾱῑδᾱc | ἕλοῑ πᾰτρῑ (probably ∼ 1716 ἐπῐ̑μἐ̆νεῑ | cἐ̆ τ' ω̄ φῐλᾱ [so Dain,
Pohlsander op. cit. 89, Dawe (Teubner ed. 1979)] ; but the antistrophe
is lacunose, and some editors mark the lacuna at the verse which
corresponds with 1690, in which case we could in theory scan Ᾱῑδᾱc |
ἕλοῑ πᾰτρῑ, with a doubly syncopated first metron ; but in the context
this is less appealing than the lekythion Ᾱῑδᾱc | ἕλοῑ πᾰτρῑ). See also
V. Schmidt, *Sprachliche Untersuchungen zu Herondas* (1968) 3–5. Against
Wilamowitz's restoration Stinton (*BICS* 22 [1975] 87) has made three
objections : (i) that resolution may not precede syncopation ; (ii) that
the sequence given by the first line (◡ – ◡ –|– ◡ –|– –) is unparalleled ;
(iii) that the sequence ἔχει μόχθον ἀθλίαϲ is a rare one. The answer
to (iii) is provided by the dozen or more instances of this sequence
allowed to Euripides by Stinton on p. 94. The answer to (ii) is to
divide πόνουϲ ἐνεγκοῦϲ' ἐν ὠδῖϲι· καὶ | νῦν τὸν ἐμὸν Ᾱῑδαϲ κτλ.

841–3   πόθεν ποθ' οἵδε διαπρεπεῖϲ εὐψυχίαι
                  θνητῶν ἔφυϲαν; εἰπέ γ' ὡϲ ϲοφώτεροϲ
                  νέοιϲιν ἀϲτῶν τῶνδ'· ἐπιϲτήμων γὰρ εἶ.

The letters -έ γ' of εἰπέ γ' were written by Triclinius during the first
stage of his correction of L. Murray reports 'πέ γ' in rasura L²:
fuit fortasse εἰπὸν'. Zuntz (*Inquiry* 76) says that 'it is perfectly possible
that L had the (non-Euripidean) imperative εἶπον', and Collard
agrees. Wecklein is silent. In fact there is no means whatever of
telling what L had here: the suggestion that it had εἶπὸν rests upon
mere guesswork and not upon anything which is visible to the eye.
The imperative εἶπον (on the accentuation, εἶπον rather than εἰπόν,
see H. W. Chandler, *Greek Accentuation* ed. 2 [1881] § 775, O.
Schroeder, *Pindari carmina* ed. 5 [1923] 41) was conjectured here by
Dobree (*Adversaria* 2. 81 [4. 79 ed. Wagner]), but it is not used by the

[1] See p. 47.

tragedians. It is found at Simon. 154 Bergk, Pi. *Ol.* 6. 92, Pl. *Men.*
71 D, Xen. *Mem.* 3. 6. 3, Men. *Dysk.* 410, *Sam.* 489, fr. 675, Theoc.
14. 11. At *Ion* 331 τίϲ εἶπον εἴ μοι ξυλλάβῃ editors rightly accept
Yxem's τίϲ; εἰ πόνου μοι ξυλλάβοι.

Is Triclinius' change any more acceptable than εἶπον? Denniston,
GP 125, lists in addition to this passage six passages in tragedy where
γε follows an imperative. 'The usage', he says, 'seems established,
though few examples of it are critically above suspicion.' Two of
his examples have a disturbing characteristic in common: S. *Ph.*
1003 ξυλλάβετέ γ' αὐτόν (A: ξυλλάβετ' αὐτόν LGRQ), *IA* 817 δρᾶ γ'
(P²: δρᾶ LP) εἴ τι δράϲειϲ. In both places γ' has been interpolated to
mend the metre: see Jackson, *Marg. scaen.* 42. At *Andr.* 589 the variants
tell their own tale: ψαῦϲόν γ' (A: δ' L: om. V: θ' MBPA²V², recte)
ἵν' εἰδῆιϲ. At *Alc.* 1126–7 οὐκ ἔϲτιν, ἀλλὰ τήνδ' ὁρᾶιϲ δάμαρτα ϲήν ::
ὅρα γε μή τι φάϲμα νερτέρων τόδ' ἦι I have some sympathy with
Denniston's ὁρῶ γε (*CR* 43 [1929] 119, ibid. 44 [1930] 214 [see also
his note on *El.* 568]; the conjecture is rejected by P. T. Stevens,
CR 60 [1946] 102, and by Dale ad loc.), but I propose instead the
simpler change to ὅρα δέ. Two remaining examples appear to be
beyond reproach: S. *El.* 345 ἔπειθ' ἕλου γε θάτερ', ἢ φρονεῖν κακῶϲ
κτλ.,[1] 411 ϲυγγένεϲθέ γ' ἀλλὰ νῦν (here ἀλλὰ νῦν makes all the difference:
see Denniston, *GP* 13). I add some further examples, in which the γε
is correctly used: *El.* 671–2 ὦ Ζεῦ πατρῶιε καὶ τροπαῖ' ἐχθρῶν ἐμῶν
. . . :: οἴκτιρέ γ' (Fix: οἰκτείρεθ' L) ἡμᾶϲ (here γε completes a prayer
begun by the previous speaker: see Denniston ad loc. and *GP* 137), *Ion*
518 ϲὺ δ' εὖ φρόνει γε (for δέ . . . γε 'in retorts and lively rejoinders'
see Denniston, *GP* 153), S. *Ai* 483 παῦϲαί γε μέντοι (see *GP* 412), S.
El. 1243 ὅρα γε μὲν δή (see *GP* 395), and probably *Rh.* 623 ἢ 'μοὶ
πάρεϲ γε (πάρεϲ γε LPO: πάρεχε (V): παράϲχεϲ Reiske; see *GP* 119).
At A. *Ch.* 130 Stanley's γ' for τ' is certainly not to be accepted (cf.
Page's note).

---

[1] Since Jebb's explanation of the force of γε here is not very convincing, I
offer with considerable diffidence a conjecture which will eliminate it. Transpose
the words to give this order, ἔπειτα θάτερ', ἢ φρονεῖν κακῶϲ, ἑλοῦ, / ἢ κτλ., assuming
γε to have been a metrical stop-gap inserted after ἑλοῦ had been transferred from its
postponed position. But ἔπειτα is suspicious. R. D. Dawe (Teubner ed. 1975)
obelizes it and records a suggestion of Page, ἐπεί γ'. I cannot believe in ἐπεί γ'
ἑλοῦ γε. But if Sophocles wrote ἐπεί γε θάτερ', ἢ φρονεῖν κακῶϲ, ἑλοῦ, / ἢ κτλ., the
corruption which my proposal postulates would be very easy indeed: ἑλοῦ transposed before γε and ἐπεί changed to ἔπειθ' in order to eliminate the hiatus. [Dawe
has now discussed the passage in *Studies* iii 57–8. For an alternative conjecture see
H. Lloyd-Jones, *CR* n.s. 28 (1978) 219.]

Collard says of *Su.* 842 that 'the emphasis on εἰπέ is strong enough for the retention of γε'. I cannot see that εἰπέ has, or needs, any emphasis at all. Elmsley's εἰπὲ δ' (*Qu. Rev.* 7 [1812] 446) should be accepted. This simple change is more plausible than Hermann's drastic expedient of writing εἴπ'· ἐπιστήμων γὰρ εἶ, with the intervening words deleted. This has been approved by P. Jachmann, *NGG* 1936, 214, and by M. D. Reeve, *GRBS* 14 (1973) 149, who remarks that 'cοφία is not required for giving information so straightforward'. On the contrary, Adrastus' cοφία is the product of ἐπιστήμη, a word which can be virtually synonymous with ἐμπειρία. It is his experience of the world which makes him a fit preceptor for the young. There is a very similar formulation at *Ph.* 529–30 ἠμπειρία | ἔχει τι λέξαι τῶν νέων cοφώτερον and in fr. 619 τὸ γῆρας, ὦ παῖ, τῶν νεωτέρων φρενῶν | cοφώτερον πέφυκε κἀcφαλέcτερον, | ἐμπειρία τε τῆς ἀπειρίας κρατεῖ. Moreover, Adrastus' speech is to be no mere recital of martial prowess. It has an ethical purpose, to explain the origin of the εὐψυχία of the dead; and to counsel the young is the privilege of older and wiser men: *Il.* 4. 322–4 κελεύcω | βουλῆι καὶ μύθοιcι· τὸ γὰρ γέρας ἐcτὶ γερόντων. | αἰχμὰς δ' αἰχμάccουcι νεώτεροι, E. fr. 508 παλαιὸc αἶνοc· ἔργα μὲν νεωτέρων, | βουλαὶ δ' ἔχουcι τῶν γεραιτέρων κράτοc, fr. 291. See also S. fr. 260, with Pearson's note.

920–2 See p. 21.

968–9   †οὔτ' ἐν φθιμένοιcιν
            οὔτ' ἐν ζωοῖcιν ἀριθμουμένη†.

968 οὔτ' ἐν ⟨τοῖc⟩ φθιμένοιc p, οὔτ' ⟨οὖν⟩ ἐν φθιμένοιc Kirchhoff (cf. *Andr.* 329, 731, *IA* 1437, οὔτ' pro οὔτ' οὖν *Hec.* 1244 cod. L), ⟨ὡc⟩ οὔτ' ἐν φθιμένοιc Page   969 οὐ ζωοῖc ἀριθμουμένα Hermann, οὔτε ζῶc' ἀρ- Wilamowitz, οὐ ζώντων ἀρ- Diggle (cf. *Ba.* 1317)

Like Stinton (*JHS* 97 [1977] 146) I do not care for Wilamowitz's ungainly collocation of participles in 969, which is accepted by Collard. If we can tolerate the non-tragic form ζωόc, then Hermann's conjecture, which Stinton supports, is likely to be right. In 968 any of the three conjectures which I have recorded is possible. Hermann's conjecture, taken with any of them, yields a negative disjunction in which the preposition is found in the first, but not the second, limb (οὔτ' ἐν φθιμένοιc, οὐ ζωοῖc). No commentator has offered a parallel (Collard and Stinton quote examples of the preposition omitted in the first limb of a positive disjunction, which is much commoner), so I

offer these: *Alc.* 973–4 οὔτ' ἐπὶ βωμοὺc . . . οὔτε βρέτας θεᾶc, *Ph.*
1555 οὐκ ἐπ' ὀνείδεcιν οὐδ' ἐπιχάρμαcιν, S. *OT* 239 μήτ' ἐν θεῶν
εὐχαῖcι μηδὲ (Elmsley: μήτε codd.) θύμαcιν, fr. 460 P οὔτε μ' ἐκ
(Meineke: εἰc codd.) Δωδῶνοc οὔτε Πυθικῶν / γυ⟨άλων⟩, Theoc. 1.
116–17 οὐκέτ' ἀν' ὕλαν, / οὐκέτ' ἀνὰ δρυμώc, οὐκ ἄλcεα, Call. *H.* 6. 72
οὔτε νιν εἰc ἐρανὼc οὔτε ξυνδείπνια πέμπον. I do not include *Ion* 507
οὔτ' ἐπὶ κερκίcιν οὔτε λόγοιc φάτιν / ἄιον, where (ἐπὶ) λόγοιc, which
troubled Wilamowitz and is paraphrased by Owen as 'at recitations
and plays', is an improbable expression. Badham's λόγων should be
accepted.

971–6

   ὑπολελειμμένα μοι δάκρυα·
   μέλεα παιδὸc ἐν οἴκοιc
   κεῖται μνήματα, πένθιμοι
   κουραὶ καὶ cτέφανοι κόμαc
   ⟨λοιβαί τε νεκύων φθιμένων⟩   974b
   ἀοιδαί θ' ἃc χρυcοκόμαc   975
   Ἀπόλλων οὐκ ἐνδέχεται.

  974b e Plut. mor. 394 B rest. Markland: om. L   τε add. Hermann: om.
Plut.   975 θ' ἃc Markland: τὰc L: ἃc ὁ Plut.

Since editors from Hermann to Collard have impugned Markland's
κάcτέφανοι κόμαι for καὶ cτέφανοι κόμαc I must explain why it is a
necessary correction. Mourners do not wear garlands, as Markland
saw, comparing Arist. fr. 101 Rose ap. Athen. 675 a ὁμοπαθείαι
γὰρ τοῦ κεκμηκότος κολοβοῦμεν ἡμᾶς αὐτοὺς τῆι τε κουρᾶι τῶν τριχῶν
καὶ τῆι τῶν cτεφάνων ἀφαιρέcει. Musgrave added Pl. *Leg.* 800 E καὶ
δὴ καὶ cτολή γέ που ταῖc ἐπικηδείοιc ὠιδαῖc οὐ cτέφανοι πρέποιεν ἄν.
Further illustration is afforded by *Alc.* 343–4 παύcω δὲ κώμους . . .
cτεφάνους τε (because of the imminent death of Alcestis), *Hi.* 1137
ἀcτέφανοι δὲ κόρας ἀνάπαυλαι / Λατοῦς (because of the death of Hippolytus).

 Hermann wrote: 'sensus est: tristia filii monumenta mihi jacent
domi detonsi crines, depositaeque coronae, et, quae mortuis libationes
feruntur, carmina non accepta Apollini. non conjecisset Marklandus
κάcτέφανοι κόμαι, si ad uerbum κεῖται attendisset.' In writing these
final words he evidently had in mind such locutions as *Ba.* 1386
θύρcου μνῆμ' ἀνάκειται, H. *Od.* 21. 40–1 (τόξον) μνῆμα ξείνοιο φίλοιο /
κέcκετ' ἐνὶ μεγάροιcι; cf. S. *Ichn.* 148–9 P. But can 'detonsi crines'
be 'monumenta' which 'jacent domi'? Surprisingly they can. Paley

refers to A. *ScT* 49–50, where the sons are said to have cut locks from their hair for their parents to keep: μνημεῖά θ᾽ αὑτῶν τοῖc τοκεῦcιν ἐc δόμουc / πρὸc ἄρμ᾽ Ἀδράcτου χερcὶν ἔcτεφον, a passage imitated by St. *Theb.* 9. 900–3 (the speaker is Parthenopaeus) '*hunc tamen, orba parens, crinem*' (*dextraque secandum / praebuit*), '*hunc toto capies pro corpore crinem . . . huic dabis exsequias*'. Similarly *IT* 820–1 τί γάρ; κόμαc càc μητρὶ δοῦcα cῆι φέρειν; :: μνημεῖά γ᾽ ἀντὶ cώματοc τοὐμοῦ τάφωι. But a decisive objection to Paley's interpretation is that the expression πένθιμοι κουραί cannot denote the cutting of the hair of the dead, whether the hair was cut before or after death. It is the shorn hair of the mourner, not of the mourned, which bears this designation: *Alc.* 512 κουρᾶι τῆιδε πενθίμωι, *Or.* 458 κουρᾶι πενθίμωι κεκαρμένοc, and for similar formulations see *Alc.* 101, 426–7, *Tr.* 141–2, *Hel.* 1053–4. In fact the hair of the mourners is already shorn, as we are told at 97. If it was Hermann's intention to refer πένθιμοι κουραί to the shorn hair not of the sons but of the mothers, then of such hair it cannot be said that 'filii monumenta . . . jacent domi', since mourners did not treasure their own shorn locks. Nor, for that matter, can such an expression as 'filii monumenta jacent domi' be predicated of 'libationes' and 'carmina'. And, finally, the translation of cτέφανοι κόμαc as '*depositae* coronae' introduces a notion for which the text gives no warrant.

Collard interprets cτέφανοι κόμαc as 'a reference to the practice of decorating the corpse's head with a garland'. To this he himself makes the decisive objection: 'in Argos there would be only ashes, not corpses to be garlanded'. And even if there had been corpses to be garlanded, we have no evidence that it was customary for the mourners to remove the garlands and keep them at home. 'The conventional and allusive vocabulary of grief leaves fact behind', we are told. I derive small comfort from such a reflection. We have two alternatives: to acquiesce in fiction and to restore fact by a slight alteration. I prefer the second alternative.

If Markland's conjecture is to be accepted, Hermann's objection to κεῖται must be answered. 'κεῖται, *sunt*, ut notaui ad uer. 665 [νεκροὺc . . . ὧν ἔκειτ᾽ ἀγών]' said Markland. One might reply that at 665 and in most of the other passages quoted by Markland κεῖcθαι is employed as the perfect passive of τιθέναι. But this is not true of *Hec.* 16 γῆc ὄρθ᾽ ἔκειθ᾽ ὁρίcματα (ἔκειτ᾽ ἐρείcματα Scaliger). Compare also *Hel.* 1125 ἄνυμφα δὲ μέλαθρα κεῖται ('the houses stand husbandless'). But perhaps we may see in κεῖται some hint of a common sense of the verb, 'to be laid down, prescribed' (cf. *Hec.* 291–2 νόμος . . . κεῖται, *Tr.* 178–9 μή με κτείνειν | δόξ' Ἀργείων κεῖται . . .; *Ion* 756 θάνατος . . . κεῖται). It would be appropriate for the mothers to refer to the various manifestations of mourning which they list in 973 ff. by a term which suggests that they are prescribed for them by law or custom, almost as a penalty to be endured. But I do not wish to press this sense. Quite a satisfactory parallel, I think, is provided by S. *OC* 1518–19 ἐγὼ διδάξω, τέκνον Αἰγέως, ἅ σοι | γήρως ἄλυπα τῇδε κείσεται πόλει ('shall be held in store').

980–3   καὶ μὴν θαλάμας τάσδ' ἐσορῶ δὴ
Καπανέως ἤδη τύμβον θ' ἱερὸν
μελάθρων τ' ἐκτὸς
Θησέως ἀναθήματα νεκροῖς.

'Non memini me alibi in eodem sententiae membro conjunctas uidisse particulas δή et ἤδη. Quare hic legerim τάσδ' ἐσορῶμεν' Blomfield (*Mus. crit.* 1 [1826] 185), forgetting perhaps that he had once attributed to Porson the conjecture πάντα γὰρ ἤδη ⟨δὴ⟩ τετέλεσται at *Alc.* 132 (*Aduers.* [edd. Monk and Blomfield 1812] 222). Hermann, for the same reason, had already proposed καὶ μὴν θαλάμας μὲν τάσδ' ἐσορῶ, although he noted that δή and ἤδη are combined at *Tr.* 233–4 δοῦλαι γὰρ δὴ | Δωρίδος ἐσμὲν χθονὸς ἤδη. Suspicion has lingered: 'δή uitiosum' Nauck, 'aut δή aut ἤδη spurium' Murray, 'δή . . . ἤδη suspectum' Collard; Wilamowitz used the obelus, and Wecklein proposed καὶ μὴν θαλάμας πάρα τάσδ' ἐσορᾶν. Even over *Tr.* 233–4 suspicion hangs: δοῦλαι γὰρ δὴ has been changed to δοῦλαι γάρ, ἰδού (Burges), μῶν δείλαιαι (Nauck), and δουριάλωτοι (Wecklein, *SBAM* 1896, 505). For a defence of the text see C. Busche, *Obseruationes criticae in Eur. Troades* (1886) 29–31.

There is not the least ground for these suspicions. δή is followed by ἤδη in the same clause at *Tr.* 1272–3 τοῦτο δὴ τὸ λοίσθιον | καὶ τέρμα πάντων τῶν ἐμῶν ἤδη (Musgrave: ἤδη τῶν ἐμῶν VP) κακῶν (even this, a quite certain conjecture, has been impugned: see Nauck, *Euripideische Studien* II [Mémoires de l'Académie Impériale des sciences de St-Pétersbourg, ser. vii, 5] 164), Ar. *Ach.* 311–12 ταῦτα δὴ τολμᾷς λέγειν | ἐμφανῶς ἤδη πρὸς ἡμᾶς; *Lys.* 523 ὅτε δὴ δ' ὑμῶν ἐν ταῖσιν ὁδοῖς φανερῶς ἠκούομεν ἤδη, Pl. *Phaedr.* 277 A νῦν δὴ ἐκεῖνα ἤδη κτλ., *Rep.* 524 E τοῦ ἐπικρινοῦντος δὴ δέοι ἂν ἤδη κτλ., *Symp.* 204 B δῆλον δή, ἔφη, τοῦτό γε ἤδη κτλ., *Leg.* 682 E καὶ δὴ ταῦτά γε ἤδη κτλ., Xen. *Oec.* 9. 6 οὕτω δὴ ἤδη κτλ. See also *Alc.* 94 (codd.). For the reverse order see *Hi.* 789 ἤδη γὰρ ὡc νεκρόν νιν ἐκτείνουcι δή. Both δή and ἤδη are found separately in clauses beginning with καὶ μήν: *Hi.* 1342 καὶ μὴν ὁ τάλαc ὅδε δὴ cτείχει, *Or.* 348 καὶ μὴν βαcιλεὺc ὅδε δὴ cτείχει, *Andr.* 1166–7 καὶ μὴν ὅδ᾽ ἄναξ ἤδη . . . πελάζει. For the position of δή (not immediately after ὅδε, as in the passages just cited) we may compare, from passages similar in content, *Alc.* 233 ἤδ᾽ ἐκ δόμων δὴ καὶ πόcιc πορεύεται, *Ion* 392–3 εἰcορῶ γὰρ εὐγενῆ πόcιν / Ξοῦθον πέλαc δὴ τόνδε. See also Denniston, *GP* 208 (for δή with ὅδε in these entrance formulas) and 227–8 (for the position of δή). Examples of ἤδη used in similar contexts, announcing a new arrival, are given below.

There is therefore no justification for the prejudice which editors display against an instance of ἤδη followed by δή which has been introduced by conjecture at 1114: τάδε δὴ παίδων †καὶ δή† φθιμένων / ὀcτᾶ φέρεται. Here καὶ δή, so placed in the middle of its clause, is indefensible, although Denniston, *GP* 251, is half inclined to defend it. Murray and Collard obelize. Musgrave proposed τάδ᾽, ἰδοῦ, παίδων ἤδη, Blomfield ἀλλὰ τάδ᾽ ἤδη παίδων, Jacobs τάδε δὴ for καὶ δή, Fix deleted καὶ δή and brought the preceding ἰώ *intra metrum* (this is accepted by Wecklein and approved by Zuntz, *Inquiry* 78 and 186), Wilamowitz proposed καὶ μὴν φθιμένων τάδε δὴ παίδων. Other proposals are recorded by Wecklein in his Appendix and by Collard in *CQ* 13 (1963) 187 and in his own Appendix, p. 432. All that we need is a half of Musgrave's conjecture, ἤδη for καὶ δή. Collard says that 'then the word-order has to be changed because of the closeness of δή' and so he changes it to τάδε δὴ παίδων ὀcτᾶ φθιμένων ἤδη φέρεται. This is surprising, since he at once quotes 980–1 ἐcορῶ δὴ Καπανέωc ἤδη. For ἤδη in a sentence announcing a new arrival see *Cycl.* 36, *Alc.* 24, *Andr.* 1166, *IT* 1222, *Ion* 516, *Ph.* 1482, S. *OT* 298, 531. The letters η and κ are constantly confused (see Jackson, *Marg. scaen.* 200), and the abbreviation of καὶ (κ᾽) is easily confused with ἤ (see Bast, *Commentatio palaeographica* 815). And so we find ἤ for καὶ in V at *Hec.* 88 and in P at *Or.* 831. At fr. 360. 31 (*Erectheus*, fr. 50. 31 Austin) Matthiae restored εἵλοντ᾽ ἤ for εἵλοντο καί. In the papyrus of Bacchyl. 9. 19 ΔΗ was written by the first hand for ΑΚΑΙ (cf. Housman, *CR* 12 [1898] 72 = *Classical Papers* 449). Note also *Herc.* 801, where καί must be a corruption either of ὡc (Musgrave) or of ἤ (Conradt).

I return to 982–3. In μελάθρων τ᾽ ἐκτὸc Θηcέωc ἀναθήματα νεκροῖc the meaning of ἀναθήματα has hardly ever been recognized, and I have seen no satisfactory interpretation of μελάθρων . . . ἐκτός. First, the normal meaning of ἀνάθημα is an offering dedicated to a god. There is no authority for the meaning 'funeral pyre' (Wilamowitz and Grégoire) or for such a paraphrase as 'the formal rites and offerings of funeral, including cremation' (Collard). The old vulgate translation 'dona dicata mortuis' was on the right lines; but the nature of the ἀναθήματα needs to be explained. It is explained by *Ion* 1141–4 λαβὼν δ' ὑφάσμαθ' ἱερὰ . . . ὀρόφωι πτέρυγα περιβάλλει πέπλων, / ἀνάθημα Δίου παιδός. They are dedicatory cloths or tapestries. And the purpose for which they are to be used was apprehended by Musgrave, who writes 'uestimenta et alia, quae cum mortuis comburi mos erat, uid. Rhes. 963 [960]'. For the same custom see *IT* 632 πολύν τε γάρ σοι κόσμον ἐνθήcω τάφωι, H. *Od.* 24. 67 καίεο δ' ἔν τ' ἐcθῆτι θεῶν, Hdt. 5. 92η. 2. We may compare the habit of putting on special clothes before death (*Alc.* 160–1, 613, 618, 631, *Herc.* 329–35, 526, 548–9, 702–3) or of clothing the corpse before burial (*Tr.* 1143, *Hel.* 1279). That this is the meaning of ἀναθήματα was recognized by Paley and Wecklein.

The early editors, adopting the translation of ἀναθήματα as 'dona dicata mortuis', were content to perpetuate the translation of μελάθρων . . . ἐκτὸς as 'extra aedes'. It has now become fashionable to explain the words by reference to 936–8, where it said that the pyre of Capaneus will be placed hard by the temple, while the communal pyre of the other heroes will be placed in a separate spot. And so Wecklein explains μελάθρων . . . ἐκτὸς with the note 'während die Grabkammer des Kapaneus sich noch innerhalb des Tempelbezirks befindet' (earlier he had conjectured μελάθρων ἐκτὸς Θηcέως τ'); and Collard writes that 'Capaneus' tomb will be where he is burned, within the τέμενος (938 f.): the others are burned outside'. And Wilamowitz translates 'jenseits der heil'gen Grenzen', Grégoire 'plus loin de ce temple'. But μελάθρων . . . ἐκτὸς means 'outside the temple'. It cannot mean 'outside the τέμενος of the temple'; for, if it could, we should have to allow that ἐντὸς μελάθρων might mean not only 'inside the temple' but also 'inside the τέμενος', that is 'outside the temple'.

I see only one way of giving point to μελάθρων . . . ἐκτὸς: to take the words closely with ἀναθήματα in the sense 'ἀναθήματα (brought) out of the temple'. For the similar use of prepositional phrases see *El.* 794 λουτροῖcι καθαροῖc ποταμίων ῥείθρων ἄπο, *Tr.* 574–6 cκύλοιc . . . ἀπὸ Τροίαc, *IT* 162 παγάc τ' οὐρειᾶν (Monk: -ῶν L) ἐκ μόcχων,

Ion 113–16 δάφνας . . . κάπων ἐξ ἀθανάτων (perhaps also *Ion* 1232–3 cπονδὰς ἐκ Διονύcου | βοτρύων, though the text is uncertain), *Ph.* 1158 γεῖc' ἐπάλξεων ἄπο, A. *Pe.* 611 βοόc τ' ἀφ' ἀγνῆc λευκὸν εὔποτον γάλα. See also p. 69. And so what the chorus see are the pyre of Capaneus and the dedicatory tapestries from the temple with which Theseus proposes to clothe the corpses.

998 ∼ 1021   See p. 72.

1025   See *PCPS* n.s. 20 (1974) 8 n. 1.

1089–93   See *GRBS* 14 (1973) 265–9. 'But D.'s own exx. show the soundness of ἐc τόδ' ἦλθον picked up by an exegetic clause (1090 here)' Collard. Between the epexegetic clauses which I quoted (consisting of an infinitive with or without ὥcτε) and the clause οἷον . . . γίγνεται (1090) there is a world of difference.

1100–2   καὶ κάρα τόδε
                   κατεῖχε χειρί· πατρὶ δ' οὐδὲν ἥδιον
                   γέροντι θυγατρός.

1101 χειρί Tr¹: χ∗∗ρί L: χερcίν Canter, χειροῖν Elmsley¹   οὐδὲν ἥδιον πατρὶ Burney

Collard, after giving a list of comparatives ending in -ίων, says 'I document this matter fully because the transposition in *Su.* 1101 to οὐδὲν ἥδιον πατρί by Burney has had an overlong life'. Examination of his list will show that it is not yet time to nail down the lid of the coffin. The only plausible example of -ίων in tragedy is κακίων in anapaests at fr. 546 (fr. 89 Austin). I call it plausible, and not certain, because (i) it can be removed by emendation ('κακίων uitiosum, χείρων coni. nescio quis' Nauck), (ii) it is attributed to Euripides only by Clement of Alexandria and Stobaeus, and we cannot have complete faith in their attribution. Comedy provides the only examples on the list which may be considered certain: Pi. fr. 89a Snell–Maehler cited by Ar. *Equ.* 1264 κάλλῖον, Ar. *Vesp.* 297 (ionics) ἥδῖον, ps.-Alexis fr. 25. 6K (cf. W. G. Arnott, *CQ* n.s. 5 [1955] 214–15) ἥδῖον, Eupolis fr. 20 Demiańczuk βελτίω. Three further instances

¹ The original accent on L was as I have shown it, not as it is shown by Zuntz, *Inquiry* 78. And Collard's suggestion that L may have had χερί is implausible: Triclinius wrote ει in the space of two letters, not one.

are adduced from the tragedians: (i) *Ba.* 877 (= 897) κάλλἷον: metre and text are alike uncertain; (ii) A. fr. 309. 3N (616. 3M) βέλτἷον: this depends on Athenaeus and is easily avoidable by Burney's βέλτερον; in any case, from satyr play, not tragedy; (iii) tr. fr. adesp. 320 (= Men. *mon.* 738 Jaekel) καλλίω: there is no reason to suppose that this is tragic. So much for the 'unshakable support' which is claimed for ἥδἷον in tragic iambics. There was no convenience, let alone compulsion, in the use of abnormal prosody at *Su.* 1101. If Euripides wrote, as I believe he did, κατεῖχε χερcίν (or χειροῖν)· οὐδὲν ἥδιον πατρί, the text was changed because someone baulked at the asyndeton and wished to introduce a connecting δέ (for other examples of this see Barrett on *Hi.* 40).

There is a further misapprehension which, lest it be perpetuated, I feel bound to dispel. Collard claims that the transmitted reading was approved by Porson and Hermann ('ἥδἷον rec. veteres edd., ex. gr. Porson ad *Or.* 499' app. crit.; 'Early edd. like Markland, Porson and Hermann, accepted L' commentary). Porson at *Or.* 499 [506] said only that this was the one exception to normal prosody 'quae speciem habet'. According to Gaisford in the 1811 edition of Markland's commentary, 'Placuit haec coniectura [Burney's], quod ex ipsius ore olim didici, . . . R. Porsono'. According to the editors of Porson's *Adversaria* (p. 245) 'Emendauit Porsonus χερcὶν οὐδὲν ἥδιον πατρί'. Hermann proposed κατεῖχε· πατρὶ δ' οὐδὲν ἥδιον πέλει, 'quum . . . haud admodum uerisimile sit, Euripidem a communi usu in tali quidem uersu locoque recessisse', adding 'dubitauit de ueritate uulgatae etiam Porsonus ad Oresten, 499'.

1114 See p. 27.

1152–7 ⟨Πα.⟩ ἔτ' εἰcορᾶν cε, πάτερ, ἐπ' ὀμμάτων δοκῶ.
　　　　　⟨Χο.⟩ φίλον φίλημα παρὰ γένυν τιθέντα cόν.
　　　　　⟨Πα.⟩ λόγων δὲ παρακέλευcμα cῶν
　　　　　　　　ἀέρι φερόμενον οἴχεται.　　　　　　　　　1155
　　　　　Χο.　δυοῖν δ' ἄχη, ματρί τ' ἔλιπεν,[1]
　　　　　　　cέ τ' οὔποτ' ἄλγη πατρῶια λείψει.

(Sons) 'I seem still to see you, father, before my eyes . . .' (Chorus) '. . . placing your loving kiss on the cheek.' (Sons) 'And the encouragement of your speech is carried away on the breeze.' (Chorus) 'And

---

[1] ματρί Hermann: ματέρι L; ἔλιπεν Tyrwhitt: -εc L.

for two of us he has left lamentation, for me his mother—and grief for a father will never leave you.'

Editors detect no oddity in 1153. But the verse contains two oddities, one serious, the other less so; together they must cast doubt on the text. Consider the second-person references in this passage. At 1152 the sons address the father with ϲε. At 1153 the chorus address ϲόν to the father. At 1154 the sons address ϲῶν to the father. At 1157 the chorus address the sons with ϲε, and in the previous line they have addressed the father in the third person (ἔλιπεν is a certain correction of ἔλιπεϲ). It is not credible that the chorus, in their first reference to the father at 1153, should address him with ϲε, and in the second should address him with the third person and address the sons with ϲε. For consistency the chorus must address the second-person pronominal adjective in 1153 to the sons. This they will do if we change ϲόν to ϲάν. Further, φίλον φίλημα is a feeble tautology (Collard says that it gives a 'special kind of emphasis . . . in a moment of pathos'; I am not persuaded), and φίλαν will give much more pointed sense.

With φίλαν . . . γένυν . . . ϲάν compare El. 1152–4 φίλαν πατρίδα . . . ἐμάν, Herc. 1281–2 ἐμαῖϲ φίλαιϲ / Θήβαιϲ. And these passages should warn us against premature alteration of Or. 1049 ὦ φίλον πρόϲπτυγμ' ἐμόν (ἐμοί Nauck). IA 630 καὶ δεῦρο δὴ πατέρα πρόϲειπε ϲὸν φίλον is not (in its present form at least) Euripidean. And I doubt Victorius' correction in El. 409 ἔλθ' ὡϲ παλαιὸν τροφὸν ἐμὸν φίλου (ἐμοῦ φίλου Victorius: ἐμοῦ φίλον Camper) πατρόϲ (see Illinois Class. Stud. 2 [1977] 110–11). We also find ϲόϲ added to the superlative φίλτατοϲ: Hi. 838 τῆϲ ϲῆϲ . . . φιλτάτηϲ ὁμιλίαϲ, Andr. 574 τῆϲ ϲῆϲ . . . φιλτάτηϲ γενειάδοϲ. But I should not entertain Hel. 899 τόνδ' εἰϲ ἐμὰϲ ἐλθόντα φιλτάταϲ (φίλτατον Cobet rightly) χέραϲ. An alternative, however, to ϲάν would be ϲοί, as Sir Denys Page suggested to me; and this is perhaps more stylish.

II. ELECTRA

57–9 See *PCPS* n.s. 15 (1969) 51–2.

116 See *Dionysiaca* 177 n. 38.

144–6 . . . γόους
οἷς ἀεὶ τὸ κατ᾽ ἦμαρ
†διέπομαι†.

λείβομαι Wecklein, Herwerden, δάπτομαι Schenkl, δεύομαι Weil, Hirschwaelder

λείβομαι, proposed in 1869 by both Wecklein (*Ars Soph. emend.* 184) and Herwerden (*Stud. Thuc.* 162) is supported by *Andr.* 532 λείβομαι δάκρυσιν κόρας and *Su.* 1119 καταλειβομένης τ᾽ ἄλγεσι πολλοῖς. Since the postulated corruption may seem a harsh one, it is worth observing how commonly Λ and Δ are confused: 180 πόδ᾽ ἐμόν Canter: πόλεμον L; 371 λιμόν L: δῆμον Π; 654 δέχ᾽ Elmsley: λέγ᾽ L; 999 τοῦδ᾽ ὄχου Victorius: τοῦ λόχου L; *Hcld.* 602 λύεται Milton: δύεται L; *Hi.* 228 ἁλίας et -α δίας codd.; *Su.* 755 λόχοις Reiske: δόμοις L; *Herc.* 19 καθόδου Reiske: καθόλου L; *Tr.* 332 ἄναγε πόδα còν PQ: ἀναγέλασον V; *Ion* 1065 λαιμῶν Scaliger: δαίμων L; A. *Pe.* 307 σποδεῖ Emperius: πολεῖ codd.; *Ch.* 566 δέξαιτ᾽ Turnebus: λέξαιτ᾽ M. The transposition of ε and ι needs no illustration; as it happens, there is a similar transposition just below: 186 εἰ πρέποντ᾽ Reiske: εἴ πέρ ποτ᾽ L. These changes will probably have happened after λείβομαι became λείπομαι.

159–62 See *PCPS* n.s. 15 (1969) 52. Compare *IA* 1102 θάνατον . . . ὃν πατὴρ βουλεύεται (also of Iphigenia's sacrifice). The word ὅδιος ('a most unfortunate word to introduce by emendation' Denniston) has been plausibly restored at *Hyps.* fr. 1. iv. 30 (see Bond ad loc.). For πικρός (art. cit., p. 52 n. 1) see Fraenkel, *Agamemnon* p. 301 n. 1.

186–7 . . . εἰ πρέποντ᾽ Ἀγαμέμνονος
κοῦραι τᾶι βασιλείαι.

186 εἰ πρέποντ᾽ Reiske: εἴ πέρ ποτ᾽ L   187 κοῦραι τᾶι Reiske: κούρας τὰ (τᾶ Tr²) L: κοῦραι 'σται Nauck

I agree with Denniston that Nauck's is the less attractive conjecture. But the objections which he formulates against it are lacking in precision. 'The prodelision . . . is highly doubtful in a lyric passage'; he knows of 'no example, in the tragic senarius, of the prodelision of any part of εἰμί except ἐcτί'. His reformulation of these objections in *CR* 53 (1939) 176 still leaves much to be desired. And Platnauer's remark on this passage in his 'Prodelision in Greek drama', *CQ* n.s. 10 (1960) 141, is based on Denniston's note. Questions which need to be asked and which are not asked by Denniston or Platnauer are whether there exists any instance of prodelision after a dative termination -αι[1] and, if any does exist, whether there appears to be any restriction on the kind of word which suffers prodelision in such circumstances. These are the instances which I should consider certain, all except the last in lyrics : *Su.* 69 ταλαίναι 'ν Wilamowitz: τάλαιν' ἐν L; *IT* 854 δέραι 'φῆκε Elmsley: δέρα θῆκε L; S. *OT* 215 πεύκαι 'πì, 866 οὐρανίαι 'ν Housman: -ίαν δι' codd.; *Tr.* 940 αἰτίαι ⟨'μ⟩βάλοι (suppl. Pearson; cf. *CR* n.s. 22 [1972] 244 n. 3). It will be seen that in each of these examples the prodelided word is a preposition or prepositional prefix. Denniston's suspicion that the only part of εἰμί which suffers prodelision in tragic iambics is ἐcτί is almost true; but there is the solitary ποῦ 'cτον at S. *OC* 1107 (he records this in *CR* loc. cit.).

209 See *Dionysiaca* 174, and p. 52 below.

216–17 ξένοι τινὲc παρ' οἶκον οἶδ' ἐφεcτίουc
εὐνὰc ἔχοντεc ἐξανίcτανται λόχου.

The much-emended ἐφεcτίουc (for the latest emendation see G. Müller, *Hermes* 106 [1978] 10) was explained by Keene as follows: 'The natural meaning of the word is "at the hearth or altar" . . . perhaps the allusion is to the stone obelisk in honour of Apollo of the Highways which usually stood in front of houses.' That ἐφέcτιοc should mean 'at the altar' is a suggestion which provoked surprise from Denniston and ridicule from Jackson (*Marg. scaen.* 94–5); but I believe that the suggestion is right.

First, as nobody disputes, ἑcτία is sometimes used as an equivalent of βωμόc: see A. *ScT* 275, *Eum.* 282, 440, S. *Tr.* 658, *OC* 1495, and

---

[1] For prodelision after -αι in forms other than the dative termination see *GRBS* 14 (1973) 243.

LSJ *s.u.* Next consider S. *OT* 32 οἵδε παῖδες ἑζόμεσθ' ἐφέστιοι. Where are they sitting? 'At the hearth', says Jebb. No, they are sitting out of doors, at the altars, as they told us plainly at 15–16: προσήμεθα / βωμοῖσι τοῖς σοῖς. This is a clear case of ἐφέστιος = ἐπιβώμιος.

Once this meaning is accepted, we can appreciate what is happening on stage and why it happens. When Orestes says to Pylades at 109 ἑζώμεσθα κἀκπυθώμεθα κτλ., the meaning of ἑζώμεσθα is suggested by the Sophoclean ἑζόμεσθ' ἐφέστιοι. They are to sit, or crouch, in the place which offers them the most natural cover for their eaves-dropping, behind Apollo's statue and altar. Had this not been their hiding-place, we may imagine that Electra's first impulse, on seeing them, would have been the same as Helen's on seeing the disguised Menelaus: *Hel.* 541 ff. ἔα· τίς οὗτος; οὔ τί που κρυπτεύομαι . . . ; οὐχ ὡς δρομαία πῶλος ἢ Βάκχη θεοῦ / τάφωι ξυνάψω κῶλον; Her natural instinct must have been to seek the security of the altar. But her way, like Helen's, is blocked: *Hel.* 550–1 ἀδικούμεθ', ὦ γυναῖκες· εἰργόμεσθα γὰρ / τάφου πρὸς ἀνδρὸς τοῦδε. Since there is no way to the altar, Electra attempts to escape indoors: 218–19 φυγῆι σὺ μὲν κατ' οἶμον, ἐς δόμους δ' ἐγώ κτλ. Orestes advances towards her with outstretched hand: 220 μέν', ὦ τάλαινα· μὴ τρέσηις ἐμὴν χέρα. Escape to the altar and to the house are now alike impossible, and she turns to Apollo's statue and appeals to it from afar: 221 ὦ Φοῖβ' Ἄπολλον, προσπίτνω σε μὴ θανεῖν. Denniston himself recognizes that Electra is here addressing 'the statue or symbol of the tutelary Apollo, standing before the house'.

The altar and statue of Apollo ἀγυιεύς were regularly seen on the Athenian stage: Poll. 4. 123 ἐπὶ δὲ τῆς σκηνῆς καὶ ἀγυιεὺς ἔκειτο βωμὸς ὁ πρὸ τῶν θυρῶν. See Pearson on S. fr. 370, Fraenkel on A. *Ag.* 1081, D. M. MacDowell on Ar. *Vesp.* 875, E. Handley on Men. *Dysk.* 659. In *CR* n.s. 29 (1979) 208 I have suggested that the ἀγυιεὺς βωμός may have served as a hiding-place for Orestes and Pylades in the *Choephori*; for a discussion of other suggested hiding-places see O. Taplin, *The Stagecraft of Aeschylus* (1977) 335–6.

238   . . . εἰ ζῆις, ὅπου τε ζῶσα συμφορὰς ἔχεις.

ὅπως Elmsley   συμφορᾶς Victorius

Since Denniston's note is confusing and inconclusive, and since Jackson's passing remark that 'Madvig's ὅπου . . . συμφορᾶς ἔχει (ἔχῃ) is far more probable than Elmsley's generally received ὅπως . . .

cυμφορᾶc ἔχειc' (*Marg. scaen.* 215) may spread yet more confusion, I must explain why ὅπωc . . . cυμφορᾶc ἔχειc is right and why Madvig's conjecture (see *Philologus* 1 [1846] 677 = *Opusc. acad.* ed. 2 [1887] 708) is wrong.

There exist two locutions which should not be confounded with each other. The first is represented by 751 πῶc ἀγῶνοc ἥκομεν; *Hel.* 313 πῶc δ' εὐμενείαc . . . ἔχειc; 857 τῆc τύχηc γὰρ ὦδ' ἔχω, S. *OT* 345 ὡc ὀργῆc ἔχω (see also KG 1. 383–4, LSJ *s.u.* ἔχω B. II. b). The second is represented by *Tr.* 685 ἔνθα πημάτων κυρῶ, *Ion* 1252 ἵν' εἶ τύχηc, *Hel.* 738 οὗ (Tyrwhitt: οἷ L; cf. *Dionysiaca* 176 n. 23) τ' ἐcμὲν τύχηc, A. *Ch.* 891 ἐνταῦθα γὰρ δὴ τοῦδ' ἀφικόμην κακοῦ, S. *Tr.* 375 ποῦ ποτ' εἰμὶ πράγματοc; 1145 ξυμφορᾶc ἵν' ἔcταμεν, *Ph.* 899 ἐνθάδ' ἤδη τοῦδε τοῦ πάθουc κυρῶ (see also KG 1. 340–1, Bruhn, *Anhang* 22–3). The verb ἔχειν (in the active) is confined to the first locution, where the interrogative or demonstrative word is πῶc, ὦδε, and the like. In the second locution, which uses ἵνα, ποῦ, and the like, ἔχειν is never used. The passive ἔχεcθαι is found in neither locution; the construction (ἐν) cυμφοραῖc ἔχεcθαι, which Jackson illustrates, has no bearing on the matter. The only way to justify ὅπου is to change ἔχειc to κυρεῖc, as Nauck implausibly proposed.

284 See p. 116.

409 See *Illinois Class. Stud.* 2 (1977) 110–11 and p. 31 above.

426–7 ἐν τοῖc τοιούτοιc δ' ἡνίκ' ἂν γνώμη πέcηι,
        cκοπῶ κτλ.

γνώμη πέcηι Schaefer: γνώμη πέcοι L: γνώμηc πέcω Stob. 4. 31. 7

By the end of the last century Schaefer's conjecture had established its rightful place in the text. But the tide has now turned. Murray follows Stobaeus. Denniston wavers between Stobaeus and a conjecture of his own. And a further conjecture, unmetrical indeed, has been proposed by G. Schiassi in *RFIC* n.s. 34 (1956) 248.[1]

In Stobaeus' reading 'it is hard to see what is the construction of the genitive', complained Paley. Denniston suggests that it may be taken as 'partitive genitive after τοῖc τοιούτοιc, "when I light upon such trains of thought"', comparing S. *Tr.* 705 ποῖ γνώμηc πέcω. I have

---

[1] I have not profited from the note of E. Merone, *Atti della Accademia Pontaniana* n.s. 12 (1963) 319–21.

illustrated the idiom ποῖ γνώμης πέσω in my note on 238 above; it cannot be used to support an alleged expression ἐν τοῖς τοιούτοις γνώμης πεσεῖν. There would not, indeed, be any fault in ἐν τῶι τοιούτωι γνώμης πεσεῖν: see ἐν τῶι συμφορᾶς Hel. 1195, S. Ant. 1229, ἐν τῶι πράγματος S. Ai. 314, ἐν τῶι τοιούτωι . . . τοῦ καίρου Thuc. 7. 69. 2 (cf. KG I. 278–9). But these passages do not justify the plural ἐν τοῖς τοιούτοις. Denniston rejects his suggestion, but for a misguided reason: 'γνώμη is surely the wrong word for "thought", "reflection" . . . γνώμη regularly means "decision", "intention".' On the contrary, the sense of γνώμη in Schaefer's conjecture ('mind', 'thoughts') is that which is found at Hi. 290 γνώμης ὁδόν ('path of your thought', Barrett; Denniston oddly quotes this line in illustration of the meaning 'decision', 'intention'), 510 ἦλθε δ' ἄρτι μοι γνώμης ἔσω. Let nobody prefer Denniston's rendering of Schaefer's conjecture as 'when my intention (of hospitality) is defeated'. IT 121 πεσεῖν ἄχρηστον θέσφατον, which he quotes, does not help such a rendering of πέσηι (the predicative adjective ἄχρηστον makes all the difference), and the implication (conveyed also by his own conjecture ἡνίκ' ἐκ γνώμης πέσω) that the Farmer was often surprised by visitors when his larder was bare does not seem at all apposite.

434 See *Illinois Class. Stud.* 2 (1977) 111–12.

453~465 See *Dionysiaca* 173.

479–86 See *Illinois Class. Stud.* 2 (1977) 112–15.

489–90 ὡς πρόσβασιν τῶνδ' ὀρθίαν οἴκων ἔχει
ῥυσῶι γέροντι τῶιδε προσβῆναι ποδί.

'One hesitates how to take the datives' (Denniston). Three ways have been suggested: (i) ῥυσῶι γέροντι τῶιδε ποδί together, 'huic rugoso et senili pedi' (so the old translators, followed by Wecklein; rejected with good reason by Denniston); (ii) ῥυσῶι with γέροντι and τῶιδε with ποδί, favoured by Denniston (' "for a withered old man to approach with this foot of mine" (probably a gouty foot)'); (iii) ῥυσῶι γέροντι τῶιδε together and ποδί by itself (so Seidler, Paley, Weil, Keene).

The last way is right. Euripides never combines τῶιδε with ποδί, but he combines ποδί (without epithet) with βαίνω or a compound at 1288 ἐμβαίνων ποδί, *Hec.* 1263 ἀμβήςηι ποδί, *Rh.* 214 ἐμβαίνω ποδί, and (if the text is sound) *Cycl.* 707 προϲβαίνων ποδί, and he combines ποδί (without epithet) with other verbs of motion at 219, *Su.* 90, *Ph.* 100, *Oeneus* 3 Page. See also V. Schmidt, *Maia* 27 (1975) 292–3 (on *Cycl.* 707). For τῶιδε applied by the speaker to himself compare 84 Ὀρέϲτην τόνδε, where Denniston gives parallels, to which add *Rh.* 646.

This, then, is the way in which Euripidean usage demands that the text should be interpreted. But Euripidean usage will equally be observed and the collocation of two independent expressions in the dative will be avoided if we write πόδα for ποδί. For the accusative with βαίνω and compounds see 94 βαίνω πόδα, 1173 βαίνουϲιν . . . πόδα, *Hcld.* 168 ἐμβήϲηι πόδα, 802 ἐκβὰϲ . . . πόδα, S. fr. 672 P ἐμβεβὼϲ πόδα, Ar. *Eccl.* 161–2 προβαίην τὸν πόδα / τὸν ἕτερον, Theogn. 283 πόδα . . . πρόβαινε. For πόδα used with other verbs of motion see Denniston on 94, and to his examples add *Med.* 729, *Ph.* 1537, *Or.* 1470, Choeril. fr. 2 (p. 719 Nauck, p. 68 Snell). At *Tr.* 455 ποῖ ποτ' ἐμβαίνειν με χρή; and *IT* 649 ὅτι ποτ' ἐμβάϲηι (Seidler: ἐπεμ- L) Elmsley proposed πόδ' for ποτ'. The change of πόδα to ποδί, after three datives have preceded, is the easiest change imaginable; an identical corruption, where no such explanation is available, is provided by 96 ἐκβάλω πόδα (Dobree: ποδί L), on which see *Illinois Class. Stud.* 2 (1977) 119. I have not seen E. Forberg, *Abhandlung über πόδα βαίνειν und ähnliche Strukturen im Griechischen* (1850).

Finally, note that προϲβῆναι does not mean 'approach', as Denniston and others translate, but rather 'climb', both here and in *Cycl.* 707: see J. I. Beare, *Hermathena* 13 (1905) 70–2.

498 See p. 50 (on *Herc.* 503).

504 See *Illinois Class. Stud.* 2 (1977) 115–16. Add H. *Od.* 3. 103 ἐπεί μ' ἔμνηϲαϲ ὀιζύοϲ, Men. *Sik.* 357–8 ἀνέμνηϲαϲ πάθουϲ / τὸν ἄθλιόν με, fr. 402 γέροντα δυϲτυχοῦντα τῶν θ' αὑτοῦ κακῶν / ἐπαγόμενον λήθην ἀνέμνηϲαϲ πάλιν κτλ.

568 See ibid. 116–17. Autopsy has now shown that the change of ει to η was made by the original scribe.

614–15 Ορ. ἥκω 'πὶ τόνδε ϲτέφανον· ἀλλὰ πῶϲ λαβῶ;
Πρ. τειχέων μὲν ἐλθὼν ἐντὸϲ οὐδ' ἂν εἰ θέλοιϲ.

For οὐδ' ἂν εἰ θέλοις 'many unattractive emendations have been proposed' (Denniston). Wecklein lists seventeen, and Denniston adds another. The score is completed by H. D. Broadhead, who proposed one emendation in *Miscellanea G. Galbiati* (1951) 1. 34, and another, without reference to the first, in *Tragica* 128–9. On the latter emendation it will be enough to remark that the presence of a bodyguard does not make a king invisible. The transmitted words have a traditional ring and should not be changed: see *Andr.* 595 οὐδ' ἂν εἰ βούλοιτό τις, *Hel.* 434 οὐδ' εἰ θέλοιεν, *Antiope* 5 Page (fr. xlviii. 5 Kambitsis) οὐδ' ἂν ἐκφύγοιμεν εἰ βουλοίμεθα.

651–2   See p. 110.

667   See p. 8.

671–2   See p. 22.

682–98   I offer four footnotes to Broadhead's treatment (*Tragica* 130–5), with which I largely agree.

(i) 685 πρὸς τάδ' (see Broadhead 131). These words generally stand at the head of an imperatival or quasi-imperatival clause ('in view of this', 'therefore': see 693, *Hi.* 304, *Andr.* 950, *Cret.* 35 Page [fr. 82. 35 Austin], A. *Pe.* 170, *ScT* 312, *Eum.* 545, S. *OT* 343; cf. Neil on Ar. *Equ.* 622). Sometimes they are used in interrogative clauses, with much the same meaning (274 [τάδ' Camper: τόδ' L; cf. *Rh.* 99, A. *Su.* 302], *Rh.* 99, S. *Ph.* 568), or with verbs of speaking ('in answer to this': *Hi.* 697, *Or.* 747, *IA* 1210, A. *Eum.* 436). A. *Pe.* 730, whose text and interpretation are open to doubt, is difficult to classify. None of these passages lends any support to the various interpretations which have been put upon the words πρὸς τάδ' at *El.* 685, where their misuse is an indication (not the only one) that the line is spurious.

(ii) The traditional division of 693 between two speakers is wrong. Such division after the third element of an iambic trimeter is found (with two exceptions) only in passages of excited dialogue, in which at least one other verse is divided (*Cycl.* 674,[1] *Herc.* 1418, *Ph.* 171, 1273, *Or.* 1598, 1607, 1611, 1617). The two instances in which

---

[1] I suggest ψεύδηι σύ for ὡς δὴ σύ. For other suggestions see *CQ* n.s. 21 (1971) 49–50, T. C. W. Stinton, *JHS* 97 (1977) 140.

division occurs in isolation are *Hi.* 310, where the speaker is interrupted, and *Hel.* 1514, where an excited question is asked.

For the expression ἄνδρα γίγνεσθαί σε χρή see Austin on Men. *Sam.* 63–4.

(iii) I see no sufficient reason to delete 690–2. Indeed, after Broadhead's transposition of 693, lines 692 and 694 are linked together in a manner which is thoroughly Euripidean: ταῦτα σοὶ (Weil: σοι L) λέγω· / ὑμεῖς δέ μοι, γυναῖκες, κτλ. Compare 1276 σοὶ μὲν τάδ᾽ εἶπον· τόνδε δ᾽ Αἰγίσθου νέκυν κτλ., *Su.* 1213 σοὶ μὲν τάδ᾽ εἶπον· παισὶ δ᾽ Ἀργείων λέγω, *Hel.* 1662 σοὶ μὲν τάδ᾽ αὐδῶ· συγγόνωι δ᾽ ἐμῆι λέγω, *Ph.* 568 σοὶ μὲν τάδ᾽ αὐδῶ· σοὶ δέ, Πολύνεικες, λέγω (I do not include *Ph.* 778: see M. W. Haslam, *CQ* n.s. 26 [1976] 7), *Antiope* 84 Page (fr. xlviii. 90 Kambitsis) Ζήθωι [τάδ᾽ εἶ]πον· δεύτερον δ᾽ Ἀμφίονα κτλ.

(iv) 693 was probably dislodged from its place after 684 because of its identical opening. Compare the loss of *Alc.* 276 (om. LP), 533–4 (om. Lac), *Su.* 974b (see p. 24) and *Hel.* 561.

784–5   νῦν μὲν παρ᾽ ἡμῖν χρὴ συνεστίους ἐμοὶ
               θοίνης γενέσθαι.

θοίνης Reiske: -ην L

'παρ᾽ ἡμῖν . . . συνεστίους ἐμοί. "In our company, as my guests." There is nothing suspicious about this' (Denniston). One might compare *Med.* 323 μενεῖς παρ᾽ ἡμῖν οὖσα δυσμενὴς ἐμοί. But how much neater is Musgrave's neglected ὁμοῦ for ἐμοί, which restores an idiomatic pleonasm, ὁμοῦ coupled with a συν-compound: see *Su.* 595, *Hel.* 104, fr. 419. 3, S. *Ai.* 1309, *Tr.* 545, 1237, Solon fr. 24 D (36 West) 16. At *IT* 765 ὁμοῦ has again been plausibly conjectured (by Badham) for ἐμοί and again (by Blaydes) at S. *Ph.* 892 συνναίειν ἐμοί (cf. 1032 ὁμοῦ Gγρ recte: ἐμοῦ codd. cett.). See also KG 2. 583 § 4, Bruhn, *Anhang* § 206, R. Renehan, *Studies in Greek Texts* (1976) 49.

862   See *PCPS* n.s. 17 (1969) 52–3.

864–5   ἀλλ᾽ ἐπάειδε
               καλλίνικον ὠιδὰν ἐμῶι χορῶι.

No editor before Keene seems to have remarked on the oddity of the compound ἐπάειδε. 'Apparently it is here only that ἐπαείδω means "to sing in accompaniment to", for in Hdt. 1, 132, quoted as a parallel by Liddell and Scott, the verb has its usual sense "to sing as an incantation".' Denniston adduces *IA* 1492 cυνεπαείδετε, 'which probably means "hymn together in accompaniment" (to our dance)', a very precarious suggestion. 'Perhaps here the force of ἐπι- is "in addition to", rather than strictly "as accompaniment to".' But ἐπάιδειν, which appears only once again in Euripides, at *IA* 1212, and ἐπωιδός and ἐπωιδή, which appear three times each, in every instance have the connotation of 'charm'. ' "Sing as accompaniment to" . . . is usually προcάιδειν.' No: it is usually ὑπάιδειν. And Blaydes's ὑπάειδε (*Adv. crit. in Eur.* [1901] 263) must be right. The verb is used of accompanying the dance at Ar. *Ran.* 366 κυκλίοιcι χοροῖcιν ὑπάιδων, Call. *h. Dian.* 240–3 ὠρχήcαντο . . . cτηcάμεναι χορὸν εὐρύν· ὑπήειcαν δὲ λίγειαι / λεπταλέον cύριγγεc, Luc. *de salt.* 30. ὑπ- and ἐπ- are often confused: to the references offered by Fraenkel on *Ag.* 69 (p. 42) add *Hi.* 1194, 1195, *Hcld.* 854, *Andr.* 906, *Hel.* 202, *Ba.* 778, A. *Pe.* 191, S. *Tr.* 931, and perhaps *Ion* 851.

894–5 See *Illinois Class. Stud.* 2 (1977) 117–18. For additions to the references in n. 14 (p. 118) see pp. 1–2 above.

962 See ibid. 119.

965–6 See p. 110.

978 See *PCPS* n.s. 20 (1974) 17 n. 1. See also P. T. Stevens, *Colloquial Expressions in Euripides* (1976) 30–1.

1013–17 See *Illinois Class. Stud.* 2 (1977) 119–21.

1045 See ibid. 121–2.

1059–60 See *PCPS* n.s. 15 (1969) 53–5.

1072–3   γυνὴ δ' ἀπόντος ἀνδρὸς ἥτις ἐκ δόμων
            ἐc κάλλοc ἀcκεῖ, διάγραφ' ὡc οὖcαν κακήν.

'A woman who, when her husband is away from home, adorns ⟨herself⟩ with a view to her beauty, write her off as wicked.'

According to Weil, 'La vulgate ἀπόντος ἀνδρὸc ἥτιc ἐκ δόμων offre un vicieux arrangement des mots', and Heimsoeth and Nauck devised four different arrangements without changing a letter. But the structure of γυνὴ δ᾽ . . . ἥτις . . . ἀϲκεῖ, διάγραφε (sc. αὐτήν) is precisely that of S. *OC* 1150–1 λόγος δ᾽ ὃς ἐμπέπτωκεν ἀρτίως ἐμοὶ / ϲτείχοντι δεῦρο, ϲυμβαλοῦ γνώμην (sc. περὶ αὐτοῦ). Similar examples are given by Jebb on S. *OT* 449 and KG 2. 413–14. For the postponement of ἥτις see *Cycl.* 128 οὐδεὶς μολὼν δεῦρ᾽ ὅϲτις οὐ κατεϲφάγη, and for the separation of cohering words by the word postponed see *Ion* 1307 τὴν ϲὴν ὅπου ϲοι μητέρ᾽ ἐϲτὶ νουθέτει. Note also *El.* 813 κἄϲφαξ᾽ ἐπ᾽ ὤμων μόϲχον ὡς ἦραν χεροῖν (i.e. ὡς ἐπ᾽ ὤμων ἦραν).

What really does appear to be vicious is the use of the verb ἀϲκεῖ in a reflexive sense. The active verb is used without an object in one sense only, 'to practise (gymnastics)', and that is not a sense which is suited to the toiletries of a Mycenaean queen. Wecklein's εὖ δέμας for ἐκ δόμων would remove the anomaly, but the corruption would be a harsh one. Perhaps a line has been lost after 1072 in which ἀϲκεῖ was given its object: e.g. ⟨δέμας χλιδαῖϲι πλουϲίοις τ᾽ ἐϲθήμαϲιν⟩ / ἐϲ κάλλος ἀϲκεῖ. Compare *Tr.* 1022–3 δέμας . . . ἀϲκήϲαϲα, *Ion* 326 ἤϲκηϲαι πέπλοις, S. *El.* 452 χλιδαῖϲ ἠϲκημένον.

1152   See *Illinois Class. Stud.* 2 (1977) 123. With the examples cited of the 'separation of noun and adjective in the vocative case' compare 796, *Hi.* 337, *Ph.* 158, S. *Ai.* 331.

1180   See ibid. 123–4.

1185   See *PCPS* n.s. 15 (1969) 55.

1233–5   ἀλλ᾽ οἵδε δόμων ὕπερ ἀκροτάτων
               φαίνουϲί τινες δαίμονες ἢ θεῶν
               τῶν οὐρανίων.

   1234 βαίνουϲι Hartung   τίνες Camper

'φαίνουϲι. "Shed radiance" ', Denniston, comparing 'for the absolute use' three passages from tragedy which by common agreement are corrupt. There is, in fact, a single place in tragedy where the verb may possibly have the required meaning, S. *El.* 1358–9 πῶς οὕτω πάλαι / ξυνών μ᾽ ἔληθες οὐδ᾽ ἔφαινες . . . ; which may be interpreted as picking up the apostrophe ὦ φίλτατον φῶς (1354). So Jebb interprets; but other interpretations, yielding a different meaning for the verb, are possible. Tragic epiphanies are not elsewhere said to be accompanied by 'radiance' (nothing should be built on the slight verbal similarity of *Ion* 1549–50 τίς οἴκων θυοδόκων ὑπερτελὴς / ἀντήλιον πρόσωπον ἐκφαίνει θεῶν;), and I doubt if an exception should be made even for the purveyors of St Elmo's Fire. Hartung's neglected[1] βαίνουσι is more natural; the recurrence of the verb at 1237 cannot be held against it (see pp. 1–2). For the confusion of β and φ see *Hel.* 673 φλέφαρον L, A. *Su.* 457 στρόβους M.

Camper's τίνες is accepted by Murray and Parmentier, and it was proposed as if new by Sandford *apud* Keene. Denniston describes it as 'more vivid than τινες: perhaps a shade too vivid for the rather formal context'. The choice between the two forms may be decided by a more objective criterion, that of word-order. ὅδε is joined with τίς and τις in these combinations: (i) τίς ὅδε, (ii) τις ὅδε, (iii) ὅδε τίς, (iv) ὅδε τις. I have investigated the occurrence of these four combinations in tragedy, Aristophanes, and Menander.

By far the commonest combination is (i) τίς ὅδε. I have found thirty-six instances in Euripides (*Cycl.* 113, 222, *Alc.* 106, *Hcld.* 658, *Hi.* 232, 369, *Hec.* 733, 740, *Su.* 104, 395, 600, *El.* 341, *Herc.* 548, 1132, 1191, *Tr.* 266, 269, 707, 1256 [Lenting], *IT* 1307 [Tournier], *Ion* 171, 223 [Musgrave], 757, *Hel.* 459, *Ph.* 915, *Or.* 333, 790, 1253, 1269 [discussed below], 1347, *Ba.* 578, 985, 1280, *IA* 6, *Rh.* 11, fr. 125[2]), eight in Aeschylus (*Pe.* 1021, *Su.* 460, *Ag.* 1101, 1114, 1162, 1407–9, *Ch.* 10, *Eum.* 209), fourteen in Sophocles (*El.* 328, 388, *OT* 2, *Ant.* 1172, *Tr.* 184, *Ph.* 201, 598, *OC* 209, 212, fr. 272 P, *Ichneutae* 118, 173, 176, 217), two (I have probably missed others) in Aristophanes (*Av.* 408, *Thes.* 1105), and one (a plausible supplement) in Menander (*Epitr.* 143 [17 Koerte]). Of (ii) τις ὅδε I know only four certain examples (*El.* 216, *IT* 267–8, *Hel.* 544–5, *Rh.* 536–7); the text of a fifth passage, fr. 74, is very doubtful.

The evidence for the combinations in which ὅδε comes first, as at *El.* 1233–4, is as follows. (iii) ὅδε τίς: *Herc.* 1181 οἱ παῖδες οἵδε τίνες ἐφ᾽ οἷς δακρυρροεῖς; (in view of the answer which this question receives, Wecklein's τίνος is probably right), *IA* 821–2 τήνδε τίνα λεύσσω ποτὲ /

---

[1] It was approved by Nauck, *De trag. graec. fr. obs. crit.* (1855) 8, although he believed that 1233 to the end were not written by Euripides.

[2] The text of this fragment reads ἔα· τίν᾽ ὄχθον τόνδ᾽ ὁρῶ περίρρυτον / ἀφρῶι θαλάσσης παρθένου τ᾽ εἰκώ τινα / ἐξ αὐτομόρφων λαΐνων τυκισμάτων (Jacobs: τειχισμάτων codd.), / σοφῆς ἄγαλμα χειρός; If the sentence is complete, we have in effect τίνα εἰκώ τινα ὁρῶ; an oddity from which Nauck's punctuation (question-mark after θαλάσσης) offers only an artificial evasion. I do not recommend that we read τίνα for τινα. I should prefer τινος.

γυναῖκα; Ar. *Ach.* 122 ὁδὶ δὲ τίc ποτ' ἐcτίν; *Vesp.* 858 ἡδὶ δὲ δὴ τίc
ἐcτιν; *Av.* 67 ὁδὶ δὲ δὴ τίc ἐcτιν ὄρνιc; *Thes.* 608 ἡδὶ δὲ δὴ τίc ἐcτιν
. . . ; conjectured at Men. *Epitr.* 576–7 (400–1 Koerte) ἀλλ' οὑτοcὶ
(ἀλλ' del. von Arnim, ἀλλ' ὁδὶ coni. Wilamowitz) / τίc ἐcθ' ὁ προcιών;
(iv) ὅδε τιc : *Alc.* 136 ἀλλ' ἥδ' ὀπαδῶν ἐκ δόμων τιc ἔρχεται, *Andr.*
879–80 καὶ μὴν ὅδ' ἀλλόχρωc τιc ἔκδημοc ξένοc . . . πορεύεται, 1228–30
δαίμων ὅδε τιc . . . ἐπιβαίνει, *El.* 107 τήνδε πρόcπολόν (Seidler : -πόλων
L) τινα, *Or.* 1269 ὅδε τιc ἐν τρίβωι †προcέρχεται† . . . τίc ὅδ' ἄρ' ἀμφὶ
μέλαθρον πολεῖ cὸν ἀγρόταc ἀνήρ; (some write ὅδε τίc at the beginning,
less plausibly), A. *Pe.* 263–4 ἢ μακροβίοτοc ὅδε γέ τιc αἰὼν ἐφάνθη,
S. *Tr.* 964 ξένων γὰρ ἐξόμιλοc ἥδε τιc βάcιc, *OC* 111 πορεύονται γὰρ
οἵδε δή τινεc, Ar. *Ach.* 1069–70 καὶ μὴν ὁδί τιc . . . ἐπείγεται, *Vesp.*
1415 ὁδί τιc ἕτεροc . . . ἔρχεται, *Av.* 1341 ὅδε τιc . . . προcέρχεται,
1414 ὅδ' αὖ μινυρίζων δεῦρό τιc προcέρχεται (note also Elmsley's
conjecture at *Lys.* 727).

There is a great disparity in numbers between the instances of
τίc ὅδε (sixty-one, of which fifty-eight are tragic) and the instances
of ὅδε τίc (at most seven, but five of these are comic, and I disbelieve
in one of the two tragic instances). We can therefore say that τίc
ὅδε is normal word-order, ὅδε τίc abnormal (in tragedy almost or
entirely non-existent). It is easy enough to see why the abnormal
order is sometimes favoured : it throws emphasis on the demonstrative
—'this person, who is he?' For this see G. Thomson, 'The Postponement of Interrogatives in Attic Drama', *CQ* 33 (1939) 147–52.
But if we look more closely at the seven instances of ὅδε τίc listed
above, we find that in each of them τίc follows immediately after
ὅδε or is separated from it only by particles; the verb is never placed
between ὅδε and τίc. This is a feature which the two instances quoted
from tragedy share with the five comic instances. It is a feature
which is not shared by *El.* 1233–5 as emended by Camper : ἀλλ'
οἵδε δόμων ὕπερ ἀκροτάτων / βαίνουcι τίνεc δαίμονεc . . . ; (Murray's
punctuation τίνεc—δαίμονεc . . . ; does not affect the issue). Let me
add here the few instances which I have found in tragedy of οὗτοc
τίc : *Ph.* 171 οὗτοc δ', ὦ γεραιέ, τίc κυρεῖ; S. *OT* 954 οὗτοc δὲ τίc ποτ'
ἐcτί . . . ; *Tr.* 242 αὗται δέ, πρὸc θεῶν, τοῦ ποτ' εἰcὶ καὶ τίνεc; *OC*
68 οὗτοc δὲ τίc λόγωι τε καὶ cθένει κρατεῖ; They show no significant
differences from the norm which I have postulated for ὅδε τίc. As
we should expect, much the commoner word-order is τίc οὗτοc :
Hec. 501, 763, *Hel.* 541, *Ph.* 119, 133, 145, 269, 418, *Or.* 1188, *IA*
1010, Men. *Mis.* 228.

By contrast, there is nothing abnormal about the transmitted οἵδε . . . τινεc. Since ὅδε τιc is found twelve times, τιc ὅδε four, we may say that οἵδε . . . τινεc represents the normal order. Further, ὅδε is sometimes separated from the following τιc by one or more words (see *Alc.* 136, *Andr.* 879, Ar. *Av.* 1414). Notice also that of the eleven instances of ὅδε τιc no fewer than nine describe (like *El.* 1233–5) the arrival of a character whose identity is unknown. And one of these instances shows a striking linguistic similarity: at *Andr.* 1228–30 a divine epiphany is announced with the words δαίμων ὅδε τιc . . . Φθίαc πεδίων ἐπιβαίνει. Similarly, but with the reverse order of words, *IT* 267–8 δαίμονέc τινεc / θάccουcιν οἵδε.

1250–1   οὐ γὰρ ἔcτι cοὶ πόλιν
τήνδ᾽ ἐμβατεύειν, μητέρα κτείναντα cήν.

κτείναντι Scaliger

Scaliger's conjecture is accepted by Murray and tacitly by Denniston. It is unnecessary; but it is not quite an accurate argument against it that 'κτείναντα is accusative in agreement with cε, understood as subject of the infinitive ἐμβατεύειν' (Keene, translating Weil). κτείναντα is clearly not a part of the infinitive construction but follows the infinitive in an independent capacity. This is different, then, from passages like *Med.* 1236–8 δέδοκται τοὖργον ὡc τάχιcτά μοι / παῖδαc κτανούcηι τῆcδ᾽ ἀφορμᾶcθαι χθονὸc / καὶ μὴ cχολὴν ἄγουcαν ἐκδοῦναι τέκνα and A. *PV* 216–18 κράτιcτα δή μοι . . . ἐφαίνετ᾽ εἶναι προcλαβόντα μητέρα . . . cυμπαραcτατεῖν; cf. *Med.* 659–61, 743–4, 886–8, *Tr.* 925–6, A. *Ch.* 1030–2 (Portus), *Eum.* 867–9, S. *El.* 959–62, *Ant.* 836–8, Fraenkel on *Ag.* 378–80. Better parallels for our passage are *Med.* 814–15 cοὶ δὲ cυγγνώμη λέγειν / τάδ᾽ ἐcτί, μὴ πάcχουcαν, ὡc ἐγώ, κακῶc, *Erectheus*, fr. 65. 95–7 Austin cοὶ . . . δίδωμι βωμοῖc τοῖc ἐμοῖcιν ἔμπυρα / πόλει προθύειν ἱερέαν κεκλημένην, A. *Ag.* 341–2 ἔρωc δὲ μή τιc πρότερον ἐμπίπτηι cτρατῶι / πορθεῖν ἃ μὴ χρή, κέρδεcιν νικωμένουc, 1610–11 οὕτω καλὸν δὴ καὶ τὸ κατθανεῖν ἐμοί, / ἰδόντα (-τι Tr) τοῦτον τῆc Δίκηc ἐν ἕρκεcιν, S. *Ai.* 1006–7 ποῖ γὰρ μολεῖν μοι δυνατόν, ἐc ποίουc βροτούc, / τοῖc cοῖc ἀρήξαντ᾽ ἐν πόνοιcι μηδαμοῦ; At *IT* 1343–4 πᾶcιν ἦν αὐτὸc λόγοc / cτείχειν ἵν᾽ ἦcαν, καίπερ οὐκ ἐωμένοιc Schaefer (*Mel. crit.* 99) proposed ἐωμένουc. And at *Alc.* 32–4 οὐκ ἤρκεcέ cοι μόρον Ἀδμήτου / διακωλῦcαι, Μοίραc δολίωι / cφήλαντι τέχνηι; Monk proposed cφήλαντα, which has the merit of eliminating a collocation of unrelated datives.

1272　See p. 112.

1319–20　　　θάρcει, Παλλάδοc ócίαν ἥξειc
　　　　　　　　　πόλιν· ἀλλ᾽ ἀνέχου.

The evidence for the sequence —ᴗᴗ ᴗᴗ— in the non-lyric anapaests of tragedy is discussed by Denniston and by Barrett, *Hippolytos* p. 404. In most of the instances the phenomenon is easily removed: A. *ScT* 827–8 δυcδαίμοναc ἀτέκνουc (spurious; see R. D. Dawe, *Dionysiaca* 88), 867–8 Ἐρινύοc ἰαχεῖν ('ἠχεῖν; in any case interpolated' Barrett; cf. Dawe, loc. cit.), *Eum.* 948 ἀκούετε πόλεωc (ἀκούειc Meineke; cf. Dawe, loc. cit.), fr. 91 N (315 M) ἐλάccονα ταχέωc (ἐλάccω Porson), E. *Tr.* 101 δαίμονοc ἀνέχου (ἄνcχου Nauck), 1252 ἐλπίδαc ἐπὶ coὶ (ἐν coὶ Porson). This leaves *Hec.* 145 ('interpolated' Barrett), *Ion* 226 ('perhaps lyric' Barrett; not prima facie lyric), *El.* 1319 (above), *El.* 1322–3 cύγγονε φίλτατε· / διὰ γὰρ ζευγνῦc᾽ ἡμᾶc πατρίων. For this last instance I have no remedy. But in this (unlike the other instances) there is a strong pause between dactyl and anapaest, a pause which may be further emphasized if we print cύγγονε φίλτατε independently as a monometer.

There is a further reason for doubting the text of *El.* 1319, besides the extreme rarity of —ᴗᴗ ᴗᴗ—. Sir Denys Page drew my attention to the rarity in tragic anapaests of a metron of the form —— —ᴗᴗ (θάρcει, Παλλάδοc). I have found only the following instances in Euripides' surviving anapaests (about 1500 metra). (i) *Andr.* 1228 δαίμων ὅδε τιc λευκὴν αἰθέρα: probably to be accepted (Klotz proposed λευκὸν ἐc αἰθέρα). (ii) *El.* 1353 ἐκλύοντεc μόχθων cώιζομεν: unemendable. (iii) *Tr.* 162 ναυcθλώcουcι πατρώιαc ἐκ γᾶc: so Biehl prints, violating the metron-diaeresis (read -cιν πατρίαc with Burges). (iv) *Tr.* 199 οὐκ Ἰδαίοιc ἱcτοῖc κερκίδα: unemendable. (v) *Ion* 866 φροῦδαι δ᾽ ἐλπίδεc, ἃc διαθέcθαι: unemendable. (vi) *IA* 122–3 εἰc ἄλλαc ὥραc γὰρ δὴ / παιδὸc δαίcομεν ὑμεναίουc. The position of γὰρ, as well as the rhythm, casts suspicion on the text. I should accept Herwerden's εἰc ἄλλαc γὰρ δὴ παιδὸc / δαίcομεν ὥραc ὑμεναίουc (cf. L. P. E. Parker, *CQ* n.s. 8 [1958] 84, Dale, *Lyric Metres* 50 n. 1, D. Bain, *CQ* n.s. 27 [1977] 22 n. 62), but even so I do not believe that these anapaests were written by Euripides. (vii) *IA* 161 θνητῶν δ᾽ ὄλβιοc ἐc τέλοc οὐδείc: again from anapaests which I do not believe to be Euripidean (cf. Bain, loc. cit. 23); (viii) *IA* 598 cτῶμεν, Χαλκίδοc ἔκγονα θρέμματα: certainly spurious (see Page, *Actors' Interpolations*

160–1). I have noticed three instances which have been introduced by emendation: at *Alc.* 81 there are better emendations available than Murray's (see Dale ad loc.); I do not know what is the truth at *Hec.* 174; and at *Or.* 1484 there is more than one reason why Biehl's text is unacceptable (cf. *CR* n.s. 28 [1978] 138). In Aeschylus I have noticed only *Eum.* 993 and two instances in the spurious part of *ScT*: 827 (quoted above) and 1068. In Sophocles I have noticed five instances: *Ant.* 129 πολλῶι ῥεύματι (ῥεύματι πολλῶι Blaydes), *Tr.* 1275 λείπου μηδὲ cύ (removable by a similar transposition), *Ph.* 1463 (not prima facie suspicious, though the text has been altered), *OC* 146 δηλῶ δ'· οὐ γὰρ ἂν ὧδ' ἀλλοτρίοιc (ἂν om. LZnZo: οὐ τἂν Nauck), 1773 δράcω καὶ τάδε καὶ πάνθ' ὁπόc' (Porson: ὅc' codd.) ἄν (perhaps it is idle to suggest καὶ τάδε δράcω).

Transposition will eliminate the incidence of —∪∪ ∪∪—. Monk proposed ἥξειc ὁcίαν, Weil ὁcίαν, θάρcει, Παλλάδοc ἥξειc. Since Weil's transposition also eliminates — — —∪∪ it is to be preferred. The cause of corruption was the parenthetical placing of θάρcει: see pp. 115–16. For neglect of synapheia at change of speakers between 1319 and 1320 see 1333, Page on *Med.* 1396, and pp. 95–7 below.

1329–30   ἔνι γὰρ κἀμοὶ τοῖc τ' οὐρανίδαιc
              οἶκτοι θνητῶν πολυμόχθων.

Tragic usage offers two reasons why οἶκτοι should be changed to οἶκτοc. First, whenever a part of the verb εἶναι is to be supplied with ἔνι (and that is the only circumstance in which ἔνι is used), ἔνι stands for ἔνεcτι, never for ἔνειcι.[1] Second, οἶκτοι means '(expressions of) lamentation'; the meaning 'pity', which we require here, is given by the singular οἶκτοc.[2] Note above all *El.* 294–5 ἔνεcτι δ' οἶκτοc ἀμαθίαι μὲν οὐδαμοῦ, / cοφοῖcι δ' ἀνδρῶν and *Or.* 702 ἔνεcτι δ' οἶκτοc, ἔνι δὲ καὶ θυμὸc μέγαc.

Emendations which fail to observe the former rule have been made at *Hcld.* 893 (Canter, Hermann, and others), *Andr.* 471 (Lenting; cf. Collard on *Su.* 282, T. C. W. Stinton, *JHS* 97 [1977] 142), *Ion* 477 (Murray), 1427 (Grégoire), *IT* 1109 (Triclinius).

[1] On the question of accentuation (ἔνι or ἐνί) see Denniston and Page on A. *Ag.* 78.   [2] See also p. 83.

III. HERACLES

63–7 See *PCPS* n.s. 20 (1974) 3–4.

93–7 See ibid. 4–6. To the illustrations of ἂν γένοιτ' ἄν on p. 6 add S. fr. 683. 1 P and Ar. *Av.* 829, and perhaps S. *Ph.* 116 θηρατέ' ἄν (Elmsley: -τέ' οὖν T: -τέα γοῦν Zo: -τέα rell.) γίγνοιτ' ἄν.

117–18 . . . ἃ τὸν Ἄιδα δόμοις
 πόςιν ἀναςτενάζεις.

Although the cretic scansion of Ἄιδα is unobjectionable (see p. 21) the expression τὸν Ἄιδα δόμοις πόςιν for 'the husband in Hades' is incredible. *Ba.* 68–9 τίς ὁδῶι; τίς μελάθροις; cited by Wilamowitz (on the punctuation of the passage see *CR* n.s. 17 [1967] 261–2, and *Phaethon*, p. 118 n. 2) is no adequate support for the dative. Closer in phraseology would be such passages as S. *OT* 900 τὸν Ἀβαῖςι ναόν, E. *Held.* 360–1 ὅ τ' Ἄργει Σθενέλου τύραννος, *Hi.* 545–6 τὰν μὲν Οἰχαλίαι πῶλον, *IT* 156 τῶν Ἄργει μόχθων, Ar. *Lys.* 1299 τὸν Ἀμύκλαις ςιόν (see also KG 1. 441–2), but in all of these the dative is the name of a place. Hermann's τὸν ⟨ἐν⟩ Ἄιδα δόμοις is inescapable: cf. *Tr.* 588–9 τὸν παρ' Ἄιδαι παῖδ' ἐμόν.

138–9 See *ZPE* 24 (1977) 291–4.

220–1 ὃς εἰς Μινύαιςι πᾶςι διὰ μάχης μολὼν
 Θήβαις ἔθηκεν ὄμμ' ἐλεύθερον βλέπειν.

220 Μινύαις ὃς εἰς ἅπαςι Elmsley (*CJ* 8 [1813] 208)   221 Θήβας Heiland

There are two reasons why it is desirable to accept Elmsley's conjecture (earlier, in *Ed. Rev.* 19 [1811] 70, he had proposed the less attractive Μινύαιςιν εἰς ὃς πᾶςι). First, and most important, Euripides admits an anapaest into the second foot of the iambic trimeter only in the case of proper names which cannot be accommodated in the verse without metrical licence: Ἐριχθόνιος *Ion* 21, 268, 1429, Ἑρμιόνη *Or.* 1314, Ἰφιγένεια *IT* 771, *IA* 416, Νεοπτόλεμος *Or.* 1655,

Παρθενοπαῖος *Su.* 889. See also Descroix, *Le trimètre ïambique* 198–9.[1]
An apparent exception is Σαλαμίς at *Hel.* 88, but I believe the passage
86–9 to be interpolated. Here briefly are my reasons. (i) repetitiveness :
86 ἀτὰρ τίς εἶ πόθεν; and 89 τούςδ' ἐπιστρέφηι γύας repeat 83 τίς δ'
εἶ; πόθεν γῆς τῆςδ' ἐπεστράφης πέδον; and 87–8 ὁ δὲ φύςας πατὴρ /
Τελαμών anticipates 92 Τελαμὼν ὁ φύςας; (ii) 86 is unmetrical and
no emendation yet proposed is convincing (Jackson's, accepted by
Kannicht, is rightly impugned by Dale). When 86–9 are removed
Teucer's remarks in 84 and 90 cohere perfectly, and they reply to the
two parts of Helen's question in 83. Others have proposed different
deletions : 85–8 Badham, 83–8 Schenkl, 84–6 Page (*Actors' Interpolations* 79). But 84–5 are faultless in diction and sense, and if genuine
they guarantee 83. Dale deletes 86–8 and marks a lacuna before 89,
in which the name of Teucer was mentioned. This does not relieve
us of the repetition in 89, and nobody, hearing 'Telamon is my father'
(92), needs to be told the speaker's name.

Second, Elmsley's conjecture has the merit of bringing together
εἰς ἅπαςι, a favourite collocation, found again at 1139 μιᾶς ἅπαντα
and 1391 ἅπαντας δ' ἑνὶ λόγωι. Numerous examples of this collocation
are listed by Lesky, *Gesammelte Schriften* (1966) 151 n. 15. For the
juxtaposition of antithetical words in general see Fraenkel on *Ag.*
1455. The corruption was caused by the postponed relative, as at
Su. 495 ὕβρις οὓς (Scaliger :[2] οὓς ὕβρις L) ἀπώλεσεν, *Ph.* 1548 παρα-
βάκτροις ἅ (ἃ παρὰ βάκτροις MAV, ἡ π- β- L), and possibly *IT* 158
μόνον ὅς (Murray : ὃς τὸν μόνον L) με.

In 221 Heiland's Θήβας should be accepted. The regular construction is τίθημί τινα (not τινι) ποιεῖν τι. For a list of examples see
Housman, *CR* 2 (1888) 243 = *Classical Papers* 25. It is surprising that
Housman did not independently light upon Heiland's conjecture
(it was published in his *Beitr. zur Textkr. des Eur.* [1887]), instead of
offering an unnatural explanation of the construction with Θήβαις.
On the expression ὄμμ' ἐλεύθερον βλέπειν I have spoken already : see
p. 13.

359–63 See *PCPS* n.s. 20 (1974) 6–8. To the examples listed on p. 7
to illustrate 'the attachment of two epithets to the governing noun
and the denial of an epithet to the noun which is governed' add

---

[1] I disregard *Cycl.*, where the licence is not confined to proper names (see Descroix 200).
[2] Not Barnes : see C. Collard, *CQ* n.s. 24 (1974) 246.

Tr. 1–2 Αἰγαῖον ἁλμυρὸν (-οῦ Burges) βάθος / πόντου, *Hel.* 1362–3 ῥόμβου (Heath: -ω L) θ᾽ εἱλισσομένα (-ου Wecklein) / κύκλιος ἔνοσις αἰθερία, S. *Ai.* 1218–19 ὑλᾶεν . . . πόντου (πόντωι Morstadt) πρόβλημ᾽ ἁλίκλυστον. The converse distribution of epithets is offered at *Hi.* 128–9 θερμᾶς . . . ἐπὶ νῶτα πέτρας / εὐαλίου, and S. *Ai.* 135–6 τῆς ἀμφιρύτου / Σαλαμῖνος ἔχων βάθρον ἀγχιάλου, where H has ἀγχίαλον, already conjectured by Bothe ('contra omnes artis criticae regulas', according to Elmsley on *Hcld.* 750); see Dawe, *Studies* i. 131. Similarly S. fr. 202 P πατρώιας γῆς ἀγνιαίου (-αῖον Meineke) πέδον.

380–4   τεθρίππων τ᾽ ἐπέβα
καὶ ψαλίοις ἐδάμασσε πώ-
λους Διομήδεος, αἳ φονίαισι φάτ-
ναις ἀχάλιν᾽ ἐθόαζον
κάθαιμα γένυσι σῖτα.

381 ἐδάμασσε Musgrave: -ασε L   384 γένυσι σῖτα Diggle: σῖτα γένυσι L

Lines 380–1 correspond with 394–5 ὑμνωιδούς τε κόρας / ἤλυθεν ἑσπέριόν ⟨τ᾽⟩ ἐς αὐ/λάν, and I have preferred to mend the syntax in 394–5 by adopting Fix's ⟨τ᾽⟩, which entails the negligible change of ἐδάμασε to ἐδάμασσε in the strophe, rather than adopt Nauck's rougher change of ὑμνωιδούς τε κόρας to ὑμνωιδῶν τε κορᾶν. The epic form ἐδάμασσε (as well as the ease of corruption) may be illustrated by *Alc.* 230 πελάσσαι (Erfurdt: -άσαι codd.), *Med.* 836 ἀφυσσαμέναν -υσαμέναν AL), *IA* 1051 ἄφυσσε, S. *Ai.* 390 ὀλέσσας (T: -έσας codd.), *Ph.* 1163 πέλασσον (-ασον pars codd.) and perhaps A. *Pe.* 289 εὔνιδας ἔκτισσαν (Boeckh: ἔκτισαν εὔνιδας codd.). At *Alc.* 397 Barnes's ὠρφάνισσε (-ισε codd.) is probably wrong; at *El.* 863 Triclinius' τελέσσας (-έσας L) is quite uncertain. See also KB 1. 270 Anmerk. 1; and for epic -σσ- in dative endings see *PCPS* n.s. 20 (1974) 22 n. 2 and p. 2 above.

In 384 κάθαιμα σῖτα γένυσι (~ 398 δράκοντα πυρσόνωτον) gives a catalectic iambic dimeter of the shape ⏑–⏑– | ⏑⏓⏑. A resolved penultimate syllable in the second metron of a catalectic iambic dimeter is a phenomenon for which tragedy provides no parallel. The simple transposition κάθαιμα γένυσι σῖτα gives ×–⏑⏓ | ⏑–⏑, which is found at 111 -δὸς ὥστε πολιὸς ὄρνις, 793 ἐμὰν πόλιν, ἐμὰ τείχη, *Tr.* 567 Φρυγῶν δὲ πατρίδι πένθος, 1084 σὺ μὲν φθίμενος ἀλαίνεις ~ 1101 μέσον πέλαγος ἰούσας, *Hel.* 1136 εἴδωλον ἱερὸν "Ηρας. 'The displacement of an adjective so that it may occupy a position next to its noun, or of a noun so that it may stand next to its adjective, is a common error, and illustration exists in abundance' (*GRBS* 14 [1973] 251–2, with references; see also *Dionysiaca* 173–4).

503 ϲμικρὰ Bothe : μικρὰ L. The evidence of the manuscripts suggests that ϲμικρόϲ should be restored in all places where metre admits either form. I have given the evidence in *Gnomon* 47 (1975) 289–90. (On p. 290 line 8 for 'thirteen' read 'fourteen' and add *El.* 407 to the list which follows.) Di Benedetto on *Or.* 462 comes to the opposite conclusion. His statement that ϲμικρόϲ is never required by the metre is, as I have shown, false.

556–7 Ηρ. κοὐκ ἔϲχεν αἰδῶ τὸν γέροντ᾽ ἀτιμάϲαι;
        Αμ. αἰδώϲ γ᾽ ἀποικεῖ τῆϲδε τῆϲ θεοῦ πρόϲω.

'Did he (Lycus) feel no shame at dishonouring the old man?' 'Shame lives far from this goddess.'

It is beyond reasonable doubt that the 'goddess' is 'Shame' (cf. *Ion* 336–7) and that the subject of ἀποικεῖ is therefore Lycus.[1] Scaliger proposed αἰδῶ γ᾽; Denniston (*GP* 130) is prepared to tolerate the γ᾽. The passages which I shall quote in a moment will show that there is no place for it here. Badham (*Philologus* 7 [1852] 165 and in the preface to his edition of *Ion* [1853] vii) proposed αἰδώϲ; It was left to Pearson (*CR* 38 [1924] 13) to perfect this conjecture by changing αἰδῶ in 556 to αἰδώϲ.

To illustrate the repetition of a single word in an indignant or incredulous question Badham had quoted only *Hel.* 460–1 Πρωτεὺϲ τάδ᾽ οἰκεῖ δώματ᾽, Αἴγυπτοϲ δὲ γῆ : : Αἴγυπτοϲ; He did not realize, as Pearson did, that the repeated word must have the same case as that in which the word was first used. Pearson added two further examples: S. *Ai.* 1126–7 δίκαια γὰρ τόνδ᾽ εὐτυχεῖν κτείναντά με; : : κτείναντα; *Tr.* 428–9 δάμαρτ᾽ ἔφαϲκεϲ Ἡρακλεῖ ταύτην ἄγειν; : : ἐγὼ δάμαρτα; The same, in essence, is *Hel.* 674–5 ἁ Διόϲ μ᾽ ἄλοχοϲ ὤλεϲεν : : Ἥρα; See also Pl. *Rep.* 328 A, Men. *Dysk.* 472–3, 819, *Epitr.* 1112–13 (754–5 Koerte), *Perinth.* 12–13. The idiom takes other forms too. Often an indignant ποῖοϲ is added: *Hel.* 566–7 ὦ χρόνιοϲ ἐλθὼν ϲῆϲ δάμαρτοϲ ἐϲ χέραϲ : : ποίαϲ δάμαρτοϲ; S. *Tr.* 425–6 ταὐτὸ δ᾽ οὐχὶ γίγνεται / δόκηϲιν εἰπεῖν κἀξακριβῶϲαι λόγον : : ποίαν δόκηϲιν; Men. *Sam.* 468, 513. Examples of this idiom with

---

[1] I have no sympathy with Parmentier, *RPh* 44 (1920) 146.

LINES 380–557 51

ποῖος are collected from the comic poets by Vahlen, *Opusc. acad.*
2 (1908) 437–9. See also P. T. Stevens, *Colloquial Expressions in
Euripides* (1976) 38–9. A verb may be used in the same way: *Ion*
951–2 τέθνηκεν, ὦ γεραιέ, θηρςὶν ἐκτεθείς : : τέθνηκ'; *IT* 548–9,
Men. *Asp.* 273–4, 310, 317–18, 501–2, *Dysk.* 503, *Sam.* 306–7 (91–2
Koerte), *fab. inc.* (i p. 90 Koerte, p. 299 Sandbach) 61–2, com.
anon., Page *GLP* 65. 54–5. The interrogative τί commonly precedes
the repeated word, whether that word is noun, verb, or any other
part of speech: *Alc.* 806–7 δόμων γὰρ ζῶςι τῶνδε δεςπόται : : τί
ζῶςιν; *Ph.* 1725–6 δεινὰ δείν' ἐγὼ τλάς : : τί τλάς; τί τλάς; *Ba.*
1181–2 τὰ Κάδμου : : τί Κάδμου; *IA* 460 τὴν δ' αὖ τάλαιναν παρθένον
. . . τί παρθένον; fr. 300 οἴμοι· τί δ' οἴμοι; A. *Ch.* 766–7 πῶς οὖν
κελεύει νιν μολεῖν ἐςταλμένον; : : τί (Canter: ἦ M) πῶς; Men. *Dis
Ex.* 55–6, *Dysk.* 320–1, *Georg.* 28, *Her.* 44–5, *Sam.* 320–1 (105–6 Koerte),
374 (159 K), fr. 11 Demiańczuk, Ar. *Ran.* 649, Diph. fr. 96 Kock.
The word-order is reversed at Men. *Dysk.* 215 κατὰ τρόπον. : : κατὰ
τρόπον τί; See also Stevens, op. cit. 40. In every one of these passages
the repeated word has exactly the same form which it had when it
was first used.

The passages which I have quoted may throw new light on four
further ones. (i) A. *PV* 971–3 χλιδᾶν ἔοικας τοῖς παροῦςι πράγμαςιν : :
χλιδῶ; χλιδῶντας ὧδε τοὺς ἐμοὺς ἐγὼ / ἐχθροὺς ἴδοιμι. We should have
expected not χλιδῶ; but χλιδᾶν; and I do not think it idle to propose
this as a conjecture. The repeated verb is infinitive at Men. *Asp.*
310 and *Sam.* 306–7 (both listed above). (ii) *Ion* 285–6 τιμᾶι ςφε
†Πύθιος† ἀςτραπαί τε Πύθιαι : : †τιμᾶ τιμᾶ†· ὡς μήποτ' ὤφελόν ςφ'
(Scaliger: ς' L) ἰδεῖν. Line 286 remains unhealed; all that we can
safely say is that τιμᾶι; would make a very suitable beginning, and
that Hermann's duplication τιμᾶι; τί τιμᾶι; (which Stevens, loc. cit.,
appears to approve) lacks analogy. (iii) *Ion* 958–9 καὶ πῶς ἐν ἄντρωι
παῖδα cὸν λιπεῖν ἔτλης; : : πῶς δ' οἰκτρὰ πολλὰ στόματος ἐκβαλοῦς'
ἔπη; In place of πῶς δ' we must write πῶς; (Matthiae) and not
πῶς δ'; which Denniston commends (*GP* 176; cf. also *CR* 43 [1929]
119). Wilamowitz (*Anal. Eur.* 25 and in the apparatus of his edition)
claims that L wrote a mark of deletion under the δ'. He is followed
by Murray; and they both make the same claim again about the
γ' at *Ion* 1591. Their supposed mark of deletion is a mark of punctuation, as Wecklein's collator, Prinz, realized. Inspection of 1614 in the
manuscript will dispel all doubt. (iv) Men. *Sam.* 587–8 (242–3
Koerte) ἀλλὰ περιπάτηςον ἐνθαδὶ / μικρὰ μετ' ἐμοῦ : : περιπατήςω;

I suggest περιπάτηcον; The repeated verb is imperative at *Dysk.*
503 and com. anon., Page *GLP* 65. 54–5 (both listed above).

581 See p. 112 n. 2.

687–90   παιᾶνα μὲν Δηλιάδες
                        ὑμνοῦς' ἀμφὶ πύλας
                        τὸν Λατοῦς εὔπαιδα γόνον
                        εἰλίccουcαι καλλίχοροι.[1]

The choriambic dimeters 687 and 689 each offer *breuis in longo*
without pause (Δηλιάδεϲ and γόνον). This is a phenomenon for which
Euripides affords no secure parallel, although there are four passages
in *Helen* which might be quoted in its support. (i) *Hel.* 1314 ἀελλόποδεϲ
~ 1332 βίοϲ. The earlier parts of the line, before the choriamb, do not
correspond. There is corruption here. Maas's solution, approved by
both Dale and Kannicht, eliminates this alleged instance. (ii) 1341
βᾶτε, cεμναὶ Χάριτεϲ, | ἴτε κτλ. The corresponding line in the anti-
strophe is 1357 οὐ cεβίζουcα θεᾶϲ. | μέγα κτλ. The full stop in the
antistrophe suggests that we have period-end here, and this will
justify the *brevis in longo* in the strophe. (iii) *Hel.* 1479 Λίβυεϲ: this
should be replaced by Λιβύαϲ (conjectured by Murray, but before
him by Wilamowitz, *Sitzb. Ak. Wiss. Berlin* 38 [1902] 875 = *Verskunst*
221). It is accepted by Kannicht, whose version of the remainder of
the line is preferable to Murray's and Wilamowitz's. (iv) 1480–1
οἰωνοὶ cτολάδεϲ | ὄμβρον λιποῦcαι χειμέριον. This appears to be in-
escapable. But in the antistrophe line 1497 παῖδεϲ Τυνδαρίδαι, which
corresponds with 1480, forms a self-contained unit and is followed
by pause (a relative clause follows; Murray's punctuation is astray).
And so we may justify the *breuis in longo* by the assumption that we
have period-end here. A further possible instance is *El.* 209 δωμά-
των πατρίων φυγὰϲ | οὐρείαϲ κτλ.; but this may be avoided by the
simple transposition δωμάτων φυγὰϲ πατρίων (Seidler), which I have
advocated in *Dionysiaca* 174.

The strophic lines to which 687–90 correspond are

                    οὐ παύcομαι τὰϲ Χάριταϲ
                    Μούcαιϲ cυγκαταμει-
                    γνύϲ, ἡδίcταν cυζυγίαν.   675
                    μὴ ζώιην μετ' ἀμουcίαϲ . . .

---
[1] καλλίχοροι Hermann: -ον L

Corresponding with γόνον in line 689 of the antistrophe is a heavy
pause at sentence-end in the strophe (675). Does this justify our
saying (as in *Hel.* 1341 ~ 1357) that we have period-end? It may
be objected that there can be no pause between γόνον and its governing verb εἱλίccουcαι. But the assumption of many editors (and of
LSJ *s.u.* ἑλίccω) that γόνον depends for its construction on εἱλίccουcαι
(like *IA* 1480–1 ἑλίccετ᾽ ἀμφὶ ναὸν . . . Ἄρτεμιν) is less than the whole
truth. As Wilamowitz says, 'Ob der Akkusativ τὸν Λατοῦc γόνον
zunächst mit παιᾶνα ὑμνοῦcι oder mit εἱλίccουcαι zu verbinden sei,
zwischen welchen Worten er steht, ist nicht zu sagen, da er mit beiden
verbunden werden kann.' He compares *IA* 1467–8 ἐπευφημήcατε . . .
παιᾶνα . . . Διὸc κόρην (I discuss this construction below, p. 58).
It would be possible to argue that εἱλίccουcαι is to be taken as intransitive ('dancing'). Such a use is attested at *Ph.* 235–6 εἱλίccων
ἀθανάταc (Σ: -ον codd.) θεοῦ | χορὸc γενοίμαν, although the verb can
be made transitive by emendation (ἀθανάτουc Wecklein, approved by
Pearson). The verb is used intransitively at *Or.* 1294 ('sc. βλέφαρον'
says Biehl, Teubner ed., absurdly), but not with the meaning 'dance'.
But it is better not to postulate an intransitive use in our passage,
since γόνον, even if it receives its construction in the first place from
ὑμνοῦcι, is still available to be understood as the object of εἱλίccουcαι.
It seems fair to say that, since γόνον is not primarily governed by
εἱλίccουcαι, the line εἱλίccουcαι καλλίχοροι may be taken as an independent unit, preceded by pause. This pause and the corresponding full-stop in the strophe justify the assumption of period-end, and
emendation is unnecessary. Note also that γόνον is supported against
any change which might be suggested by the almost identical expression at *IT* 1234 εὔπαιc ὁ Λατοῦc γόνοc.

But I believe emendation to be necessary in 688. T. C. W. Stinton
(*CQ* n.s. 27 [1977] 59) has suggested Δηλιάδεc ⟨γ᾽⟩, where the particle
is otiose. I suggest that we write ⟨ναῶν⟩ ὑμνοῦc᾽ ἀμφὶ πύλαc. In the
corresponding strophic line (674) we can gain the extra syllables
needed by reverting to what is in fact the best attested reading.
Editors print Μούcαιc, which is merely a conjecture by Tr² designed
to give the line the same length as the line to which it responds.
Dio offers the same reading (32. 100), but he is not a reliable witness,
since he also offers μὴ παυcαίμην for οὐ παύcομαι and ἀναμιγνύc for
cυγκαταμειγνύc. What is offered by L and by four other witnesses
(Plut. *mor.* 243 A, Stob. 2. 4. 6, Σ Hes. *Th.* 64, Agath. *hist.* 3. 1) is
ταῖc Μούcαιc. And so I suggest ταῖc Μούcαιc⟨ιν⟩ or ταῖc⟨ιν⟩ Μούcαιc.

It is greatly to the benefit of the sense that the location of the πύλαι should be specified by the addition of ναῶν. For the linking of these two words compare *Ion* 79 πρὸ ναοῦ . . . πυλώματα, *IT* 1227 ναῶν πυλωρός. The word ναός is used in similar contexts at *Ion* 495–8 χοροὺς cτείβουcι . . . πρὸ Παλλάδοc ναῶν and *IA* 1480–1 ἑλίccετ' ἀμφὶ ναὸν . . . Ἄρτεμιν.

738 See *PCPS* n.s. 20 (1974) 8. Similarly A. *Ch.* 160 ἴτω Bothe: ἰὼ M, E. *Phaethon* 101 ιτω C: ιω P.

807 See ibid. 8–9.

875–9 See ibid. 9–13; to the list of pairs of verbs in asyndeton (p. 10) add *Hel.* 371 ἐκελάδηcεν ἀνοτότυξεν (Wilamowitz: κελάδηcε κἀνοτό-τυξεν L; see Kannicht ad loc. and p. 65 below). Of the 'two instances' of dochmiacs with two shorts for initial anceps which had so far defied emendation (p. 11) I have now emended one: see *Illinois Class. Stud.* 2 (1977) 123. To the parallels quoted (p. 11) for μανιάcιν λύccαιc add *IA* 547 μανιάδων (Wecklein: μαινόμεν' L) οὔcτρων and perhaps Ar. *Thes.* 680 μανιάcιν . . . λύccαιc (Meineke: μανίαιc . . . λύccῃι R). For the 'active sense' of φόβοc (p. 12) note also *Rh.* 308, and A. *PV* 355 cυρίζων φόβον (φόνον pars codd.), which also provides a parallel for the corruption postulated at *Herc.* 1218 (p. 12 n. 5). Other parallels are *IT* 1037 (see p. 88), A. *ScT* 45 and 132 (cf. R. D. Dawe, *The Collation and Investigation of Manuscripts of Aeschylus* [1964] 249 and 253); note also *Andr.* 962 φόβωι codd.: φ]θονω P. Oxy. 2335: φόνωι Lenting (cf. Dawe, op. cit. 142 n.), and *Ion* 601.

1016–24 See ibid. 13–16.

1060–3 Aμ. cῖγα, πνοὰc μάθω· φέρε, πρὸc οὖc βάλω.
     Xo. εὕδει; Aμ. ναί, εὕδει ὕπνον ὕπνον ὀλόμενον,
          ὃc ἔκανεν ἄλοχον, ἔκανε δὲ τέκεα
          τοξήρει ψαλμῶι τοξεύcαc.

If we do not omit the second ὕπνον as an error of dittography, as editors used to do (without thereby amending the metre), then Dobree's ὕπνον ⟨ἄ⟩υπνον, an expression which also appears at S. *Ph.* 848, is the likeliest change.[1] Dobree's conjecture is generally

---

[1] There is no likelihood whatever in Hermann's ὕπνοι τ' ἄυπνοι for ὕπνοι τ' ἐκεῖνοι at *Tr.* 1118: see Jackson, *Marg. scaen.* 87, and *Dionysiaca* 162.

accepted; but the metre of the passage remains faulty. Although ὕπνον ⟨ἄ⟩υπνον ὀλόμενον, ὃς ἔκανεν ἄλοχον gives two fully resolved dochmiacs, there are faults on either side of this verse. First the hiatus εὕδει ὕπνον is intolerable: see N. C. Conomis, *Hermes* 92 (1964) 42–3.[1] Second, the words ἔκανε δὲ . . . τοξεύσας have no metre. Wilamowitz in his first edition (1889) printed without argument ἔκανε ⟨μὲ⟩ν, to produce four dochmiacs ὕπνον ⟨ἄ⟩υπνον ὀλόμενον, ὃς ἔκανε ⟨μὲ⟩ν ἄλο/χον, ἔκανε δὲ τέκεα τοξήρει ψαλμῶι, deleting τοξεύσας with Madvig (*Adv. crit.* 1 [1871] 248). The simplicity of this is attractive; but I believe that ἔκανε μὲν ἄλοχον, ἔκανε δὲ τέκεα is foreign to the style of tragic lyrics, as I must attempt to show.

According to Denniston (*GP* 163), 'In Anaphora, when δέ is in the second limb, μέν is usually in the first (see p. 370). But there are numerous exceptions to this principle in serious poetry.' This is misleading. I have found the following instances in tragedy of μέν and δέ linking verbs in anaphora: *Cycl.* 363–4, *Hcld.* 491, *Hi.* 453–4, 473–4, *Ph.* 521, *Rh.* 906–7, fr. 898. 7–9, A. *Pe.* 694–5, 700–1, *Ag.* 508, *Ch.* 935–7, S. *Ai.* 506–7, *OT* 25–6, 259–60, *Ant.* 200–1, *OC* 279–80, 610. (I do not include passages where μέν and δέ introduce a pair of contrasted clauses, as *Hcld.* 494 λέγει μὲν οὐ σαφῶς, λέγει δέ πως, *Hi.* 1091.) Of these seventeen passages twelve are in spoken iambics. Of the five lyric passages four have a striking feature in common. These four are: *Cycl.* 363–4 χαιρέτω μὲν αὖλις ἅδε, / χαιρέτω δὲ θυμάτων, *Rh.* 906–7 ὄλοιτο μὲν Οἰνείδας, / ὄλοιτο δὲ Λαρτιάδας, A. *Pe.* 694–5 σέβομαι μὲν προσιδέσθαι, / σέβομαι δ' ἀντία λέξαι, 700–1 δίομαι μὲν χαρίσασθαι, / δίομαι δ' ἀντία φάσθαι. In these four passages the formal balance between the two clauses is emphasized not only by μὲν . . . δέ but also by the use of an identical rhythm in both lines (and in three of the passages the balance is fortified by concluding rhyme; for isometric rhyming cola see *CR* n.s. 18 [1968] 3–4 and *Phaeth.* 99 n.). The fifth passage is A. *Ch.* 935–8 ἔμολε μὲν Δίκα Πριαμίδαις χρόνωι, / βαρύδικος ποινά. / ἔμολε δ' ἐς δόμον τὸν Ἀγαμέμνονος / διπλοῦς λέων. Here ἔμολε μὲν and ἔμολε δ' are well separated; more important, they signal an important antithesis. None of these five passages resembles ἔκανε μὲν ἄλοχον, ἔκανε δὲ τέκεα, in the middle of a run of dochmiacs. In anaphora, with verbs at least, μέν is more commonly omitted.

---

[1] I persist in calling this instance intolerable, in spite of T. C. W. Stinton's attempt to undermine Conomis's conclusions (*CQ* n.s. 27 [1977] 45–7). The hiatus in the dochmiac εὕδει; ναί, εὕδει is defended by *Or.* 148 βοάν : : ναί, οὕτως (see Conomis 42), a passage containing several echoes of this passage from *Herc.* (see Bond for details).

Denniston himself lists from tragedy thirteen examples besides ours (I have subtracted *El.* 311–12: see Denniston's note in his edition), and we may add seven more, *Alc.* 108, *Hel.* 667–8, fr. 153. 3, A. *Pe.* 403, S. *El.* 987–8, *Ph.* 779, *OC* 1389–91. Of these twenty passages eight are lyric or anapaestic: *Alc.* 108 ἔθιγες ψυχᾶς, ἔθιγες δὲ φρενῶν, *Med.* 99 κινεῖ κραδίαν, κινεῖ δὲ χόλον, 131 ἔκλυον φωνάν, ἔκλυον δὲ βοάν, *Hel.* 667–8 πετομένας κώπας, | πετομένου δ' ἔρωτος, *Ba.* 142–3 ῥεῖ δὲ γάλακτι πέδον, ῥεῖ δ' οἴνωι, ῥεῖ δὲ μελισσᾶν | νέκταρι, *IA* 16–17 ζηλῶ σέ, γέρον, | ζηλῶ δ' ἀνδρῶν κτλ., fr. 153. 3 νεύει βίοτος, νεύει δὲ τύχα, S. *Tr.* 517 ἦν χερός, ἦν δὲ τόξων. These passages show that ἔκανεν ἄλοχον, ἔκανε δὲ τέκεα represents the normal style of lyrics.

In his second edition Wilamowitz printed ὕπνον ⟨γ' ἄ⟩υπνον ὀλόμενον, ὃς ἔκανεν ἄλο/χον κτλ., four dochmiacs again, and this is accepted by Murray. But if the corruption of ὕπνον ἄυπνον to ὕπνον ὕπνον is easy, the corruption to ὕπνον ὕπνον of ὕπνον γ' ἄυπνον is correspondingly less easy by a degree not commensurate with the slenderness of the letter γ. Furthermore, the dochmiac ὕπνον γ' ἄυπνον ὀλο- is of a shape (∪ — ⌢ ∪ ⌢) unparalleled in Euripides (see Conomis, loc. cit. 24). Nor, indeed, does either of Wilamowitz's conjectures help to eliminate the hiatus after εὕδει.

Perhaps we should use the γε to eliminate the hiatus: ναί, εὕδει ⟨γ'⟩ | ὕπνον ⟨ἄ⟩υπνον κτλ. For γε following upon ναί see Denniston, *GP* 136, who quotes *Cycl.* 586 ναὶ μὰ Δί', ὃν ἁρπάζω γ' ἐγώ, Pl. *Theaet.* 193 A ναί, ἀληθῆ γε, and we may add Ar. *Plut.* 904 ἀλλ' ἔμπορος; : : ναί, σκήπτομαί γ', Plat. *Rep.* 415 E, 422 B, *Prot.* 347 B, *Soph.* 226 E.[1] The objection may be made (it has been made to me by Mr Bond) that γε is less naturally placed after the repeated εὕδει than after ὕπνον, where it 'adds detail to an assent already expressed' (Denniston, loc. cit.). The objection is a fair one, but it is difficult to know how strong it is. I can give no example of γε placed after a repeated verb where ναί precedes. But if ναί had not preceded, there could be no objection to the placing of γε after the repeated word: this would be the straightforward use of γε in an 'affirmative answer to a question or statement' (Denniston, *GP* 130).

Metre can be restored to ἔκανε δὲ κτλ. by a change of word-order: ἔκανε δὲ ψαλμῶι τέκεα τοξήρει, two dochmiacs of the common shape

---

[1] At S. *Tr.* 425 the use of γε is rather different, and it may be that ναί is best deleted (so Dindorf). At E. *Andr.* 242 ναί (followed by γε) is omitted by P and is usually deleted by editors; but I agree with Stevens that deletion is unwarranted.

◡ ◡̃ – – —. The change of order arose from the cause which I have spoken about earlier (see pp. 49–50). I accept Madvig's deletion of τοξεύϲαϲ, for, although a molossus is possible as a tail-piece to dochmiacs, the participle 'ignauissime adhaeret', as Madvig says. For the interpolation of an otiose participle see *Med.* 981.

1181 See p. 42.

1218 See p. 54.

1228 See *PCPS* n.s. 20 (1974) 32 n. 7.

IV. TROADES

1 See p. 49.

59–60   ἦ πού νιν, ἔχθραν τὴν πρὶν ἐκβαλοῦσα, νῦν
ἐς οἶκτον ἦλθες πυρὶ κατῃθαλωμένης;

59 νιν V: νυν P: νῦν Q

In 59 read οὔ πού (*olim* Wecklein [*SBAM* 1895, 535]). We want incredulity (Denniston, *GP* 492) not open-minded acquiescence (ibid. 286). For the supplanting of οὔ που by ἦ που in the manuscripts of Euripides see Page on *Med.* 695, Zuntz, *Inquiry* 196 n. § and Kannicht on *Hel.* 135.

Defenders of the sequence νιν . . . ἐς οἶκτον ἦλθες . . . κατῃθαλωμένης speak of anacoluthon. 'He was going to say, ἦπου νιν οἰκτίζεις; but changes the construction to εἰς οἶκτον ἦλθες αὐτῆς', Paley. A similar explanation is offered by Schiassi and Lee. It carries no conviction. In place of νιν Markland proposed γάρ, Lenting cύ γ' (so also Madvig, *Advers.* 1 [1871] 271),[1] Nauck ποτ'. Burges proposed (and Wecklein accepted) πόλεος for πού νιν, Heimsoeth ἔλαβες . . . -μένην for ἦλθες . . . -μένης. No such radical changes are needed. As Tyrrell saw, νιν is governed by ἐς οἶκτον ἦλθες, the periphrasis standing as the equivalent of a transitive verb: see KG 1. 321, Page on *Med.* 206, Dodds on *Ba.* 1288, R. Renehan, *Studies in Greek Texts* (1976) 51, and add *Phaethon* 69–70 ὀρθρευομένα γόοις "Ἴτυν. (These examples show that no change is needed at *IT* 1091 ἔλεγον οἶτον [οἰκτρὸν Barnes] ἀείδεις, whose construction Renehan, op. cit. 36, appears to interpret differently.) But it is unthinkable that Euripides should have abandoned the construction by adding κατῃθαλωμένης as a 'genitive absolute' (Tyrrell). Elmsley's κατῃθαλωμένην (on *Med.* 1275 [1308]) is inescapable, although I find it approved only by Hartung and Herwerden (*RPh* 18 [1894] 87).

95–7   μῶρος δὲ θνητῶν ὅστις ἐκπορθεῖ πόλεις
ναούς τε τύμβους θ', ἱερὰ τῶν κεκμηκότων,
ἐρημίαι δοὺς αὐτὸς ὤλεθ' ὕστερον.

---

[1] It was accepted by Wilamowitz, *Griechische Tragödien*, xi, ed. 2 (1920) 101.

A literal translation, with the order of the Greek expressions retained, will show what is wrong. 'It is a foolish man who sacks cities and shrines and tombs, holy places of the dead, having devastated he himself perishes later.' To make sense of this one must take τε in 96 as connecting not ναούς with πόλεις but clause with clause: 'It is a foolish man who sacks cities, and having devastated shrines . . .' The scholiast recognized that this is a contrivance against which the natural inclination of the reader rebels, and accordingly he punctuated with a strong stop after τύμβους θ'. This punctuation is as inept as the colon which Biehl claims credit for placing after πόλεις, but which had already been placed there by Kirchhoff and Blaydes (*Adu. crit. in Eur.* 157). Reiske's ἐκπέρσας (approved by Wecklein, *SBAM* 1896, 465) and Hartung's ἐκπορθῶν (accepted by Dindorf) do great harm to the style.

Neither Wecklein nor any editor known to me records the conjecture δέ for τε in 96. This conjecture was first made by Blomfield on p. 611 of the fifth volume of the variorum edition of Euripides published by A. and J. M. Duncan at Glasgow in 1821 (see the editors' preface, vol. i, p. 7). Hartung made it afresh only to reject it. And it was proposed again by Headlam, *JPh* 23 (1895) 287. This conjecture causes Poseidon to make not one point but two: to sack cities is folly, but to devastate temples and tombs is suicide. Headlam remarks that 'sacrilege does not necessarily accompany the sack of a town'. For the confusion of δέ and τε see 31, 365, 398, 407, 438, 480, 596, 711, 731, 744, 927, 1040, 1130, 1183.[1]

This is not a bad solution. But Sir Denys Page convinced me that it is not quite good enough. 'If two points are made, and the second is stronger than the first, the contrast and stress are not well expressed by μῶρος δέ ἐστι . . . αὐτὸς δὲ ὤλετο. Euripides could so easily have said μῶρος μὲν ἀνδρῶν instead of μῶρος δὲ θνητῶν. I would rather contemplate 97 as a new sentence in asyndeton, preferably with the object of δούς expressed, δούς ⟨σφ'⟩.' The omission of σφ' could easily have happened after it had been corrupted to σ' (as at *Hcld.* 103, *Su.* 1168, *Ion* 286; cf. *Hcld.* 506, *Hel.* 1201, A. *Ag.* 216). For a parallel omission cf. *Herc.* 398 ὅς ⟨σφ'⟩ ἄπλατον (Hermann).

98–9 See pp. 64, 96.

101 See p. 45.

[1] I have listed instances in *Herc.* in *PCPS* n.s. 20 (1974) 3 n. 4 (add 193 τε L: δὲ P).

133   See p. 96.

156   See p. 72.

170–1   See p. 96.

218   See p. 6.

233–4   See p. 26.

329–30   . . . κατὰ còν ἐν δάφναις
                    ἀνάκτορον θυηπολῶ.

These words are usually misinterpreted. 'In laureto, in tuo sacello'
Melanchthon; 'in tuo lauris-cincto templo' Musgrave; 'ἐν δάφναις,
because his temple was surrounded by bay-trees' Paley; 'O shrine
in the laurels' Murray; 'dans ton temple parmi les lauriers' Parmentier. Similarly Lee: 'The bay tree was sacred to Apollo and for this
reason his temples are often surrounded by them. Cf. *Ion* 76, where
Hermes goes into δαφνώδη γύαλα near Apollo's temple; *Andr.* 296 f.
παρὰ θεσπεσίωι δάφναι βόασε Κασσάνδρα.'

That is not a meaning which ἐν δάφναις, in this sentence at least,
can bear. A few have interpreted correctly: the scholiast (μετὰ
δαφνῶν χορεύω), Wilamowitz ('Durch deine Hallen wall' ich keusch
im Lorbeerschmuck'),[1] Pohlenz, *Die griechische Tragödie: Erläuterungen*,
ed. 2 (1954) 150, and Lattimore ('I wear your laurel, I tend your
temple').[2] It is Cassandra herself who is ἐν δάφναις, 'crowned with
bay-leaves', as at *IA* 757–60 τὰν Κασσάνδραν ἵν' ἀκούω ῥίπτειν ξανθοὺς
πλοκάμους χλωροκόμωι στεφάνωι δάφνας κοσμηθεῖσαν. These will be
among the garlands which she flings down at 451 (cf. 256–8).[3] For
the use of ἐν ('equipped with', 'clothed in') see KG 1. 463, Denniston on *El.* 321, and my note on *Cycl.* 360 in *CQ* n.s. 21 (1971) 46.
Similar are *Herc.* 677 ἐν στεφάνοισιν, *Ion* 1310 ἐν στέμμασιν, and above
all Call. fr. 194. 26 καὶ Πυθίη γὰρ ἐν δάφνηι μὲν ἵδρυται, quoted by
Pohlenz. Note also *Ion* 25–6 ὄφεσιν ἐν χρυσηλάτοις / τρέφειν ('bring up
wearing'), which explains the meaning of ἐντρέφειν at 1428.

[1] op. cit. (p. 58 n. 1 above).
[2] In Grene and Lattimore, *The Complete Greek Tragedies* 3 (1959). Perhaps
Heath should be added to the list: 'ἐν δάφναις potest uel ad ipsam Cassandram
referri, uel ad Apollinis templum.'
[3] Musgrave on 451 mentions St. *Theb.* 7. 784 (Amphiaraus) *accipe commissum
capiti decus, accipe laurus.*

335–7   †βοάϲατε τόν† ὑμέναιον ὤ
μακαρίαιϲ ἀοιδαῖϲ
ἰαχαῖϲ τε νύμφαν.

βοάϲατε τόν V: βοάϲατ᾽ (βάϲατ᾽ P) εὖ τόν PQ

The strophic line corresponding to 335 is 319 ἐγὼ δ᾽ (δ᾽ PQ: τόδ᾽ V)
ἐπὶ γάμοιϲ ἐμοῖϲ, and we must begin by assessing the rival claims of
δ᾽ and τόδ᾽ (for the confusion cf. 1053 δ᾽ P: τάδ᾽ V). Many editors
have preferred τόδ᾽, and the latest of them is Lee, although the
reason which he gives for his preference cannot be upheld. He
believes that in the sentence (315 ff.) ἐπεὶ ϲύ, μᾶτερ, . . . καταϲτένουϲ᾽
ἔχειϲ, ἐγὼ δ᾽ κτλ. the δ᾽ will have to be apodotic, a usage which
he rightly finds unacceptable.[1] But ἐπεί does not have to introduce
a protasis: it may simply mean 'for', as at 1145, 1224, and often
elsewhere. The sentence may therefore be translated: 'For you are
grieving, while (δ᾽) I . . .' Lee, like the scholiast and others, para-
phrases the text with τόδ᾽ in this way: 'Since you are engrossed in
your lamentation, I shall perform your duty.' This makes Cassandra
say very plainly what the other text allows her to say more subtly.
What I find most disagreeable is the asyndeton, which causes the
sentence to begin very abruptly.

Of the conjectures which are offered in 335 the most popular is
Fix's βοᾶτε τόν. The definite article is thoroughly undesirable; but no
less undesirable is the plural imperative. Consider the imperatives in
this antistrophe. At the beginning there are singular imperatives
addressed to Hecuba, followed by a brief imperatival address to
Apollo. Immediately before 335–7 there is a series of singular imperatives addressed to Hecuba: χόρευε, μᾶτερ, κτλ. Immediately after
335–7 there is a plural imperative addressed to the chorus, who
are named in the vocative: ἴτ᾽, ὦ καλλίπεπλοι Φρυγῶν / κόραι, μέλ-
πετε. If, between a singular imperative with vocative attached and
a plural imperative with vocative attached, there is interposed an
imperative without vocative, that imperative must be addressed to
the same person as were the imperatives which went before. Therefore the imperative in 335 must be addressed to Hecuba. And so we
can reject not only βοᾶτε τόν but also Burges's βοάϲαθ᾽, which is
printed (with δ᾽ in 319) by Murray and Biehl, and Schiassi's βοᾶτε δ᾽.
The answer must be βόαϲον ὑμέναιον ὤ (∼ ἐγὼ δ᾽ ἐπὶ γάμοιϲ ἐμοῖϲ).

[1] Arguments in favour of an apodotic use are offered by C. Busche, *Obs. crit.
in Eur. Troades* (1886) 17.

Whether the metre should be interpreted as ∪-⌣|∪-∪- or as
∪-∪⌣|-∪- is a question which I have discussed on pp. 19-20. The
former rhythm recurs at 564.

Fix remarks that 'ubique in hoc carmine sunt praesentis imperatiui
usurpati'. True; but present and aorist imperatives may be found in
close proximity with no discernible difference of meaning: *Hi.*
473-4 λῆγε μὲν . . . λῆξον δ' ('the variation is not a matter of subtle
nuance but of mere metrical convenience' Barrett), *Med.* 1258-9
κάτειργε κατάπαυσον, *Hcld.* 635 ἔπαιρέ νυν ϲεαυτόν, ὄρθωϲον κάρα,
Andr. 1227 λεύϲϲετ' ἀθρήϲατε, S. *OC* 1499 ϲπεῦϲον ἅϲϲ'. See also
J. Donovan, *CR* 9 (1895) 145-9. The aorist βόαϲον is used at *Alc.* 234,
ἀμβόαϲον at A. *Pe.* 572. And for an aorist imperative with the sense
'sing a song' we have ἆιϲον (ἄειϲον codd.) at 513 below.

Beware of writing Ὑμέναιον, as most editors do. The proper name
has no place here. For the construction βόαϲον ὑμέναιον . . . νύμφαν
see p. 58.

456-7   οὐκέτ' ἂν φθάνοιϲ ἂν αὔραν ἱϲτίοιϲ καραδοκῶν,
            ὡϲ μίαν τριῶν Ἐρινὺν τῆϲδέ μ' ἐξάξων χθονόϲ.

I have not found anyone who has apprehended Cassandra's meaning.
First we must dispose of an unreal problem. 'It is interesting that
Eur. specifies that there were *three* Furies. In Aeschylus and even in
the *IT* (cf. 79), they appear to be unlimited in number' (Lee).
This is to forget that Euripides specifies three Erinyes at *Or.* 408 and
1650 and causes three to attack Orestes at *IT* 285 ff. Other evidence
for the trinity of Erinyes is given by E. Wüst, *RE* Suppl. VIII (1956)
122-3.

There is therefore no reason why Euripides should not call Cassandra
one of three Erinyes. But he did not do anything so pointless here.
Cassandra is saying that three Erinyes will take vengeance on Agamemnon when he arrives home (she has already predicted this
vengeance at 356-64). And these three will be herself, Clytemnestra,
and Aegisthus. The last two are coupled in a comparable expression
at S. *El.* 1080: Electra is ready to die διδύμαν ἑλοῦϲ' Ἐρινύν, 'when
she has destroyed the twofold Erinys'.

V has ἐρινὺν, P ἐρινῦν, Q ἐρινvῦν. Editors used to print Ἐρινὺν,
'quod saltem esse debuerat Ἐρινννύων trisyllabum', said Seidler,
who preferred the accusative. Modern editors print Ἐρινύν. But since
Ἐρινύων is used as a trisyllable at *IT* 931, 970, 1456, there is no less

probability in Ἐρινύων here. It was proposed by Burges and again by Blaydes (*Adu. crit. in Eur.* 161). Compare *IA* 1137 εἰς τριῶν δυςδαιμόνων.

538–41   κλωςτοῦ δ᾽ ἀμφιβόλοις λίνοιο ναὸς ὡςεὶ
                 ςκάφος κελαινὸν εἰς ἕδρανα
                 λάϊνα δάπεδά τε φόνια πατρί-   540
                 δι Παλλάδος θέςαν θεᾶς.

540 φόνια Musurus: φοίνια PQ: φοίνιά τε V: φονία τε Σ lemma¹ (ἀντὶ τοῦ φονίως ἢ τὰ φοινιχθέντα Σ)

Everyone now prints the text as I have given it. The object of the sentence is πεύκαν οὐρείαν, ξεστὸν λόχον Ἀργείων.² 'They brought it, like a ship's dark hull, with ropes of spun flax to the stone temple and floors φόνια πατρίδι of the goddess Pallas.' Musurus's φόνια restores metre but not acceptable Greek. δάπεδα . . . φόνια πατρίδι cannot mean 'solum letale patriae' (Melanchthon), 'floor fateful to the fatherland' (Tyrrell), 'soon to run with their country's blood' (Paley), 'her hallowed floor, who lusted for her people's blood' (Murray), 'où devait couler le sang des nôtres' (Parmentier), 'blood-stained to their country's disadvantage' and so 'red with their country's blood' (Lee). Apart from the impossible s   m placed on the language, the sense is preposterous. τοῦτο δὲ ἀπὸ τοῦ cυμβεβηκότος λέγει, said the scholiast. 'Eur. calls it red by prolepsis to emphasise the inevitability of the coming destruction', says Lee. This is sheer sophistry. Kirchhoff, alone of editors known to me, damns 540 as 'uersus corruptissimus'.³

Wilamowitz seems to have taken φόνια πατρίδι not with δάπεδα but in apposition to the object of the verb. In *Verskunst* 172 he punctuates δάπεδά τε, φόνια πατρίδι, Παλλάδος κτλ., and in *Griech. Tragödien*, xi. 66, he translates 'Und der Taue Schlingen schleppten / auf die Burg wie ein Schiff / auf zum Heiligtum / unsre Mörder'. But, even divorced from δάπεδα, the words φόνια πατρίδι cannot mean 'bringing bloodshed to our country'. We can, however, get that meaning if we accept Wilamowitz's punctuation and change a single letter: δάπεδά τε, φονέα πατρίδι, Παλλάδος κτλ. Compare *El.* 1229

_____

¹ Not φόνιά τε as Wecklein, Murray, Parmentier, and Biehl report.
² For the text of this line see Jackson, *Marg. scaen.* 200–1. His conjecture was anticipated by Dobree (*Advers.* 2. 90 [ed. Wagner 4. 87]).
³ Wecklein has the note ' "in litteris φόνια πατρίδι unum subest adiectiuum compositum ad δάπεδα aptum" Madvig | πραπίδι olim coniciebam'.

φονέας ἔτικτες ἆρά coι, and below, 813–14 χερὸς εὐстοχίαν ἐξεῖλε
ναῶν, Λαομέδοντι φόνον. For similar datives see KG 1. 426–8.

542–8

> ἐπὶ δὲ πόνωι καὶ χαρᾶι
> νύχιον ἐπεὶ¹ κνέφας παρῆν,
> Λίβυς τε λωτὸς ἐκτύπει
> Φρύγιά τε μέλεα, παρθένοι δ'   545
> ἀέριον ἀνὰ κρότον ποδῶν
> βοάν τ' ἔμελπον εὔφρον', ἐν
> δόμοις δὲ . . .

The old editors translated παρθένοι δ' | ἀέριον ἀνὰ κρότον ποδῶν |
βοάν τ' ἔμελπον εὔφρον' as 'per plausum aereum pedum laetam can-
tionem canebant' (Melanchthon) or 'aereo cum plausu pedum . . .'
(Barnes), giving to ἀνὰ a sense unexampled and ignoring τ'. When
these faults were noticed two explanations were devised. The first
was to suppose that ἀνὰ might stand for a verb: 'ἀνὰ κρότον. Elliptice
pro ἀνὰ κρότον ᾖcαν uel ἐcτρέφοντο' Musgrave; 'ἀνὰ κρότον, i.e.
ἀνήειρον, as above, v. 99, ἀνὰ πεδόθεν κεφαλήν' Paley. This needs no
refutation. (At 99 read with Musgrave ἄνα, δύcδαιμον· πεδόθεν
κεφαλὴν | ἐπάειρε δέρην ⟨τ'⟩. Lee has the strange idea that τ' 'destroys
the metron diaeresis'. What of 1120? See also p. 96 below.) The
second explanation was to suppose that ἀνὰ . . . ἔμελπον is an example
of tmesis, and that κρότον ποδῶν βοάν τ' ἀνέμελπον is an example of
zeugma (so, among others, Tyrrell, Parmentier, Biehl). This puts a
strain on our credulity. 'ἀναμέλπω is not tragic and ἀναμέλπω κρότον is
odd and not paralleled by the Homeric meanings of μολπή to which
T. refers', remarks Lee.

The remedy now much favoured is Burges's deletion of the τ'
after βοάν. But those who adopt this remedy are still unable to make
sense of ἀνὰ κρότον ποδῶν. 'uelim . . . ἀνὰ κρότον ποδῶν interpretari
comitante pedum strepitu' Matthiae; on which Paley remarks 'this is
hardly a right use of ἀνά'. According to Lee 'we can take ἀνά in a
local sense (LSJ C. I. 3) = "amidst the beating of feet raised in the
air".' Recourse to LSJ yields the following alleged analogies: ἀνὰ
θυμὸν φρονεῖν, ἀνὰ cτόμα ἔχειν, ἀν' Αἰγυπτίους ἄνδρας, ἀνὰ πρώτους
εἶναι.

There is a further oddity, and only Wecklein has noticed it. When
the Greeks raised their feet or their voices on high they raised them

¹ ἐπεὶ Reiske: ἐπὶ codd. This conjecture (which Parmentier, Biehl, and Lee,
among others, reject) is self-evidently correct.

not to the ἀήρ but to the αἰθήρ or, more commonly, to the οὐρανός:
325 πάλλε πόδ' αἰθέριον, 519–20 οὐράνια βρέμοντα, *El.* 860–1 οὐράνιον
πήδημα, A. *Pe.* 573 ἀμβόασον οὐράνι' ἄχη, *Su.* 808–9 οὐράνια μέλη,
S. *El.* 752–3 οὐρανῶι / σκέλη προφαίνων, Ar. *Nub.* 357 οὐρανομήκη . . .
φωνήν, *Vesp.* 415–16 μὴ κεκράγετε / : : νὴ Δί' ἐς τὸν οὐρανόν γ',
1492 σκέλος οὐρανίαν (Meineke: -ον codd.) ἐκλακτίζων, 1530 ῥῖπτε
σκέλος οὐράνιον. Similarly *Med.* 440 αἰθερία δ' ἀνέπτα (sc. αἰδώς),
Andr. 830–1 ἔρρ' αἰθέριον πλοκαμῶν ἐμῶν ἄπο / λεπτόμιτον φάρος,
Tr. 1064 σμύρνας (-ης VP)[1] αἰθερίας, A. *ScT* 81 αἰθερία κόνις. The
expression ἀέριος κρότος ποδῶν is no happier than 'an airy tapping of
feet'. Wecklein proposed αἰθέριον.

I suggest that we change ἀέριον to ἄειρον and ἀνὰ to ἅμα:

> παρθένοι δ'
> ἄειρον ἅμα κρότον ποδῶν
> βοάν τ' ἔμελπον εὔφρον' . . .

The verb ἀείρω is a particularly suitable verb to have 'tapping of feet'
as its object, since one can ἀείρειν both a foot and a noise. For the
former see 342 μὴ κοῦφον ἄρηι (Wecklein: αἴρηι uel sim. codd.)
βῆμ', *Hel.* 1627 ποῖ σὸν πόδ' αἴρεις; S. *Ant.* 224 κοῦφον ἐξάρας πόδα,
for the latter Ar. *Equ.* 546 αἴρεσθ' αὐτῶι πολὺ τὸ ῥόθιον, Dem. 18. 291
ἐπάρας τὴν φωνήν.

ἄειρον must be looked upon as a borrowing from Homer (ἄειρεν
Il. 11. 637, cf. ἤειρεν 10. 499). Elsewhere the tragedians use the form
ἦιρον not ἤειρον in the imperfect. But it is relevant to note that, while
in the aorist they use ἦρα and ἠράμην and not ἤειρα and ἠειράμην,
they readily use the longer form when it is not augmented: ἀείρας
S. *Ant.* 418, ἀειράμενοι *Phaeth.* 81, ἀερθῶ *Andr.* 848, ἀερθέν A. *Ag.* 1525.
And so in the imperfect Euripides may have felt that the unaugmented
form was permissible while the augmented form would not have been.
He has no objection to dropping the temporal augment: see 518
ὀλόμαν (Musgrave: ὀλοίμαν codd.), *Med.* 1413 ὄφελον (V: ὤφ- rell.),
Hi. 167 αὔτευν, 362 ἄιες, 1129 ἔναιρεν (Blomfield: ἐναίρων codd.),
Andr. 109 ἀγόμαν (ἄγομαι VB), *Su.* 821 ἔναρον, *IT* 150 ἰδόμαν (Tri-
clinius: εἰδ- L), 153 ὀλόμαν (Heath: ὠλ- L), *Hel.* 348 κατόμοσα
(Elmsley: -ώμοσα L), 367 ὄλεσαν (Murray: ὤλ- L), 371 ἐκελάδησεν
ἀνοτότυξεν (Wilamowitz: κελάδησε κἀνοτότυξεν: see Kannicht ad loc.),
Ph. 663 ὄλεσε (Hermann: ὤλ- codd.), *Or.* 200 ὀλόμεθα, *Ba.* 131

---

[1] I have restored the Doric form: cf. *Hyps.* fr. 58. 2 c]μύρνας καπν[. See also
p. 94, n. 1.

ἐξανύσαντο, 563 cύναγεν, *IA* 218 ἰδόμαν (Dindorf: εἶδ- L), 1051 ἄφυccε, 1066 ἐξονόμαζεν (Monk: ἐξωνόμαcεν L). At *Andr.* 289 Murray's ἔλε for εἶλε is probable. See also O. Lautensach, *Grammatische Studien zu dem griech. Tragikern und Komikern: Augment und Reduplikation* (1899) 179–80.

For the corruption of ἅμα to ἀνὰ see *Ion* 41 ἅμ' ἱππεύοντος Musgrave: ἀνιππ- L; also *Hel.* 587 πῶc οὖν; ἅμ' (ἂν L) ἐνθάδ' ἦcθ' ⟨ἄρ'⟩ ἐν Τροίαι θ' ἅμα; On the text of this latter passage see Kannicht. For the repeated ἅμα see Bruhn, *Anhang* § 214.

594 See p. 11.

640 See p. 3.

694–5   οὕτω δὲ κἀγὼ πόλλ' ἔχουcα πήματα
              ἄφθογγόc εἰμι καὶ παρεῖc' ἐῶ cτόμα.

ἐῶ] ἔξω Reiske, ἔχω Burges

'Verbum ἐῶ sollicitari non debuerat', said Valckenaer, *Diatribe in Eur. fragmenta* 72, quoting fr. 187. 2 τὰ μὲν κατ' οἴκουc ἀμελίαι παρεὶc ἐᾶι, S. *OC* 361–3 τὰ μὲν . . . παρεῖc' ἐάcω, tr. fr. adesp. 353. 2 τὰ μικρὰ δ' ἄλλοιc δαίμοcιν παρεὶc ἐᾶι. These passages do not prove that παρεῖc' ἐῶ can govern cτόμα in the sense 'I let speech be' (Lee's translation), for cτόμα cannot be used as a mere synonym of λόγος. This point was established by Housman, *AJP* 13 (1892) 156–7 = *Classical Papers* 196. His punctuation of S. *OC* 981 coῦ γ' ἐc τόδ' ἐξελθόντος, ἀνόcιον cτόμα (ignored by editors but approved by Jackson, *Marg. scaen.* 194) may be mentioned in support of Burges's punctuation (also ignored by editors) of *Tr.* 1180 ὦ πολλὰ κόμπουc ἐκβαλών, φίλον cτόμα, | ὄλωλαc (ἐκβαλὼν P: -ὸν V edd.).

Editors are content with ἐῶ, but we should certainly accept Burges's ἔχω. Compare *Hi.* 660 cῖγα δ' ἕξομεν cτόμα, *Hec.* 1283 οὐκ ἐφέξετε cτόμα; *Su.* 513 cῖγ', Ἄδραcτ', ἔχε cτόμα, *Herc.* 1244 ἴcχε cτόμ', *Phaeth.* 104–5 ἔχειν χρὴ cτόμ' ἐν ἡcυχίαι, S. *Tr.* 976–7 ἴcχε δακὼν cτόμα cόν. Similarly *Andr.* 250 cιωπῶ κἀπιλάζυμαι cτόμα. Does the collocation of ἔχουcα and ἔχω seem objectionable? Then see *El.* 40 εἰ γάρ νιν ἔcχεν ἀξίωμ' ἔχων ἀνήρ, *Hel.* 759–60 τοὺc θεοὺc ἔχων τιc ἂν | φίλουc ἀρίcτην μαντικὴν ἔχοι δόμοιc, *Or.* 9–10 κοινῆc τραπέζηc ἀξίωμ' ἔχων ἴcον | ἀκόλαcτον ἔcχε γλῶccαν, *IT* 338–9 τὸν cὸν 'Ελλὰc ἀποτείcει φόνον | δίκαc τίνουcα τῆc ἐν Αὐλίδι cφαγῆc, fr. 362. 7–8

(*Erectheus*, fr. 53. 7–8 Austin) διδοὺϲ . . . δίδου, A. *Ag.* 1608–9 καὶ
τοῦδε τἀνδρὸϲ ἠψάμην . . . πᾶϲαν ξυνάψαϲ μηχανήν, S. *El.* 580–1 ὅρα
τιθεῖϲα τόνδε τὸν νόμον βροτοῖϲ | μὴ πῆμα ϲαυτῆι καὶ μετάγνοιαν τιθῆιϲ
(R. D. Dawe, *PCPS* n.s. 14 [1968] 14, and *Studies* i. 181–2, suggests
κτίϲηιϲ for τιθῆιϲ, unnecessarily in view of the passages quoted).
There is therefore no need for Hartung's πόλλ' ὁρῶϲα (ἰδοῦϲα Schenkl)
πήματα . . . ἔχω, which he supported by the negligible authority of
Chr. Pat. 630–1 οὕτωϲ δὲ κἀγὼ δείν' ὁρῶϲα πήματα | ἄφθογγοϲ κτλ.
(the speaker is the chorus and ἔχουϲα would not suit).[1]

747 See p. 13.

817–18   δὶϲ δὲ δυοῖν πιτύλοιν τείχη περὶ
         Δαρδανίαϲ φοινία κατέλυϲεν αἰχμά.

817 περὶ V: παρὰ P   818 δαρδανίαϲ V: -δάναϲ P   φονία Musurus

The corresponding strophic lines are 806–7 *"Ιλιον "Ιλιον ἐκπέρϲων*
πόλιν | *ἀμετέραν τὸ πάροιθεν* (V: *πάροιθ'* P) *ὅτ' ἔβαϲ ἀφ' 'Ελλά-*
δοϲ. The last four words were deleted by Dindorf (the words which
immediately follow are ὅθ' 'Ελλάδοϲ), and the original text is beyond
recovery. We cannot therefore be sure what was the metre of 807 ∼
818; but the minimal change of φοινία to φονία (cf. 540 discussed on
p. 63) restores a praxillean (a rhythm which recurs at 1070 ∼ 1080,
the second of which lines contains a clear echo of 818: ἂν [sc. πόλιν]
πυρὸϲ αἰθομένα κατέλυϲεν ὁρμά), and it is at least a reasonable assumption that this is the right metre. Dale (*BICS* Suppl. 21. 1 [1971] 84)
prefers *"Ιλιον "Ιλιον ἐκπέρϲων πόλιν ἀμετέραν* (the rest marked as
corrupt) ∼ δὶϲ δὲ δυοῖν πιτύλοιν τείχη περὶ Δαρδανίαϲ | φοινία κατέλυϲεν
αἰχμά. This is less natural.

Many editors imagine that τείχη περὶ Δαρδανίαϲ means 'the walls
around Troy'. But this is scarcely possible: περί with the genitive
is all but unexampled in this connection (see LSJ *s.u.* A. I). A second
objection which springs to mind is that, since Δαρδανία (sc. γῆ) is
the land of Troy, not merely the city, the walls should not be said to be
'around' it. But this objection collapses in the face of 4–5 ἀμφὶ τήνδε
Τρωϊκὴν χθόνα . . . πύργουϲ πέριξ. Here indeed F. W. Schmidt proposed to replace χθόνα with πόλιν, Wecklein with πλάκα. Against
these proposals E. L. B. Meurig-Davies, *REG* 61 (1948) 361, quotes
Hec. 17, *Ph.* 287.

---

[1] On the value of *Chr. Pat.* in *Troades* see A. Döring, *Philologus* 25 (1867) 246–51.

In place of τείχη περὶ Heimsoeth (*Krit. Stud. zu den griech. Tragikern* [1865] 293) proposed πυργώματα, Parmentier τειχίςματα. These are heavy changes. Murray deleted φοινία and αἰχμά, so that Δαρδανίας κατέλυςεν might correspond with ἁμετέραν τὸ πάροιθεν. The deletions are arbitrary, and Murray was still obliged to obelize περὶ, in whose place he suggested 'π̄ρ̄ i.e. πατήρ, metro epitritis conueniente'. The designation of Zeus by the bald πατήρ is inept; and in the strophe it would be most unnatural to have to take the last syllable of πόλιν as *breuis in longo* in what gives every appearance of being a straightforward run of dactyls (″Ιλιον ″Ιλιον ἐκπέρςων πόλιν / ἁμετέραν τὸ πάροιθεν). And so we can reject other iambic substitutes for περὶ (παρὰ), such as Reiske's πόλεως and (with Murray's deletions) Robert's πρόμοι (*Hermes* 56 [1921] 310–11; for a more elaborate proposal see J. Mesk, *WS* 45 [1926/7] 14–15). Also accepting these deletions Scheidweiler (*Hermes* 82 [1954] 251) proposed δόρυ, but this is not a likely corruption. Biehl too accepts the deletions but retains περὶ. What his citation of *Il.* 21. 446 ἤτοι ἐγὼ Τρώεςςι πόλιν πέρι τεῖχος ἔδειμα is intended to prove I do not know. Seidler's πυρὶ is inapposite. Lee's proposal to retain τὸ πάροιθ' ὅτ' ἔβας ἀφ' Ἑλλάδος in responsion with αἰχμὰ κατέλυςε φοινία is ill conceived.

I suggest that we do no more than change the accent on περὶ and add a letter to Δαρδανίας:

> δὶς δὲ δυοῖν πιτύλοιν τείχη πέρι
> Δαρδανί⟨δ⟩ας φονία κατέλυςεν αἰχμά.

The descendants of Dardanus, fighting for their city, naturally met their deaths 'around the walls': cf. *Il.* 6. 327–8 λαοὶ μὲν φθινύθουςι περὶ πτόλιν αἰπύ τε τεῖχος / μαρνάμενοι. The Trojans are called Δαρδανίδαι at *Rh.* 230. The verb καταλύω is properly used of destroying things (as at 1080 quoted above), but to apply it to the destruction of people is an easy extension.

1033–5 Μενέλαε, προγόνων τ' ἀξίως δόμων τε ςῶν
τεῖςαι δάμαρτα κἀφελοῦ πρὸς Ἑλλάδος
ψόγον τὸ θῆλύ τ', εὐγενὴς ἐχθροῖς φανείς.

1033 τ' ἀξίως Seidler: ἀξίως τε P: ἀξίως V   1034 τεῖςαι Herwerden: τῖςαι P: τί- V   1035 ψόγον om. P

Criticism of these verses begins with Musgrave, who first restored ψόγον in place of the makeshifts by which editors had supplemented

the omission in **P**. That the omission of ψόγον was an accident is
suggested by the following passages: 219 ἐλθεῖν V: om. PQ; 266 τί
VQ: om. P; 312 βασιλικοῖς λέκτροις V: om. PQ; 322 διδοῦς᾽ V: om.
PQ; 455 με VQ: om. P; 490 Ἑλλάδ᾽ V: om. PQ; 711 τ᾽ V: om. P;
804 τῶι V: om. P; 827 δ᾽ V: om. P; 965 coι V: om. P; 1073 παν-
νυχίδες θεῶν V: om. P; 1132 τ᾽ V: om. P; 1296 τε V: om. P.

Musgrave translated 'et auferas ex Graecia probrum et mollitiem,
inimicis animosum te praebens'. But Helen's conduct (or Menelaus'
failure to punish it) does not lay Greece open to the charge of 'molli-
ties'. Nor is πρός with the genitive used with verbs meaning 'take
away from' but rather with verbs meaning 'receive from' (LSJ
s.u. A. II. 1).[1] Further, it is not clear what Musgrave understood by
'inimicis animosum te praebens' (he is modifying Melanchthon's
'inimicis apparens animosus'). The words εὐγενὴς ἐχθροῖς φανείς
have caused surprising difficulty to interpreters. Quite wrong are
translations like 'fortem te praebens contra inimicos' (Fix), 'not
weak, but iron against the wrong' (Murray), 'après t'être montré si
brave devant les ennemis' (Parmentier). The meaning is '(by doing
this) proving your nobility to your enemies'.[2]

Hermann (apud Seidler) translated 'auerte a te reprehensionem
Graeciae et mores effeminatos'; similarly Paley, 'Remove from
yourself the reproach you bear from Greece, and the charge of
effeminacy'. The first part of this is unexceptionable: πρὸς Ἑλλάδος
ψόγον may be compared with Hcld. 624 δόξα πρὸς ἀνθρώπων, S. El.
562 πειθὼ κακοῦ πρὸς ἀνδρός, OC 73 πρὸς ἀνδρός . . . ἄρκεσις, Pi. Ol.
7. 89–90 αἰδοίαν χάριν καὶ ποτ᾽ ἀςτῶν καὶ ποτὶ ξείνων, Hdt. 4. 144. 1
ἀθάνατον μνήμην πρὸς Ἑλλησποντίων, 7. 139. 1 γνώμην ἀποδέξαςθαι
ἐπίφθονον μὲν πρὸς πλεόνων ἀνθρώπων. For other examples of prepositional phrases dependent on a noun see pp. 28–9. But is ψόγον
τὸ θῆλύ τ᾽ an acceptable expression for 'blame and (the charge of)
effeminacy'? 'ψόγον τὸ θῆλύ τε accipio per ἓν διὰ δυοῖν dictum pro
ψόγον τῆς θηλύτητος', said Matthiae. Tyrrell compared Med. 218
δύσκλειαν ἐκτήσαντο καὶ ῥαιθυμίαν, 'where the meaning is δύσκλειαν
ῥαιθυμίας'; but there the language lends itself much more naturally
to the figure of hendiadys.

Furthermore, although 'effeminacy' is a natural enough taunt to

[1] Hence Blaydes's lamentable γ᾽ ἀφ᾽ for πρός (Adu. crit. in Eur. 168).
[2] Herwerden's ἔργοις for ἐχθροῖς (Mélanges Graux [1884] 197) removes an important detail. As Lee says, 'ἐχθροῖς is stressed: "noble even in the eyes of your
enemies".' The point is also missed by F. W. Schmidt, Krit. Stud. zu den griech.
Dramatikern 2 (1886) 400.

level against Menelaus (cf. *Andr.* 590 ff., *Or.* 754, *IA* 945), we may wonder whether such a taunt is best suited to this context. In the speech which precedes these lines Hecuba ended by appealing to Menelaus to punish Helen and so set an example to *women*: 1031–2 νόμον δὲ τόνδε ταῖς ἄλλαισι θὲς / γυναιξὶ κτλ. It would follow with much more point if the chorus were to appeal to Menelaus to remove from *women* the blame which, because of Helen's conduct, Greece has heaped upon them. This was recognized by W. R. Paton, *REG* 27 (1914) 37, who proposed κἀφελοῦ πρὸς Ἑλλάδος / ψόγον τὸ θῆλύ γ' ('délivre de la part de la Grèce notre sexe du reproche qui pèse sur lui'). But γε is here a pointless particle. Perhaps we should write as follows:

κἀφελοῦ πρὸς Ἑλλάδος
ψόγον τὸ θῆλυ κεὐγενὴς ἐχθροῖς φανῆι.

The changes which I have introduced are Dobree's, although his own proposal (*Advers.* 2. 92 [4. 89 ed. Wagner]) was rather different. His words are 'κἀφελοῦ, πρὸς Ἑλλάδος, ψυχῆς τὸ θῆλυ, κεὐγενὴς— *per Graeciam obtestamur, animo pelle muliebrem misericordiam, et sic apparebis*, etc. Sic Iph. A. 1208'. This interpretation of πρὸς Ἑλλάδος goes back to Reiske, and Murray's punctuation shows that he too accepted it. But the Trojan women may not appeal to Menelaus 'in the name of Greece'. Rather, take πρὸς Ἑλλάδος in the way I have illustrated above, with ψόγον. Herwerden's τὸν for πρὸς is unnecessary.

Although Dobree does not explicitly propose φανῆι for φανείς (and Wecklein does not attribute it to him), he made clear that this was what he intended by his reference to *IA* 1208 μὴ . . . κτάνηις / τὴν σήν τε κἀμὴν παῖδα καὶ σώφρων ἔσηι. For similar turns of phrase see 726 ἀλλ' ὡς γενέσθω καὶ σοφωτέρα φανῆι, *Med.* 600 οἶσθ' ὡς μετεύξηι (μέτευξαι Elmsley) καὶ σοφωτέρα φανῆι, *El.* 226 μεῖνας ἄκουσον καὶ τάχ' οὐκ ἄλλως ἐρεῖς, fr. 188. 3 τοιαῦτ' ἄειδε καὶ δόξεις φρονεῖν, A. *ScT* 261 λέγοις ἂν ὡς τάχιστα καὶ τάχ' εἴσομαι, S. *OT* 1517 λέξεις καὶ τότ' εἴσομαι κλύων, Men. fr. 417. 6 πείσθητε κοὐ μέμψεσθέ με. For the crasis κεὐγενής see *Cycl.* 530 κεὐθύμει, *Alc.* 292 κεὐκλεῶς, *Andr.* 888 κεὐτυχοῦσα, *Ion* 264 κεὐτυχοῦμεν, S. *El.* 902 κεὐθύς, *Ph.* 780 κεὐσταλής.

1064 See p. 65.

1079–80 See p. 94.

1087 ~ 1105   See p. 20.

1100–4   εἴθ᾽ ἀκάτου Μενέλα
μέcον πέλαγοc ἰούcαc
δίπαλτον ἱερὸν ἀνὰ μέcον πλατᾶν πέcοι
Αἰγαίου κεραυνοφαὲc πῦρ.

1100 εἴθ᾽ Stephanus: ἔνθ᾽ VPΣ   μενέλαε P   1102 δίπλατον P   πλατᾶν
Burges: πλάταν VPΣ

'As the ship of Menelaus sails in mid-ocean, may there fall between its banks of oars the holy fire of the lightning flash hurled by the two hands of Zeus.' This translation ignores Αἰγαίου, which the order of words forbids to be constructed with πέλαγοc and which a good many commentators forlornly construct with πῦρ ('Αἰγαίου πῦρ = "lightning such as commonly occurs over the Aegean" ' Lee). With Jacobs's verdict (*Animadu. in Eur. trag.* [1790] 101) 'Αἰγαίου somniculoso debemus librario' it is hard not to agree.

Αἰγαίου has sometimes been replaced with a trisyllable, and sometimes with a disyllable, since the corresponding ἀίccον in the strophe at 1086 may equally well be written as ᾇccον (Hermann, *De locis aliquot Eur. Troadum* 15 = *Opusc.* 8 [1877] 216). Wilamowitz once proposed to write Αἰγαῖον for δίπαλτον and δίπαλτον for Αἰγαίου (*Verskunst* 171), and no better proposal exists, even though it is hard to see why such an interchange, if it occurred, should have entailed a change in the termination of Αἰγαῖον. The long list of conjectural substitutes for Αἰγαίου has nothing that appeals, whether of two syllables or three: 'Ιδαίου Musgrave, 'Ιδαῖον Hermann (*apud* Matthiae), ἀνταῖον Jacobs, Αἰγαῖον Reiske, Ἀργείαν (with πλάταν) Heath, λυγαιῶc Burges, 'Ολύμπου Schenkl, ἀγαῖον Headlam (*CR* 15 [1901] 18); ἁγνὸν Hermann (*De locis* 16 = *Opusc.* 217), Ζηνὸc or Δῖον Schenkl, διπλᾶν Wilamowitz (*Verskunst* 172). But there is an adjective whose appeal lies not only in its bearing a more than superficial resemblance to αἰγαίου but also in its having been applied to the lightning by Hesiod (*Th.* 72, 504, 707, 854 αἰθαλόεντα κεραυνόν), by Aeschylus (*PV* 992 αἰθαλοῦccα φλόξ), and also by Euripides himself (*Ph.* 183 κεραυνῶν [Nauck: -νιον codd.: -νοῦ Hermann] τε φῶc αἰθαλόεν). For the contraction of -όειc see *Phaethon* 214 n. (p. 143): add κεροῦccα S. fr. 89 P and [E.] fr. 857. 2. See also V. Schmidt in *Kyklos: Festschrift R. Keydell* (1978) 38–53.

In the strophe we may scan ἀίccον with its first syllable long. There is only one other place in tragedy where this, the epic scansion, is found: *Tr.* 156 διὰ δὲ cτέρνων φόβος ἄιccει. Here Wecklein has revived a proposal made but rejected by Seidler, τάρβος ἄιccει. Murray prints ἄιccεν, Wilamowitz, objecting to the imperfect, preferred ἄιξεν.[1] There are two reasons why Murray's and Wilamowitz's proposals are improbable. First, tragic usage demands ἤιccεν and ἤιξεν: there is no warrant for the Doric forms. Second, the tragic poets use the trisyllabic form of the verb only in the present tense; in the imperfect and aorist tenses they use only the disyllabic ἄιccω. The imperfect ἦιccον is used by Euripides four times, by Aeschylus once. The aorist ἦιξα and compounds are used by Euripides nineteen times,[2] by Aeschylus three,[3] by Sophocles twelve. The evidence is presented, and the restriction of the trisyllabic form to the present tense is noted, by Lautensach (cited p. 66) 71–3.[4]

It must be acknowledged that a disyllabic substitute for Αἰγαίου (together with disyllabic ἄιccον) would yield a much commoner form of colon. The closest parallel to the colon restored by ἄιccον and αἰθαλοῦν (−⌣−⌣|−⌣⌣−|−) is S. *Ai.* 181 ∼ 191 (−⌣−⌣|−⌣⌣−|−). At *Alc.* 595 ∼ 604 the best remedy may be to read πόντιον δ' Αἰγαῖον ἐπ' ἀκτάν ∼ πρὸς δ' ἐμᾶι ψυχᾶι θράcος ἧcται (−⌣−−|−⌣⌣−|−), as Dale ad loc. advocates. We might also compare *El.* 434 ∼ 444 (−−−⌣̲|−⌣⌣−| −−). If the colon αἰθαλοῦν κεραυνοφαὲς πῦρ is acceptable, as it clearly is, then we may even be entitled to scan ἄιccον in 1086 with its first syllable short and to accept the responsion ⌣̲⌣−⌣|−⌣⌣−|−. This responsion has been restored with probability at *Su.* 998 ἐπύργωcε καὶ γαμέτα ∼ 1021 χρῶτα χροΐ (Hermann: χρωτὶ L) πέλαc θεμένα. And for a similar freedom of responsion before the choriamb see S. *Ph.* 1125 ∼ 1148 (⌣̲⌣|−⌣⌣−|−) and 1126 ∼ 1149 (⌣⌣̲|−⌣⌣−|⌣−).

1173–7   δύστηνε, κρατὸς ὥς c' ἔκειρεν ἀθλίως
τείχη πατρῶια, Λοξίου πυργώματα,
ὃν πόλλ' ἐκήπευς' ἡ τεκοῦcα βόcτρυχον   1175
φιλήμαcίν τ' ἔδωκεν, ἔνθεν ἐκγελᾶι
ὀcτέων ῥαγέντων φόνος, ἵν' αἰcχρὰ μὴ λέγω.

'. . . a head from whose shattered bones blood smiles forth, not to

---

[1] op. cit. (p. 58 n. 1 above) 102.

[2] I include fr. 1110a Snell and *Ion* 997 (ἦιξεν Paleii amicus: ἦλθεν L).

[3] It is therefore unlikely that at *Pe.* 470 ἵηc' should be replaced by ἦιξ' (Hermann and some manuscripts) or ἦιcc' (G. C. W. Schneider). Cf. the conjectures of Blomfield and Broadhead at *Pe.* 505.

[4] Pindar, however, has μεταΐξαντα (*N.* 5. 43) and Bacchylides ἄιξε and ἄιξαν (10. 23, 13. 144).

say anything shocking.' Lee says that in the qualification ἵν' αἰςχρὰ μὴ λέγω 'Hecuba tones down the force of her startling expression by implying the words used are not as shocking as the words she might have used'. I should like to know what could be more shocking than an image in which 'the white strip of bone between two strips of blood is compared to a set of teeth smiling between two red lips' (Denniston, *CR* 50 [1936] 116). According to Athenaeus 66a, Apollodorus of Athens believed that for the sake of politeness Hecuba had omitted to use the word ἐγκέφαλος; indeed, he claimed that οὐδ' ὀνομάζειν τινὰ τῶν παλαιῶν . . . ἐγκέφαλον. His claim is false (I need cite only *Hi.* 1352) and his belief is foolish, although he has the following of the scholiast and Paley. Athenaeus himself believed that Euripides wished only to avoid τὸ τῆς προσόψεως εἰδεχθὲς καὶ αἰςχρὸν . . . ἐναργῶς ἐμφανίςαι. As an attempt to avoid 'the visually repulsive' Hecuba's words are not well chosen.

According to Tyrrell, ἵν' αἰςχρὰ μὴ λέγω is apotropaic in function. 'This phrase always introduces an apology *for something said or about to be said*, and does not refer to a phrase suppressed lest it should prove offensive; it does not explain the reason why the phrase used is employed and another avoided, but asks the indulgence of the hearers for the phrase used: the words ἵνα μηδὲν ἐπαχθὲς εἴπω in Dem. always *introduce* some phrase which he fears may possibly offend some of his audience.' These are vapid and tendentious words. 'This phrase always introduces . . .' But where else does it occur? 'The words ἵνα μηδὲν ἐπαχθὲς εἴπω in Dem. always . . .' These words occur in Demosthenes once, and they have the opposite meaning from that which Tyrrell alleges: 18. 10 μηδενὸς τῶν μετρίων, ἵνα μηδὲν ἐπαχθὲς λέγω, χείρονα, '(I am) inferior to none of the respectable citizens, to say nothing offensive' ('i.e. *quite as good as any of our respectable citizens*: this moderate expression is made more effective by ἵνα . . . λέγω' Goodwin ad loc.).

Hecuba's language is shocking. Language more shocking would be hard to find. And for Hecuba to imply that she might have found it, had she wished, is pointless and absurd. It is equally pointless for her to apologize for the use of shocking language. Why should she mince her words? Now is no time for euphemisms. Denniston, though in the end he decided that the text was defensible, suggested δὴ for μὴ. Much stronger point is given to Hecuba's words if we write ἵν' αἰςχρὰ μὴ ςτέγω. In neither the literal nor the figurative sense does Hecuba wish to cloak the horror of the wounds. For the figurative sense see *Ph.* 1214 κακόν τι κεύθεις καὶ στέγεις ὑπὸ σκότωι, S. *OT* 341 ἥξει γὰρ αὐτά, κἂν ἐγὼ σιγῆι στέγω, fr. 679 P σύγγνωτε κἀνάσχεσθε σιγῶσαι· τὸ γὰρ / γυναιξὶν αἰσχρὸν σὺν γυναῖκα (Meineke: σὺν uel ἐν γυναικὶ Stob.) δεῖ στέγειν, S. *Tr.* 596–7 μόνον παρ' ὑμῶν εὖ στεγοίμεθ'· ὡς σκότωι / κἂν αἰσχρὰ πράσσηις, οὔποτ' αἰσχύνηι πεσῆι. The same alteration has been made with great probability at *IA* 872 ἐκκάλυπτε νῦν ποθ' ἡμῖν οὕστινας λέγεις (στέγεις F. W. Schmidt) λόγους.

1180 See p. 66.

1188 See p. 54 n. 1.

1252 See p. 45.

1287 (= 1294) See p. 106.

V. IPHIGENIA IN TAURIS

3–4 ἐξ ἧς Ἀτρεὺς ἔβλαστεν· Ἀτρέως δὲ παῖς
Μενέλαος Ἀγαμέμνων τε· τοῦ δ᾽ ἔφυν ἐγώ . . .

According to Platnauer, παῖς is 'difficult with a plural subject.
It is better to accept Badham's ἄπο or παῖδε δ᾽ Ἀτρέως.' The former
conjecture was accepted by Weil, England, and Wecklein. But
objections to the singular παῖς are invalid. See *Med.* 734–5 Πελίου δ᾽
ἐχθρός ἐστί μοι δόμος / Κρέων τε, *Ion* 64–5 χρόνια δὲ σπείρας λέχη /
ἄτεκνός ἐστι καὶ Κρέους᾽, *Hel.* 412–13 ἐσώθην μόλις ἀνελπίστωι τύχηι /
Ἑλένη τε, *Or.* 462–4 καὶ γάρ μ᾽ ἔθρεψε . . . Λήδα θ᾽ ἅμα, fr. 149. 22–3
Austin (Page, *GLP* 3. 22–3) κἀ[γ]ὼ μέν . . . / ἥκω στρατός τε Μ[υρ]-
μιδών.

6 See p. 80.

15 See *CQ* n.s. 22 (1972) 242. To the examples cited add *Hi.* 803,
Hel. 800, 1516.

34–41 See *PCPS* n.s. 15 (1969) 56–9. A few addenda.

(i) For the position of μέν (p. 58) see also *Cret.* 9–10 Page (fr. 82.
9–10 Austin) νῦν δ᾽, ἐκ θεοῦ γὰρ προσβολῆς ἐμηνάμην, / ἀλγῶ μὲν κτλ.

(ii) A parallel for Herwerden's conjecture in 35 (νόμοισιν οἷσιν
for νόμοισι τοῖσιδ᾽) is provided by *Herc.* 1300 (ἐν οἷσιν L marg.: ἐν
τοῖσι δ᾽ L).

(iii) To the examples quoted (pp. 58–9) to illustrate the proposition
that Euripides uses the article for the relative pronoun in iambic
trimeters only for metrical necessity add fr. 853. 1. Three exceptions
are presented by the manuscripts, but they are to be emended: *Su.*
858 τῶν (ὧν Pierson), *Herc.* 252 λόχευμα τοὺς (λοχεύμαθ᾽ οὓς Pierson),
Ba. 338 τὸν (ὃν Tr). On the use of the article for the relative in Aeschylus
and Sophocles see M. D. Reeve, *GRBS* 11 (1970) 285.

(iv) For repetition of the same syllable in contiguous words (p. 59)
see also Housman, *CR* 20 (1906) 41 = *Classical Papers* 644, Page, *Actors'
Interpolations* 124, Handley on Men. *Dysk.* 735 f., Kannicht on *Hel.*

1292 and Addenda, G. Luck, *HSCP* 65 (1961) 260, R. Führer, *Maia* 27 (1975) 217–20. Markland's comment on *IT* 710, 'sonus suaderet ἐνέγκας potius quam ἐνεγκὼν τῶν ἐμῶν ἄχθη κακῶν' is misguided.

(v) A partly different arrangement of these lines is proposed by T. C. W. Stinton, *JHS* 97 (1977) 149–51.

70 See pp. 110–11.

113 See p. 87 n. 2.

116–19   *Ορ.*   οὔτοι μακρὸν μὲν ἤλθομεν κώπηι πόρον
          ἐκ τερμάτων δὲ νόστον ἀροῦμεν πάλιν.
          ἀλλ' εὖ γὰρ εἶπας, πειστέον· χωρεῖν χρεών[1]
          ὅποι χθονὸς κρύψαντε λήσομεν δέμας.

Orestes ended his previous speech by saying 'let us flee before we are put to death' (102–3). Can he begin his next speech by saying 'We have not sailed all this way merely to turn back again on reaching our destination'?[2] No: he may not speak as if he had never doubted the wisdom of the course which Pylades has taken pains to commend in the intervening lines.[3] Some particle of agreement, at least, is necessary. Furthermore, what is the meaning of ἀλλά in 118? 'We shall not turn back. *But*, since your advice is sound, you must be obeyed.' This is quite unsatisfactory. In the 'complex' use of ἀλλά . . . γάρ (Denniston's expression, *GP* 98) 'ἀλλά and γάρ fulfil their normal functions independently'. Instances where the second verb is an imperative or quasi-imperative (like πειστέον) may be divided into two classes: (i) in the great majority the function of ἀλλά is to break off the train of thought (for a reason supplied by the γάρ-clause), and this is different from the adversative function alleged here; (ii) in a few (S. *El.* 256–7, *Ph.* 81–2, *OC* 755–7) ἀλλά does have an adversative function, but these show little resemblance to our passage. The words ἀλλ' εὖ γὰρ εἶπας, πειστέον cry out to be taken as the opening words of Orestes' speech, for the use of ἀλλά falls into the category neatly defined by Denniston (*GP* 16 § 6b) as that in which 'agreement is presented, not as self-evident, but as wrung from the speaker *malgré*

---

[1] χωρεῖν χρεών Scaliger: χώρει νεκρῶν L.
[2] For the structure of 116–17, which many have misunderstood, see Denniston, *GP* 371.
[3] Markland's attempt to evade the difficulty by printing 102–3 as a question is ineffectual.

lui. ἀλλά then points the contrast between the assent given and the considerations which have militated against the giving of it.' Compare above all S. *El.* 1470–2 αὐτὸς cὺ βάcταζ᾽· οὐκ ἐμὸν τόδ᾽ ἀλλὰ cὸν / τὸ ταῦθ᾽ ὁρᾶν τε καὶ προcηγορεῖν φίλωc. / : : ἀλλ᾽ εὖ παραινεῖc κἀπιπεί-coμαι.

That Orestes should begin his speech at 118 was first proposed by Hardion (*Histoire de l'Académie Royale des Inscriptions et Belles-Lettres* 5 [1729] 116–18) and independently by Markland. They attached 116–17 to the end of Pylades' speech. Modern editors reject this proposal; in the last century most editors accepted it. But some, while making Orestes begin his speech at 118, have dealt differently with 116–17. Dindorf deleted the lines (see his *Poetae scenici*, ed. 5 [1869]). He is followed by Wilamowitz (*Anal. Eur.* 244) and Page (*Actors' Interpolations* 77). For a defence of the lines see C. Schulze, *De versibus suspectis et interpolatis Iph. Taur. fab. Eur. pars prior* (1881) 25–6. Camper gave the lines to Pylades (see his note on *El.* 111 [p. 119]; he also wrote τί δ᾽ εἰ for οὗτοι), but placed them after 105. He is followed by England and Wecklein (1904 ed.). Bergk (*RhMus* 17 [1862] 592–3) placed them after 103 and gave them to Orestes (taking the previous sentence, with Markland, as a question).[1] Mähly,[2] accepting this transposition, gave them to Pylades. Wecklein once proposed (*Jahrb. f. cl. Phil., Supplbd.* 7 [1874] 391–2) to place them after 112; while A. Y. Campbell (*CQ* 32 [1938] 135) placed them after 119. It has to be admitted that οὗτοι provides a rather abrupt introduction to lines 116–17 when they are added to the end of Pylades' speech, although, in themselves, these lines make an excellent conclusion to the speech. But the lines fit no better in any of the other positions proposed for them. (The best place for them would be after 103, at the beginning of Pylades' speech, since οὗτοι commonly starts a speech. But then we should need γὰρ for μὲν in 104; and it would be a pity to separate φεύγωμεν 103 from φεύγειν 104.) If the transition between 115 and 116 should be considered to be excessively abrupt, then we might either accept Dindorf's deletion of 116–17 (but it would be a pity to lose the lines) or write οὐ γὰρ for οὗτοι, as Sir Denys Page suggested to me.

147 See p. 96.

[1] See the preceding note.
[2] *Neues Schweiz. Museum* 6 (1866) 217. Similarly Tournier, *RPh* n.s. 3 (1879) 28–9 (with Badham's οὗτω . . . ; for οὗτοι).

155   See p. 96.

157–8   See p. 97.

161   See *PCPS* n.s. 22 (1976) 42, where I failed to observe that
ὑγραίνειν had been proposed already by Blaydes (*Adv. crit. in Eur.*
[1901] 427).

186–8   οἴμοι τῶν Ἀτρειδᾶν οἴκων.
                     ἔρρει φῶς σκήπτρων οἴμοι
                     πατρώιων οἴκων.

186–202 choro contin. Hermann: Iphigeniae trib. L   187 φῶς Heath:
φόως L:]ως Π   σκηπ[Π

'The sceptre-brilliance of ⟨your⟩ ancestral home', translates Platnauer with misgivings. φῶς σκήπτρων is an extraordinary expression;
the addition of πατρώιων οἴκων makes it unbearable. Some prefer to
punctuate ἔρρει φῶς σκήπτρων· οἴμοι / πατρώιων οἴκων. But οἴμοι
πατρώιων οἴκων can hardly mean 'alas for *your* ancestral home'.
Accordingly Musgrave attributed οἴμοι πατρώιων οἴκων and all that
follows up to 202 to Iphigenia. This reduces the lamentations so
impressively promised by the chorus at 179 ff. to the unimpressive
exclamation οἴμοι . . . σκήπτρων. And a further obstacle is σοι in 202,
which, since it must refer to Iphigenia not to Orestes, cannot be
spoken by Iphigenia. Koechly, followed by England and Platnauer,
gives 186–91 to Iphigenia. But then the promised lamentations are
nowhere to be found. Platnauer, indeed, says that 'the ἀντιψάλμους
ᾠιδάς promised by the chorus must be taken as beginning at l. 192',
but he has forgotten how the chorus defined these ᾠιδαί in 182–3.
Another difficulty is that πατρώιων οἴκων is a metrically defective
verse. This difficulty, like the former, can be removed by adding
⟨τῶν σῶν⟩ before πατρώιων with Hermann. But neither Hermann's
addition nor the deletion of οἴμοι πατρώιων οἴκων (Dindorf) or that of
πατρώιων οἴκων (Hartung, approved by Wilamowitz *apud* Bruhn,
and by Strohm) touches the expression φῶς σκήπτρων.

Elmsley neatly removed all difficulties with ἔρρει φῶς, ⟨ἔρρει⟩
σκῆπτρον, / οἴμοι, πατρώιων οἴκων (*Mus. crit.* 2 [1826] 281). Orestes
is aptly described both as the light and as the sceptre of his ancestral
home. The former description is applied to him again at 849 and
S. *El.* 1354; for the image in general see Wilamowitz on *Herc.* 531

and D. Tarant, *CQ* n.s. 10 (1960) 181–7. For the application of
cκῆπτρον to a person see S. *OC* 848, 1109. Orestes is called cκηπτοῦχοc
at 235. The *breuis in longo* in cκῆπτρον is no obstacle: see p. 97.
But the same result can be achieved more economically by writing
ἔρρει φῶc cκῆπτρόν ⟨τ'⟩, οἴμοι, / πατρίων οἴκων. The conjecture
cκῆπτρόν ⟨τ'⟩ was made silently by Burges (ed. *Tr.* p. 140) and has
never been noticed; πατρίων was proposed by Mekler.

207–9   See p. 96.

212–13   See p. 97.

219–20   See p. 96.

231   See p. 97.

257   See *PCPS* n.s. 15 (1969) 59.

288   ἡ δ' ἐκ χιτώνων πῦρ πνέουcα καὶ φόνον . . .

I wish only to add a pedestrian footnote in support of Jackson's
brilliant ἡ 'κ γειτόνων δὲ (*Marg. scaen.* 146–8). Illustration of this
locution (which has been described by Platnauer, *CR* n.s. 6 [1956]
114, as 'far too colloquial' for Euripides) is given in Austin's note on
Men. *Asp.* 122. For the order of words (article, preposition, noun,
δέ) see *El.* 74, *Ion* 256, 622, *Or.* 427, 1664, *IA* 740, A. *PV* 442, S. *El.*
7, 924 (Canter), and Denniston, *GP* 186. The change of γειτόνων
to χιτώνων, prompted by the transfer of δέ to what was considered
its natural place, may be illustrated in all its elements. Jackson has
given examples of the confusion of o and ω. The confusion of χ and γ
is found at *Andr.* 1037, *El.* 654, 904, *Tr.* 231, A. *ScT* 114 (δογμ- Y),
Su. 677. The confusion of ι and ει, which is widespread, is found in
this very word at Men. *Asp.* 122 (γιτονων Π). It is also found below at
1462, where Pierson's λείμακαc must replace κλίμακαc, a reading
traditionally defended (even in LSJ Suppl. *s.u.*) with futile parallels. I
hope that we have now seen the last of notes like that of K. J. McKay,
'The Fury's Coats', *Mnemos.* ser. iv 17 (1964) 384–5.

300   ὡc αἱματηρὸν πέλαγοc ἐξανθεῖν ἁλόc.

On Markland's necessary ὥcθ' for ὡc see p. 8. Since Platnauer

describes πέλαγοc . . . ἀλόc as 'odd', and many editors have accepted
p's absurd πελανὸν (from αἱματηρὸc πελανὸc *Alc.* 851, *Rh.* 430), it is
worth showing how frequently phrases like this one are found:
πέλαγοc (πελάγη) ἀλόc *Tr.* 88, H. *Od.* 5. 335, *h. Ap.* 73, *h.* 33. 15,
Archil. 8. 1 West, Men. *Perik.* 809 (379 Koerte), ἅλιον πέλαγοc
Andr. 1011, *Hec.* 938, 950, ἅλc πελαγία A. *Pe.* 427, 467, πόντοc ἀλόc
H. *Il.* 21. 59, πόντου πέλαγοc Pi. fr. 140b. 16 Snell–Maehler, *maris
pontus* V. *Aen.* 10. 377 (see Housman, *JPh* 25 [1897] 244 = *Classical
Papers* 437).

On ἐξανθεῖν used of the frothing sea see E. K. Borthwick, *JHS*
96 (1976) 5–7.

338–9 On ἀποτείcει . . . τίνουcα (in order to avoid the repetition
Koechly proposed διδοῦcα, Nauck deleted 339) see p. 66.

394 See *Dionysiaca* 176 n. 30.

442–5   . . . ἵν᾽ ἀμφὶ χαί-
                   ταν δρόcον αἱματηρὰν
                   ἑλιχθεῖcα λαιμοτόμωι
                   δεcποίναc χειρὶ θάνηι . . .

442 χαίταν Musurus: -τα L   444 ἑλιχθεῖcα Tr²: εἱλ- L   445 χειρὶ
Monk: χερὶ L   θάνοι Seidler

Everyone used to print χαίταν, assuming it to be the transmitted
reading. Kirchhoff was perhaps the first editor to report L correctly
and to print χαίται, which everyone now accepts. I have not seen the
dative defended, except by England, who refers merely to ἀμφὶ
δίναιc in line 6, where tragic usage prescribes Monk's neglected
δίναc (cf. *Or.* 1310), for Iphigenia did not meet her slayer in the
Euripus. Perhaps someone will draw attention to *Med.* 980 ἀμφὶ
κόμαι and 1160 ἀμφὶ βοcτρύχοιc, which describe the placing of a
crown 'on the head'. What our passage describes is different—
'the lustral water being poured on the victim's head with a circular
motion' (Platnauer), and the accusative is needed, just as at 622
χαίτην ἀμφὶ cὴν χερνίψομαι, where the same activity is described. For
ἑλίccειν ἀμφί with accusative see also *Ph.* 1622 ἑλίξαc γ᾽ ἀμφὶ còν
χεῖραc γόνυ. And I should expect that an accusative has been lost at
Hyps. fr. 60. 74 εἵλιξεν ἀμφ[ὶ.

But ἑλιχθεῖcα is itself in need of vindication. Badham calls it 'prorsus absurdum', Kirchhoff 'uox corrupta', Platnauer 'strange'. In its place Badham proposed φοινιχθεῖca (repudiated in his note), Bergk (*RhMus* 18 [1863] 206) χερνιφθεῖca, Rauchenstein (*Disputatio de locis aliquot Eur. Iph. Taur.* [1860] ix) εὖ ῥανθεῖca, Koechly (*Emendationum in Eur. Iph. Taur. pars iv* [1861] 6–7) ἁγνιcθεῖca, Mekler παλαχθεῖca, and Sarros (reported in *REG* 35 [1922] 458) μειλιχθεῖca. The word is faultless. The image which it conveys is well expressed by Weil: 'Les eaux lustrales, répandues autour de la tête, sont comme une autre couronne à côté de la couronne de fleurs que portait la victime.' For a similar use of the passive verb see Hdt. 7. 90 τὰς μὲν κεφαλὰς εἱλίχατο μίτρῃcι ('they had had their heads encircled with turbans'). For the accusative δρόcον after the passive verb Weil and England compare 456–7 χέρας . . . cυνερειcθέντες, where χέρας is no more a parallel for δρόcον than is κεφαλάς in Hdt. 7. 90 just cited. The construction of δρόcον ἑλιχθεῖca is that of the familiar *suspensi loculos* (Hor. *serm.* 1. 6. 74) and is exemplified from tragedy by S. *Tr.* 157–8 δέλτον ἐγγεγραμμένην / ξυνθήματ': see KG 1. 125 § 7, W. H. D. Rouse, *CR* 29 (1915) 140. The same verb is used of making lustration at *Herc.* 926–7 ἐν κύκλωι δ' ἤδη κανοῦν / εἵλικτο βωμοῦ.

To the instances quoted by Platnauer of a subjunctive (θάνηι) retained in a final clause when an optative has preceded add *Andr.* 845, *Ion* 672, *Hel.* 178, *Ba.* 1258; see also F. Johnson, *De coniunctiui et optatiui usu Eur. in enuntiatis finalibus et condicionalibus* (1893) 37–8.

482–9 Op. τί ταῦτ' ὀδύρηι κἀπὶ τοῖc μέλλουcι νῶιν
   κακοῖcι λυπεῖc, ἥτις εἶ ποτ', ὦ γύναι;
   οὔτοι νομίζω cοφόν, ὃc ἂν μέλλων θανεῖν
   οἴκτωι τὸ δεῖμα τοὐλέθρου νικᾶν θέληι,   485
   οὐχ ὅcτιc Ἅιδην ἐγγὺς ὄντ' οἰκτίζεται
   cωτηρίας ἄνελπιc· ὡc δύ' ἐξ ἑνὸc
   κακὼ cυνάπτει, μωρίαν τ' ὀφλιcκάνει
   θνήιcκει θ' ὁμοίωc.

483 κακοῖc cε (potius cὲ) Housman apud Platnauer   484 θανεῖν L et Stob. 3. 8. 6: κτανεῖν Seidler   486 οὐδ' Hermann   u. del. Reiske, Markland

In *Prometheus* 2 (1976) 83 I commended κακοῖc cε λυπεῖc, giving parallels for the expression.[1] Additional point is given to this conjecture

---

[1] It is also accepted by Strohm. As a further parallel for the reflexive use of cε see A. *ScT* 255, with Stinton's note in *PCPS* n.s. 13 (1967) 49. See also Men. *Sam.* 3, with Austin's note.

if we accept Kvičala's hesitant proposal, which has been wholly neglected, μέλουϲι for μέλλουϲι (*Sitzb. d. k. Ak. d. Wiss. Wien* 29 [1859] 244). The sentence τί . . . ἐπὶ τοῖϲ μέλουϲι νῶιν | κακοῖϲ cὲ (rather than cε) λυπεῖϲ; rings true and Euripidean. The verb μέλειν is regularly used in sentences where roles or responsibilities are apportioned. Such sentences are commonly antithetical in nature: 'something μέλει (is the concern of) A; but B . . .'; or 'A will do something; but what μέλει (is the concern of) B is . . .'. So 40 κατάρχομαι μέν, cφάγια δ᾽ ἄλλοιϲιν μέλει, *Hcld.* 711 ἀνδρῶν γὰρ ἀλκή· coὶ δὲ χρῆν τούτων μέλειν, *El.* 1342–3 τοῖϲδε μελήϲει γάμοϲ· ἀλλὰ . . . cτεῖχε, *Ion* 35–6 ('you must do certain things') τὰ δ᾽ ἄλλ᾽ (ἐμὸϲ γάρ ἐϲτιν, ὡϲ εἰδῆιϲ, ὁ παῖϲ) | ἡμῖν μελήϲει, 414 ἡμεῖϲ τά γ᾽ ἔξω, τῶν ἔϲω δ᾽ ἄλλοιϲ μέλει, *Rh.* 983–4 οὗτοϲ μὲν ἤδη μητρὶ κηδεύειν μέλει· | cὺ δ᾽ . . . , fr. 522 εἰ κερκίδων μὲν ἀνδράϲιν μέλοι πόνοϲ, | γυναικὶ δ᾽ ὅπλων ἐμπέϲοιεν ἡδοναί, *Men. Sam.* 112–13 καὶ ταῦτα μὲν | ἑτέροιϲ μέλειν ἐῶμεν· ὑπὲρ ὧν δ᾽ ἐλέγομεν κτλ. In these passages the two roles or responsibilities are kept separate. But what concerns A may also be the legitimate concern of B: *Rh.* 647 μέλει δ᾽ ὁ cόϲ μοι πόλεμοϲ, 665 μέλειν γὰρ πάντ᾽ ἐμοὶ δόκει τὰ cά. Yet sometimes such concern, far from being legitimate, may amount to a meddlesome curiosity, which must be repudiated: *Ion* 433–4 ἀτὰρ θυγατρὸϲ τῆϲ Ἐρεχθέωϲ τί μοι | μέλει; προϲήκει γ᾽ οὐδέν. Just as Ion concludes that Creusa's behaviour is her own affair and resolves to inquire no more into its causes, so Orestes resolves to answer no questions from Iphigenia about his family or his mission, for these are his own business, and a distressing business at that. Indeed (he reasons) the sympathetic interest which Iphigenia displays is nothing but a polite charade by which her inhumanity attempts to mask itself. Let her cut their throats and stop prying. μέλειν is corrupted to μέλλειν twice elsewhere in this play: at 909 and 1051, even against the metre in both places; and the corruption is very common elsewhere.

We should accept Seidler's κτανεῖν in 484 and Hermann's οὐδ᾽ in 486. The alternative, to keep θανεῖν and delete 486, is more commonly adopted: cf. Schulze (cited on p. 77) 42–3. Platnauer, who favours it, raises four objections against the former solution, and I shall answer them in turn. (i) 'It ignores the fact that Stobaeus . . . quotes l. 484 as ending in θανεῖν.' The objection itself ignores the fact that the two words are perpetually confused: 553, 1017 (κτανεῖν P), *Andr.* 661, 686, 810, 824, *Or.* 1611, *Rh.* 635. See also Dawe, *Studies* i. 236. (ii) 'It puts into Orestes' mouth what Weil reasonably

calls "un langage fort déplaisant".' Since neither Weil nor Platnauer explains what is unpleasant, the objection must be disregarded.
(iii) 'It involves translating τὸ δεῖμα νικᾶν as "to overcome ⟨the victim's⟩ fear".' No reason is offered why we should not translate in this
way; nor can I imagine any reason. (iv) 'It introduces a sentiment
inconsistent with the following sentence, ὡc δύ', κτλ.' But ὡc δύ' κτλ.
may quite naturally be taken as a comment on only the second of the
two clauses (οὐδ' ὅcτιc κτλ.). The chief obstacle against accepting
θανεῖν is that it really does put into Orestes' mouth unpleasant
language. According to Platnauer, 'We can take οἴκτωι δεῖμα νικᾶν
either as "to drown his fear in pitiful cries" or "to overcome his
fear by the help of others' pity".' Against the former interpretation
it may be held that crying pitifully is a preposterous way of drowning
one's fear of death. The latter interpretation, in which the victim is
represented as '*wishing* to overcome his fear of death with the help
of another's pity' is no less absurd. It may be added, as an objection
against the deletion of 486, that cωτηρίαc ἄνελπιc follows much less
naturally after 485 than it does after 486.

507   χάριν δὲ δοῦναι τήνδε κωλύει τί cε;

Monk proposed cε τί; So too did Cobet (*Var. lect.* ed. 2 [1873] 597),
'ut τί ictum habeat et sua sede sit collocatum'. Murray objects that
'τι indefinitum esse uidetur'. Monk, Cobet, and Murray have all
assumed that if τί is interrogative its proper place is at the end of the
line. An investigation of the passages in which the tragic poets,
Aristophanes, and Menander place a pronoun and a form of τίc
or τιc in the last foot of the iambic trimeter will show whether there
is any justification for this assumption.

Consider first the placing of the enclitic forms. So far as concerns
the enclitic τι and the accusative pronoun, either order (cέ τι or τί cε)
is metrically possible and both are found: cέ τι A. *PV* 835, S. *OT*
644, Men. *Epitr.* 433 (257 Koerte), 574 (398 K.), τί με (cε) S. fr.
176 P, Ar. *Nub.* 38, *Lys.* 656, *Plut.* 22 (and in a trochaic tetrameter
at *Pax* 330), Men. *Sam.* 702, *Dysk.* 107, *Phas.* 53. Whether the words
are the last in the sentence or appear in the middle of the sentence is
not a factor which determines the choice of order. When τιc is used
with the accusative pronoun, or when τι is used with the pronoun
in the genitive or dative, the order is dictated by metre: μέ (cέ) τιc
Hcld. 248, *El.* 559, *Hel.* 1615, *Ba.* 649, *IA* 849, Ar. *Plut.* 1014, Men.

Dysk. 142, τί μοι (coι, μου, cου) *Cycl.* 175, *Hec.* 992, *IT* 582, *Ba.* 658, *IA* 1188, A. *Eum.* 442, S. *El.* 902, *Ph.* 761, *OC* 1414, *GLP* 32. 4 Page, Ar. *Au.* 51, *Lys.* 861, *Ran.* 44, 175 (and in a trochaic tetrameter at A. *Pe.* 705), Men. *Asp.* 173 (coni.), 420, *Dis Ex.* 62, *Dysk.* 299 (suppl.), 877 (suppl.), *Epitr.* 264 (88 Koerte), 1070 (712 K.), *Perik.* 485 (235 K.), fr. 97. 1.

Now consider the placing of the interrogative forms τίc and τί. I can find no example of τί με (cε). But this is of no significance, since I am equally unable to find an example of με (cε) τίc (τί). Metrical necessity dictates the order at *Ion* 433 ἀτὰρ θυγατρὸc τῆc Ἐρεχθέωc τί μοι / μέλει; and at *Ba.* 832 τὸ δεύτερον δὲ cχῆμα τοῦ κόcμου τί μοι; cf. Men. *Mis.* 216 (18 Koerte), if Handley's supplement is right. And so these passages tell us nothing. And it would be doubly irrelevant to adduce in evidence passages where the interrogative is the opening word of its clause, since here again the alternative order is excluded: *Andr.* 1104–5 ὦ νεανία, τί coι / θεῶι κατευξώμεcθα; A. *PV* 83, S. *El.* 352, 887, *Ph.* 559, 753, *OC* 1420, Men. *Mis.* 308. I have therefore found no evidence either in tragedy or in Aristophanes or Menander to justify the assumption that, when the interrogative form is used, a trimeter will more naturally end with cε τί than with τί cε. The assumption may have been prompted by the very common occurrence of δὲ τίc (τί) at the end of the line, which I have illustrated in *Dionysiaca* 170.

691–2 ... τὸ μὲν γὰρ εἰc ἔμ' οὐ κακῶc ἔχει,
πράccονθ' ἃ πράccω πρὸc θεῶν, †λήcειν† βίον.

λήcειν L: λήγειν L^sl: λύcειν P: λιπεῖν Badham, λῦcαι Schenkl

The easiest course is to accept the supralinear λήγειν and change βίον to βίου with Markland (Maas, *Textual Criticism* [1958] 27, retains βίον because 'λήγειν transitive recurs at *Ion* 1404', a remarkable aberration). But although in support of the expression we may quote Xen. *Ap.* 8 λῆξαι τοῦ βίου, neither this nor Badham's λιπεῖν βίον has the idiomatic colour of Schenkl's λῦcαι βίον (*Philologus* 20 [1863] 328; Elmsley, *Quart. Rev.* 7 [1812] 464 and *Mus. crit.* 2 [1826] 292–3, had already suggested λύειν). Compare *Su.* 1004–5 καταλύcουcα ... βίοτον, fr. 994 καταλυcαμένουc βίον, Xen. *Ap.* 7 καταλῦcαι τὸν βίον, Bacchyl. 1. 153 αἰῶν' ἔλυcεν, S. *Ant.* 1268 ἔθανεc ἀπελύθηc, 1314 ποίωι δὲ κἀπελύcατ' (κἀπελύετ' Pearson, *CQ* 22 [1928] 190) ἐν φοναῖc τρόπωι; *OC* 1720–1 ἔλυcεν τὸ τέλοc ... βίου, Kaibel, *Ep. gr.* 218. 8

(1871. 8 Peek) τερπνὸν ἔλυσε βίον, Prop. 2. 9. 39 *soluite uitam*, Sen. *ep.* 22. 3.

The change of λῦσαι to λήςειν was not difficult. P's λύςειν, a happy error, shows how readily υ and η are confused: see also *Su.* 952, *Herc.* 185, *El.* 647, *Ion* 173). Equally common is the confusion of -αι and -ειν: 938, 1041 (see Madvig, *Adv. crit.* 1 [1871] 171), *Alc.* 657, *Med.* 748, *Andr.* 311, *Ion* 1348, and perhaps *Herc.* 946.

719–20   ἀτὰρ τὸ τοῦ θεοῦ ς᾽ οὐ διέφθορέν γέ πω[1]
            μάντευμα· καίτοι γ᾽ ἐγγὺς ἔςτηκας φόνου.

Denniston, *GP* 564, quotes besides this one five examples of καίτοι γε in verse. Four evaporate on scrutiny. (i) Hippon. fr. 31 (44 West) καί τοί γ᾽ (i.e. the pronoun). (ii) E. fr. 953. 10 καίτοι γ᾽, ὦ πάτερ, breaking Porson's law into the bargain (Denniston admits that this fragment is 'spurious': see p. 104 below). (iii) Ar. *Nub.* 876 καίτοι γε (RV: καίτοι cett.) ταλάντου, giving a split anapaest in the second foot of the iambic trimeter and rejected for that reason by Dover (who rejects another instance of καίτοι γε presented by some of the manuscripts at 1254). (iv) Ar. *Lys.* 1035, described by Denniston as 'doubtful', would more correctly be described as unmetrical (γε del. Florens Christianus). This leaves only Ar. *Ach.* 611 καίτοι γ᾽ ἐςτί, which Dover (on *Nub.* 876) calls 'certain' but which was simply emended by Elmsley to καίτοὐςτίν γε (for the crasis see *Vesp.* 599), and this is accepted by both Starkie and R. T. Elliott (see his edition [1914] p. 162 for a useful discussion). Denniston overlooks another instance in the manuscripts of Euripides, at *Tr.* 1015, καίτοι γ᾽ ἐνουθέτουν ςε, where Burges's καίτοι ς᾽ ἐνουθέτουν γε is to be accepted.[2] It is hard to disagree with Porson's verdict (on *Med.* 675 [677]) that 'Atticis non licuisse γε post τοι ponere, nisi alio vocabulo interjecto' (for poetry, at least, I believe this to be true; I say nothing of prose).

Write therefore καίτοι κἀγγὺς with Erfurdt. καίτοι καί is found at A. *PV* 642. For καί emphasizing verbs see Denniston, *GP* 320–3. There is a very similar corruption at *Su.* 879: ἐπεί τοι κοὐδὲν Stob.: ἐπεί τοί γ᾽ οὐδὲν L. Another example of καί in crasis corrupted to γ᾽ is *Med.* 1367 ςφε κἠξίωςας LP: ςφέ γ᾽ ἠξ- AVB.

I see no reason to evade the difficulty by deleting 720 with Herwerden (*Versl. en Mededeel. der k. Akad. van wetensch. Afd. Letterk.*

---

[1] ς᾽ . . . γέ Nauck: γ᾽ . . . μέ L: γ᾽ . . . ςέ apogr. Par.
[2] See the preceding note and *Hel.* 118 (ςέ γ᾽ Tr² rightly: γέ ςε L).

1874, 103), approved by Bruhn and by G. Jachmann, *NGG* 1936, 201.

736   See p. 110.

765   See p. 39.

786–7   αἵδ' ἐπιστολαί,
         τάδ' ἐcτὶ τὰν δέλτοιcιν ἐγγεγραμμένα.

787 τάδ' L: ταῦτ' Plut. mor. 182 E   ἐcτὶ τὰν Plut.: ἐcτιν ἐν L

Paley preferred ταῦτ' since 'οὗτοc and ὅδε were elegantly used, in two consecutive clauses, of the very same thing or person'. This is not in dispute: for examples see Page on *Med.* 1046, Barrett on *Hi.* 194. What has escaped notice is that, when these two words are used in anaphora, as they would be here, the variation may always be imputed to metrical necessity: *Hec.* 279–80 ταύτηι γέγηθα κἀπιλήθομαι κακῶν, / ἥδ' ἀντὶ πολλῶν κτλ., fr. 670. 4 τήνδ' ἀροῦμεν, ἐκ ταύτηc βίοc κτλ., 941. 3 τοῦτον νόμιζε Ζῆνα, τόνδ' ἡγοῦ θεόν, S. *El.* 981 τούτω φιλεῖν χρή, τῶδε χρὴ πάντας cέβειν, Ant. 296–7 τοῦτο καὶ πόλεις / πορθεῖ, τόδ' κτλ., 673–4 αὕτη πόλεις ὄλλυcιν, ἥδ' ἀναcτάτουc / οἴκουc τίθηcιν, ἥδε κτλ., *Ph.* 841 τοῦδε γὰρ ὁ cτέφανοc, τοῦτον θεὸc εἶπε κομίζειν.

811   See p. 110.

829–30   See *Dionysiaca* 175 n. 18.

832–3   See p. 20.

854   See p. 33.

859   See *Illinois Class. Stud.* 2 (1977) 123 n. 28.

861   See *Dionysiaca* 162.

870–6   See *PCPS* n.s. 22 (1976) 42–4. To the illustrations adduced in support of my conjecture at S. *El.* 853 add A. *Ag.* 1653.

986   See *PCPS* n.s. 20 (1974) 32 and p. 112 below.

1004 On the word-order see *CQ* n.s. 27 (1977) 236.

1010–11 ἥξω δέ γ', ἥνπερ καὐτὸς ἐνταυθοῖ πέcω,
πρὸς οἶκον, εἴ cου κατθανὼν μενῶ μέτα.

1010 ἄξω δέ c' Canter   ἐντεῦθεν περῶ Seidler   1011 εἴ L: ἤ L^{sl}   cοῦ
apogr. Par.

I have recorded the four changes which are needed to set these lines
right. They are accepted by Badham, Bruhn, and Schulze (cited
on p. 77) 76–7. No other remedy will satisfy save deletion, an
expedient first advocated by Dindorf and last by Page, *Actors' Interpolations* 78. The lines as emended mean 'I shall take you (for ἄξω
cf. 1001), if *I myself* travel from here to home (πρὸς οἶκον should be
taken ἀπὸ κοινοῦ with ἄξω and περῶ), or I shall stay with you in death'.

The problems of these lines have attracted a good deal of tiresome
and meandering discussion,[1] and my own remarks will be brief.
First, δέ γ' will not do: see Denniston, *GP* 155.[2] Second, ἐνταυθοῖ is
not a tragic form. The corruption of ἐντεῦθεν to ἐνταυθοῖ is paralleled
at fr. 497. 1 (Elmsley, *Mus. crit.* 2 [1826] 302 n. 1). Another instance
of ἐνταυθοῖ generated by corruption may be found in Dawe's apparatus
criticus at S. *El.* 1496. More commonly ἐντεῦθεν means 'thence';
but the meaning 'hence' is clear at S. *OT* 1521 ἄπαγέ νύν μ' ἐντεῦθεν.
The καί in καὐτὸς, which according to Platnauer 'has no point at all',
may be interpreted in the way that my translation suggests or in the
way suggested by Denniston, *GP* 304 (the two suggestions are not
incompatible). The verb περῶ, which according to Weil 'ne convient
pas ici', has the meaning illustrated by LSJ *s.u.* II. 3, '*pass to* or *from*
a place'.

The most popular alternative method of emendation is to accept
Markland's μὴ αὐτὸς for καὐτὸς, in the hope of restoring some such
sense as 'I shall take you, if I myself do not fall (here), to our home,
or I shall stay with you in death'. To this I make three objections.
(i) the synecphonesis μὴ αὐτὸς is not Euripidean; (ii) ἐνταυθοῖ still
needs emendation, and the emendations offered are not attractive:
among others are ἐν Ταύροιc Goram (*RhMus* 20 [1865] 466), ἐν

---

[1] Particularly from J. Meunier, *MB* 33 (1929) 132–3 and J. C. Kamerbeek,
Mnemos. ser. iii 10 (1942) 48–53, J. D. Meerwaldt, ibid. 11 (1943) 228–32, Kamerbeek, ibid. 12 (1945) 44–6.
[2] No more will δέ γ' at 113, a point usually overlooked in discussions of
this line (most recently in those of D. Sansone, *Mnem.* ser. iv 29 [1976] 79, and
M. Marcovich, ibid. 30 [1977] 288–9).

ταύτηι Platnauer; (iii) as Seidler saw, the sense is unacceptable: 'proxima ἤ coῦ κατθανὼν μενῶ μέτα ... parum accuratam oppositionem faciunt: *nisi hic occubuero, ducam te domum, aut (i.e. si occubuero) manebo tecumque moriar.* sane quidem manebit, si occubuerit.'

1035-7   Ιφ. ὡc οὐ θέμιc cε λέξομεν θύειν θεᾶι.
Ορ. τίν' αἰτίαν ἔχουc'; ὑποπτεύω τι γάρ.
Ιφ. οὐ καθαρὸν ὄντα· τὸ δ' ὅcιον δώcω φόνωι.

1035 cε Reiske: γε L   1036 ἔχονθ' Reiske   1037 φόνωι Musurus: φόβω L

Commentators, if they trouble to explain the construction at all, accept Hermann's explanation that 'cohaerent haec sic: λέξομεν ὡc οὐ θέμιc ἐcτί cε θύειν θεᾶι οὐ καθαρὸν ὄντα, τὸ δ' ὅcιον δώcω φόνωι, ita ut etiam δώcω ex ὡc pendeat'. This is unnecessarily complicated. I take ὡc to be an instance of the use exemplified by Elmsley on *Med.* 596 [609]: "Ὡc fortiter affirmantis est, ut ἴcθι ὡc.' Similarly *Cycl.* 473, *Andr.* 255, 587, *Hec.* 400, *Su.* 294, 1056, *Herc.* 62, *Ion* 935, *Hel.* 126, 831, *Ph.* 625, 720, 1664, *IA* 863, 1367, *Hyps.* fr. 60. 1. 8, and perhaps 1214 below.

δώcω κτλ. was satisfactorily explained by Markland: '*dicam me daturam,* ut mox [1039] βουλήcομαι est *dicam me uelle.*' For the confusion of φόνωι and φόβωι see p. 54.

1041   See p. 85.

1091   See p. 58.

1109   See p. 46.

1218   Ιφ. πέπλον ὀμμάτων προθέcθαι.   Θο. μὴ παλαμναῖον λάβω.

'παλαμναῖον: here the neut. of the adj., sc. τι', says Platnauer, echoing the common opinion (the strange misapprehension of LSJ *s.u.* is corrected in the Supplement). To 'understand' τι is impossible. It does not help to quote passages in which a neuter adjective or participle is used (*a*) in apposition, as in *Med.* 1034-5 κατθανοῦcαν ... περιcτελεῖν, / ζηλωτὸν ἀνθρώποιcι, *Su.* 1070, *Or.* 30, 624, S. *Ant.* 44, or (*b*) in phrases which are almost adverbial, as S. *OT* 1312 ἐc δεινὸν οὐδ' ἀκουcτὸν οὐδ' ἐπόψιμον, *Ph.* 83 εἰc ἀναιδέc. On S. *OT* 517 see

Dawe, *Studies* i. 235–6. W. Bauer's παλαμναίουc βλέπω may well be right.[1]

1318–21   Αγ.   cώιζουc' 'Ορέcτην· τοῦτο γὰρ cὺ θαυμάcηι.
      Θο.   τὸν ποῖον; ἆρ' ὃν Τυνδαρὶc τίκτει κόρη;
      Αγ.   ὃν τοῖcδε βωμοῖc θεὰ καθωcιώcατο.   1320
      Θο.   ὦ θαῦμα, πῶc cε μεῖζον ὀνομάcαc τύχω;

Thoas is informed that Iphigenia has saved the life of her victim, and that the victim was Orestes. 'O marvel!' he cries, 'how may I correctly call you by a greater name?' (For the use of τυγχάνω in this sense see Barrett on *Hi.* 826–7, Fraenkel on *Ag.* 622.) There are two difficulties here.

First, to what do ὦ θαῦμα and the pronoun cε refer? Commentators refer ὦ θαῦμα to the circumstances just described, and they refer cε to θαῦμα. But if ὦ θαῦμα is an exclamation, then cε is oddly used, since it is not very natural to make a direct address to an exclamation; cφε would be more natural (for the corruption of cφε to cε see p. 59), but cφε in the singular is masculine or feminine, not neuter (it is neuter, but plural, at Theoc. 15. 80).

Second, is the question πῶc cε μεῖζον ὀνομάcαc τύχω; an appropriate sequel to the exclamation ὦ θαῦμα? Commentators suppose that the king, having exclaimed 'O marvel!', decides that 'marvel' is too mild a description for the messenger's revelations. 'What greater name' (they suppose him to inquire) 'may I find?' The name he seeks (we shall have to suppose) will describe what is, in the common phrase, 'beyond marvels': 839–40 θαυμάτων / πέρα καὶ λόγου πρόcω τάδ' ἀπέβα (Reiske: ἐπ- L), *Hec.* 714 ἄρρητ' ἀνωνόμαcτα θαυμάτων πέρα, *Ba.* 667 δεινὰ δρῶcι θαυμάτων τε κρείccονα. That θαῦμα is a name which may do its recipient less than his fair credit is confirmed by *Hel.* 601 (the text is not quite certain) θαυμάcτ' (θαῦμ' ἐcτ' Scaliger), ἔλαccον τοὔνομ' ἢ τὸ πρᾶγμ' ἔχον (p: ἔχων L). Note also *Ph.* 389 ἔργωι δ' ἐcτὶ μεῖζον ἢ λόγωι, 407 οὐδ' ὀνομάcαι δύναι' ἂν ὡc ἐcτὶν φίλον.

There is, then, no reason why the king should not proceed to search for *le mot le plus juste*. But is the question πῶc cε μεῖζον ὀνομάcαc τύχω; the right way to proceed? Questions with πῶc and the subjunctive can sometimes be taken as real and open questions to which an answer

[1] In his 1873 ed. (knowledge of which I owe to Wecklein, *Bursian* 1 [1873] 122–3).

is expected (as A. *Ch.* 88 πῶς εὔφρον' εἴπω; πῶς κατεύξωμαι πατρί;), but usually such a question is no question at all but rather an admission of helplessness (as *Alc.* 912–13 ὦ σχῆμα δόμων, πῶς εἰσέλθω; / πῶς δ' οἰκήσω . . . ; *Ion* 859–60 πῶς σιγάσω; πῶς δὲ σκοτίας ἀναφήνω / εὐνάς; S. fr. 196 P πῶς οὖν μάχωμαι θνητὸς ὢν θείαι τύχηι;). The run of the words ὦ θαῦμα, πῶς σε μεῖζον ὀνομάσας τύχω does not read very naturally as a genuine inquiry after a more suitable name (it would perhaps read more naturally with σφε for σε).[1] The run of the words might more naturally suggest that the question ought to express the speaker's inability to find any name more suitable than the one he has already found: 'O marvel! ⟨I use this name because⟩ how can I call you (σε) by any name more suitable?' We then have an apostrophe followed by an explanation for the choice of words used in the apostrophe, as at *Med.* 465–6 ὦ παγκάκιστε, τοῦτο γάρ σ' εἰπεῖν ἔχω / γλώσσηι μέγιστον εἰς ἀνανδρίαν κακόν, *Andr.* 56–7 δέσποιν', ἐγώ τοι τοὔνομ' οὐ φεύγω τόδε / καλεῖν σ' . . ., 64 ὦ φιλτάτη σύνδουλε, σύνδουλος γὰρ εἶ, *Hel.* 1193 ὦ δέσποτ', ἤδη γὰρ τόδ' ὀνομάζω σ' ἔπος, fr. 666 ὦ παγκακίστη καὶ γυνή· τί γὰρ λέγων / μεῖζόν σε τοῦδ' ὄνειδος ἐξείποι τις ἄν; cf. Ar. *Vesp.* 1297–8, *Thes.* 582–3.[2]

The only obstacle to so taking the sentence is μεῖζον. 'Potius putarem μεῖον. quo enim *minore nomine recte te possim appellare?*' writes Markland. He may be right: μείων is corrupted to μείζων at S. fr. 86. 2 P, μεῖζον to μεῖον at E. fr. 1025. 2. But while the conjecture μεῖον may solve the second of our difficulties, it leaves untouched the first, the difficulty of σε. A possible answer to that difficulty is, instead of writing πῶς ὄλειζον (Wecklein) or πῶς γε μεῖον (Platnauer),[3] to refer ὦ θαῦμα and σε to Iphigenia: 'O you marvel! how may I correctly call you by a lesser name?' θαῦμα is used of persons in H. *Od.* 9. 190 θαῦμ' ἐτέτυκτο πελώριον (Polyphemus), E. *IA* 202 Μηριόνην . . . θαῦμα βροτοῖσιν, S. *Tr.* 961 ἄπετόν τι θαῦμα (Heracles), Bacchyl. 17. 123 θαῦμα πάντεσσι (Theseus), Melanipp. *PMG* 762 κλῦθί μοι ὦ πάτερ, θαῦμα βροτῶν. For the use of an abstract noun in an apostrophe cf. ὦ μῖσος at 525, *Med.* 1323, *Hcld.* 52, 941; see also p. 5 above.

---

[1] Other emendations which aim to restore this type of sentence are not appealing: πῶς δ' ὁ μεῖζον Mekler, πῶς δὲ (or γὰρ) μεῖζον Paley.

[2] On *Hi.* 88–9, which is usually taken in this way, see *CR* n.s. 17 (1967) 133–4.

[3] This conjecture is accepted by Strohm. Platnauer, muddled though his note is, shows a better awareness of the problems of this passage than his reviewer in *CR* 52 (1938) 220.

In order that ὦ θαῦμα and ϲε may refer to Iphigenia, it is desirable, perhaps indispensable, that Iphigenia should be mentioned immediately before. For this reason we might accept (as everyone did before Markland) Musurus's θεᾶι for θεά in the preceding line. In that line the meaning of καθωϲιώϲατο is far from certain. According to Hesychius Euripides used the active verb καθωϲίωϲε in the sense κατέθυϲε in his *Meleager* (fr. 539). In prose, much later, the active means 'dedicate' (statues and the like). The passive is found at Ar. *Plut.* 660–1 ἐπεὶ δὲ βωμῶι πόπανα καὶ προθύματα / καθωϲιώθη πελανὸϲ Ἡφαίϲτου φλογί, a passage clearly parodying the language of tragedy (cf. Men. *Sam.* 674 [329 Koerte]), where the sense seems to be 'were dedicated to (i.e. consumed by) Hephaestus' flame on the altar'. Neither LSJ nor TLG cites any other authority for the middle than the present passage. If θεά is kept, we may follow Paley's explanation : 'whom the goddess had just had consecrated (by her priestess) to the altar here', except that '(for a sacrifice) at the altar' will be preferable, as in Ar. *Plut.* 660. For this use of the middle ('to have consecrated', like *Med.* 295 ἐκδιδάϲκεϲθαι 'to have taught') see KG 1. 108, Schwyzer 1. 232. With θεᾶι the meaning would be 'whom she dedicated to the goddess as a sacrifice at her altar'. (Monk unnecessarily objected to the two datives and proposed θεᾶϲ.) The middle is used often enough in tragedy without any perceptible difference from the active : see KG 1. 102, Pearson on S. fr. 941. 16, Broadhead on A. *Pe.* 48.

We might be tempted to compare 1194 ὁϲιώτεροι (Tournier : -ον L) γοῦν τῆι θεῶι πέϲοιεν ἄν (sc. after the purification) and to refer καθωϲιώϲατο to the actual purification of Orestes which Iphigenia has pretended to perform on the sea-shore. But this seems less plausible, since the messenger has not yet given us the details of that pretended act. Instead compare, for the sense and the dative, *Hcld.* 600–1 θεάν, / ἧι ϲὸν κατῆρκται ϲῶμα, 'the goddess to whom your body has been dedicated', where κατῆρκται refers only to the intention to offer the body as a sacrifice and not to any ritual dedication. No less comparable is A. *Eum.* 304 (the Erinyes speaking of their victim Orestes) ἐμοὶ τραφείϲ τε καὶ καθιερωμένοϲ.

If this version of 1320 is not accepted, then perhaps the best solution is to write ϲφε for ϲε, and to refer the pronoun (as well as ὦ θαῦμα) to Iphigenia : 'O marvel! How may I correctly call her by a lesser name?'

1344 See p. 44.

1348–53   . . . ἐκ δεϲμῶν δὲ τοὺϲ νεανίαϲ
ἐλευθέρουϲ πρυμνηθεν ἑϲτῶταϲ νεώϲ.
κοντοῖϲ δὲ πρῶιραν εἶχον, οἱ δ' ἐπωτίδων   1350
ἄγκυραν ἐξανῆπτον, οἱ δὲ κλίμακαϲ
ϲπεύδοντεϲ ἦγον διὰ χερῶν πρυμνήϲια,
πόντωι δὲ δόντεϲ τῆι ξένηι καθίεϲαν.

1349 νεώϲ Musurus: νεῶν L   1351 ἄγκυραν Scaliger: -ραϲ L   1353 τῆι
ξένηι Musgrave: τὴν ξένην L (τὴν ξένοιν P): τοῖν ξένοιν Seidler

'And (we saw) the young men free from their bonds standing on the
stern of the ship.' Why they are standing on the stern is explained by
J. S. Morrison and R. T. Williams, *Greek Oared Ships 900–322 B.C.*
(1968) 201–2. Commentators usually translate 'astern of the ship',
i.e. on the shore; but no satisfactory parallel has been offered for
such a use of πρύμνηθεν. '⟨Some of the sailors⟩[1] were holding the prow
with poles, others were fastening the anchor to the catheads, others . . .'
What were the others doing? According to the text printed above
(and so it is printed by, among others, Markland, Hermann, Paley,
Murray, and Grégoire), 'others were carrying stern-cables in their
hands while hurrying ladders (κλίμακαϲ ϲπεύδοντεϲ), and after putting
them into the sea were letting them down for the foreign girl'.

Before I tackle the more serious problem in these lines, let me
briefly commend τῆι ξένηι (1353) in preference to τοῖν ξένοιν, a
conjecture which gains no support from P's itacistic error. I have
assumed above that Orestes and Pylades are on board the ship. If
this assumption is right, then τοῖν ξένοιν is impossible. But assume,
for the sake of argument, that they are on the shore. The decisive
objection to τοῖν ξένοιν would be not that agile young men have no
need of a ladder (M. L. Earle, *AJP* 13 [1892] 87–8 = *Classical
Papers* [1912] 116–17) but that the dual would exclude Iphigenia.
That τῆι ξένηι excludes her companions is as it should be.

Two things are clear: κλίμακαϲ is not the object of ϲπεύδοντεϲ,
and the aorist participle δόντεϲ has no place among these imperfect
main verbs. Kirchhoff proposed ἢ πρυμνήϲια / ϲπεύδοντεϲ ἦγον διὰ
χερῶν καὶ κλίμακα / πόντωι διδόντεϲ. This, as a whole, is violent and
unsatisfactory, but one element of it is plausible: πόντωι διδόντεϲ
neatly eliminates the aorist, and κλίμακα(ϲ) provides the participle
with a suitable object. Several proposals for effecting a juncture of
κλίμακαϲ . . . πόντωι διδόντεϲ have relied upon the removal of 1352,

---

[1] For the ellipse see Wilamowitz on *Herc.* 635, Denniston, *GP* 166 (ii).

which interrupts these words. But each of these proposals entails the further assumption of a lacuna or other corruption. Bergk (*RhMus* 18 [1863] 221–4) transposed 1352 after 1353, but was obliged to mark a lacuna between 1353 and 1351. Earle, adopting this transposition, changed ϲπεύδοντεϲ ἦγον to ϲπουδῆι τ᾽ ἐϲῆγον. Koechly (*Emendationum in Eur. Iph. Taur. pars ii* [1860] 91–3), who is followed by Weil and approved by Platnauer, transposed 1352 after 1349. But he was then obliged to mark a lacuna in 1349 between ἐλευθέρουϲ and πρύμνηθεν (England, who also follows him, prints an impossible asyndeton) and to change ἑϲτῶταϲ to ἑϲτῶτεϲ. Bruhn, adopting the same transposition, marks a lacuna after 1349. Wecklein (*Jahrb. f. cl. Phil.* Suppl. Bd. 7 [1874] 348–9), who is followed by Strohm, simply deleted 1352. But why should such a line have been interpolated?

The simplest way to achieve the connection κλίμακαϲ . . . πόντωι διδόντεϲ is to change πρυμνήϲια to πρύμνηϲ τ᾽ ἄ⟨πο⟩ with Bauer (cited p. 89 n. 1 above), a proposal foreshadowed by Musgrave's πρύμνηϲ τ᾽ ἄπο / πόντου διδόντοϲ. 'They hurriedly carried ladders in their hands and let them down for the foreign girl, putting them into the sea from the stern.'

1371　See p. 9.

1462　See p. 79.

1486　　αἰνῶ· τὸ γὰρ χρεὼν ϲοῦ τε καὶ θεῶν κρατεῖ.

The verse was deleted by Nauck. For χρεὼν Dindorf proposed χρῆν, Wecklein χρὴ: cf. *Hec.* 260 πότερα τὸ χρῆν (χρή Nauck, χρεών Scaliger) ϲφ᾽ ἐπήγαγ᾽ . . . ; *Herc.* 828 τὸ χρή (χρῆν L marg.) νιν ἐξέϲωιζεν. Monosyllabic χρεὼν is defended by fr. 733. 3 πάντεϲ· τὸ γὰρ χρεὼν μεῖζον ἢ τὸ μὴ χρεών, where Nauck remarks 'uitiosum est χρεών monosyllabum'. The variation of scansion in this line is no more vicious than the variations in the scansion of θεόϲ at *Cycl.* 231, *Andr.* 1258, *Tr.* 1280, *Hel.* 560, *Ph.* 608, *Or.* 418, fr. 292. 7, S. *Ai.* 1129. And the synizesis is paralleled by νεώϲ *Cycl.* 144, ἀνεωιγμέναϲ *Hi.* 56, τεθνεώτων *Su.* 273, ἀνεώιχθη *Ion* 1563, ἵλεωϲ *Hel.* 1007, λεωφόρου *Rh.* 881, λεώϲ fr. 360. 7 (50. 7 Austin), τεθνεῶτα A. *Ch.* 682, ἕωϲ(περ) S. *Ai.* 1117, *El.* 571 (ἕωϲ Walter: ὡϲ codd.), *Ph.* 1330 (ἕωϲ Q, coni. Lambinus: ὡϲ cett.), *OC* 1361. For τὸ χρεὼν see *Hi.* 1256, *El.* 1301, *Hel.* 1636.

VI. ION

84–5   ἄστρα δὲ φεύγει πυρὶ τῶιδ' αἰθέρος
             ἐς νύχθ' ἱεράν.

φεύγει] φλέγει L^sl   τῶιδ' P^ac ut uid.: τόδ' L

'The stars are put to flight into the holy night by this fire of aether.'
So the words are to be translated. All other attempts to explain the
construction of αἰθέρος (they are listed by Owen) are to be rejected.
The words πυρὶ τῶιδ' αἰθέρος, described by Owen as 'a picturesque,
but not very easy phrase', are a straightforward echo of pre-Socratic
cosmology, particularly that of Anaxagoras, whose μαθητής Euripides
was often alleged to have been (e.g. Diog. Laert. 2. 10 [DK 59 A 1]).
Anaxagoras identified αἰθήρ with πῦρ (DK 59 A 43, A 73, A 84)
and said that the sun and other heavenly bodies were fiery stones
(DK 59 A 1, et alibi). The identification of αἰθήρ and πῦρ had already
been made by Empedocles (DK 31 B 115 [p. 356. 22]), who said also
that the stars were fiery (DK 31 A 53). Parmenides had spoken of
φλογὸς αἰθέριον πῦρ (DK 28 B 8. 56) and had said that the sun was
fiery (DK 28 A 41). And αἰθήρ had probably been identified with
πῦρ by Heraclitus (see Kirk and Raven, *The Presocratic Philosophers*
[1962] 200). Euripides echoes these ideas again at El. 991 φλογερὰν
αἰθέρα and *Tr.* 1079–80 αἰθέρα τε πόλεος ὀλομένας, / ἂν πυρὸς αἰθομένα
κατέλυσεν ὁρμά, where there is an allusion to the etymological connection which was current in the fifth century (some attributed it to
Anaxagoras: see DK 59 A 73) between αἰθήρ and αἴθω (cf. Σ ad loc.
ὁ Δίδυμος τὸν ἐμπυρισμὸν ἀπὸ τοῦ αἴθεσθαι).[1] On the etymological connection see C. H. Kahn, *Anaximander and the Origins of Greek Cosmology*
(1960) 140–54, and for further literature on αἰθήρ and fire in the
pre-Socratics see M. Griffith, *Dionysiaca* 132 n. 73. Whether Euripides
intended πυρὶ τῶιδ' αἰθέρος to refer to the fiery aether or to the sun is
a question which cannot be answered and need hardly be asked.

Owen remarks that 'πυρί is instrumental. The stars do not flee
before the light, but are dimmed by it'. The remark appears incom-

---

[1] Σ *Tr.* 1064 offers the same explanation, absurdly, of σμύρνης αἰθερίας. For
the right explanation see p. 65, and cf. *Ion* 89–90.

prehensible or at best inconsequential. Owen is, in fact, translating and apparently misunderstanding Wilamowitz. The stars regularly flee before the light in poetry: see *Phaethon* 66 n. Further elucidation is offered later at 1148 ff. by the Delphic tapestry, which depicts a procession through heaven comprising, in this order, Sun, Evening Star, Night, Stars, Dawn. Dawn pursues the stars (1158 *Έως διώκους'* ἄςτρα), who, it is to be supposed, flee over the western horizon, beneath which Night has already gone. The region beneath this horizon must be imagined as dark, since Night is now there. And for that reason the stars are described at 85 as fleeing ἐc νύχθ' ἱεράν. Similar conceptions are found in H. *Od.* 3. 335 ἤδη γὰρ φάος οἴχεθ' ὑπὸ ζόφον, A. *Su.* 769 ἐc νύκτ' ἀποcτείχοντοc ἡλίου, and Stes. 8 P, where Helios, on setting, crosses the ocean ποτὶ βένθεα νυκτὸc ἐρεμνᾶc (i.e. the East, because 'cum sol occidit profundissima est in oriente caligo', Page ad loc.). At Aratus 580 the lesser half of the constellation Arctophylax is visible; the greater half, beneath the horizon, is described as ἔννυχος. See, further, H. D. Jocelyn, *PCPS* n.s. 17 (1971) 66-7 and 71, who, however, explains ἐc νύχθ' ἱεράν differently.

The use of φεύγειν as if it were a passive is exemplified by H. *Il.* 18. 149-50 ὑφ' Ἕκτοροc . . . φεύγοντεc, Hdt. 4. 125. 4 φεύγονταc ὑπὸ Σκυθέων.

98-101 See p. 10.

167-9 See p. 97.

174-6   οὐ πείcῃι; χωρῶν δίναc
                   τὰc Ἀλφειοῦ παιδούργει
                   ἢ νάποc Ἴcθμιον . . .

174-5 δίναc / τὰc Badham: -αιc ταῖc L, quibus seruatis ἢ ⟨'c⟩ 176 Beck

If we wished to avoid the hiatus παιδούργει / ἢ we might accept Badham's παιδουργεῖν, constructed like *Andr.* 233 πείθου . . . cυμβῆναι and S. *Ph.* 624-5 πειcθήcομαι . . . ἀνελθεῖν (see Barrett on *Hi.* 950-1). Or we might change the word-order: οὐ πείcῃι; τὰc Ἀλφειοῦ / παιδούργει χωρῶν δίναc. But is it necessary to avoid the hiatus? Here is the evidence which I have found for hiatus in anapaests.

(*a*) In non-lyric anapaests hiatus is permitted after a paroemiac followed by a heavy pause; very occasionally it is found after a paroemiac where the following pause justifies punctuation no heavier than a comma: *IT* 460, A. *Pe.* 15, *Su.* 7, *Ag.* 356 (in this instance

also with *breuis in longo*). (*b*) In lyric anapaests hiatus is permitted
after a paroemiac followed by a heavy pause: *Tr.* 172, *IT* 152, 154,
166, *Ion* 886, 911. Very occasionally it is found after a paroemiac
where the following pause justifies punctuation no heavier than a
comma: *Tr.* 225 (but the text is doubtful), *IT* 131, S. *El.* 193. At
IT 207–9, if 208 is placed after 220 (Scaliger), as I believe it should be,
then hiatus exists between 207 and 209 (unless we accept Elmsley's
τὰν for ἂν). After *IT* 219 there is a change of metre (220 is an iambic dimeter, like 232 and *Ion* 889).[1] (*c*) In lyric anapaests hiatus is
attested after a paroemiac, where there is no pause at all, in three
places, two of which are textually secure: *Ion* 860, 907 (this cannot be
considered certain: see *PCPS* n.s. 20 [1974] 25), *Hec.* 191. (*d*) Hiatus
is attested after a lyric dimeter followed by light pause at *El.* 112 = 127
(the interjection at the end of the dimeter makes this a special case)
and followed by heavy pause at 113 = 128 (also *breuis in longo*;
change of metre follows). It is also attested after a non-lyric dimeter
at *Tr.* 98 (pars codd., accepted by Murray, wrongly; see p. 64)
and after a lyric monometer at *Tr.* 170 (avoidable by Murray's
transposition of 170 after 171). If we accept Wilamowitz's conjecture
at *Hi.* 1381, we have hiatus without pause after a lyric monometer
isolated among iambics. (*e*) Hiatus is permitted at change of speaker
(see Page on *Med.* 1396).

The hiatus at *Ion* 175 seems to be vindicated by the instances of
hiatus at *Hec.* 191 and *Ion* 860 ((*c*) above).

It is worth while to investigate the incidence of *breuis in longo* in
anapaests, since this has a bearing on the text of two other passages
in *Ion*. (*a*) In non-lyric anapaests *breuis in longo* is permitted in a
paroemiac followed by a heavy pause; very occasionally it is found
in a paroemiac where the following pause justifies punctuation no
heavier than a comma: A. *Su.* 36, *Ag.* 356 (also with hiatus), *Ch.* 862
(*IA* 600 is not Euripidean). (*b*) In lyric anapaests *breuis in longo*
is found in a paroemiac followed by a heavy pause at *Hec.* 164, *Ion*
901, and possibly *IT* 147 (the word at the beginning of 148 is corrupt
and need not have begun with a vowel) and 155 οἴμοι ⟨μοι⟩ φροῦ-
δος γέννα (γενεά Elmsley; cf. *Phaethon* 235 n.). Possible or probable
instances of *breuis* in a paroemiac followed by a pause which justifies
punctuation no heavier than a comma are *Tr.* 133 δύσκλειαν (δυσκλείαν
Nauck) and 193 (there is corruption, but it seems beyond serious

---

[1] I cannot accept Dale's analysis of these lines (*Lyric Metres* 64–5), and I retract
what I said about the metre of *Ion* 889 in *PCPS* n.s. 20 (1974) 22 n. 2.

doubt that *breuis in longo* exists). At *Hec.* 72 there is change of metre.
I do not count *IT* 212, since 213 is corrupt. Note also Elmsley's
conjecture at *IT* 187, discussed on pp. 78–9. (*c*) *Breuis in longo* is attested
in a lyric monometer followed by a heavy pause at *Hec.* 83 (certain)
and in a non-lyric monometer followed by a heavy pause at *Hec.* 147
(but Porson's γαίαc may be right). It is also attested in a lyric monometer followed by a light pause at *Hi.* 1372 (suspicious, but possibly
right; see Barrett ad loc.) and *IT* 157–8 ἰὼ δαῖμον, / ὃc τὸν μόνον με
κτλ. (but here Murray's μόνον ὅc με is probably right). (*d*) *Breuis in
longo* is attested in a lyric dimeter followed by a heavy pause at *Hi.*
1377 (certain) and *El.* 113 = 128 (but here there is change of metre).
It is also attested in a lyric dimeter followed by a light pause at *Hec.*
159–60 τίc ἀμύνει μοι; ποία γέννα, / ποία δὲ πόλιc κτλ., where Porson's
γενεά is perhaps best accepted (cf. *IT* 155, under (*b*) above). After *IT*
231 (lyric dimeter, followed by a light pause) there is change of
metre (see (*b*) above in the section on hiatus). (*e*) *Breuis in longo* is
permitted at change of speaker (see Page on *Med.* 1396).

  In the light of this evidence we may judge the permissibility of the
two instances of *breuis in longo* which are transmitted at *Ion* 167 and
898. (i) 167–9 λίμναc ἐπίβα τᾶc Δηλιάδοc· / αἰάξειc (Nauck: αἱμάξειc
L, the defence of which by K. H. Lee, *CR* n.s. 19 [1969] 13–14, is
misguided), εἰ μὴ πείcῃι, / τὰc καλλιφθόγγουc ὠιδάc. Although we
might avoid the *breuis in longo* by transposing 168 and 169, the *breuis*
is probably justified by the pause, as it was in the case of the lyric
monometer *Hec.* 83 ((*c*) above) and the lyric dimeter *Hi.* 1377
((*d*) above). (ii) 898–9 κοῦρον, τὸν φρίκαι ματρὸc / εἰc εὐνὰν βάλλω
τὰν cάν. Here there is no pause, and since I have found no parallel
for *breuis in longo* in a paroemiac unaccompanied by pause (except
where metre changes) I should accept βάλλω τὰν cὰν εἰc εὐνάν (H.
Buchholtz, *De Eur. uers. anap.* [1864] 18).

206 τείχεccι Murray: τείχεcι L. For the epic termination see *PCPS*
n.s. 20 (1974) 22 n. 2, and above, p. 2. For the expression τείχεccι
λαΐνοιcι see *Tr.* 1087–8, *Ph.* 797. And for the responsion (⌣ – after the
choriamb in a glyconic) see *Hi.* 741 ~ 751, *Ba.* 867 ~ 887, S. *OT*
1187 ~ 1197, *Ph.* 1128 ~ 1151, and Barrett, *Hippolytos* p. 299.

251   οἴκοι δὲ τὸν νοῦν ἔcχον[1] ἐνθάδ' οὐcά που.

Attempts to defend οἴκοι (see most recently A. D. Skiadas, *Festschrift
Merentitis* [1972] 378–9) are not successful. Burges (on *Tr.* 662 [653])

---

[1] ἔcχον Stephanus: ἔcχομεν L

proposed ἐκεῖ. Preferable is Owen's ἐκεῖσε, already considered and
rejected by Herwerden. For parallels see *Phaethon* 265 n. Add *Ion* 1370
ἐκεῖσε τὸν νοῦν δούς, *Or.* 1181 δεῦρο νοῦν ἔχε, Sappho 96. 2 LP τυίδε
[ν]ῶν ἔχοισα.

Better than που (which Skiadas forlornly takes with οἴκοι) is περ,
ascribed by editors to Hermann (1827) but already proposed by
Dobree, who died in 1825 (published in his *Adversaria* 2 [1831]
111 = ed. Wagner 4 [1883] 109). For the confusion of these two
words see Bast, *Commentatio palaeographica* 763.

258–61   Ιων   τίς δ' εἶ; πόθεν γῆς ἦλθες; ἐκ ποίας πάτρας
πέφυκας; ὄνομα τί σε καλεῖν ἡμᾶς χρεών;

Κρ.   Κρέουσα μέν μοι τοὔνομ', ἐκ δ' Ἐρεχθέως   260
πέφυκα, πατρὶς γῆ δ' Ἀθηναίων πόλις.

'Qui Creusae responsa eorumque ordinem attendit non dubitabit quin
uerissime L. Dindorfius ποίου πατρὸς pro ποίας πάτρας legerit',
remarks Badham (1853 ed.). The conjecture is more logical and
almost everyone has accepted it. But it appears not to conform with
Greek usage. One inquires not ποίου πατρός or ποίας μητρὸς πέφυκας;
but τίνος πατρός and τίνος μητρός; See 540 ἐκ (Bothe: ἔα L) τίνος δέ
σοι πέφυκα μητρός; *Alc.* 497 τίνος δ' ὁ θρέψας παῖς πατρὸς κομπάζεται;
IT 1360 τίνος τίς ὤν . . .; fr. 1. 3 τοῦ κεκήρυξαι πατρός; S. *OC* 571
κἀφ' ὅτου πατρὸς γεγώς, Men. *Carched.* 33 τίνος πατρὸς λέγε, *Sam.*
314 (99 Koerte) πατρὸς δὲ τοῦ; By contrast, in inquiries about
πάτρα, χθών, and the like, ποῖος is the normal interrogative: *Hcld.*
133, *El.* 780, *IT* 495, *Ph.* 278, *Rh.* 278, 702, fr. 1. 1, *Antiope* 21 Page
(fr. xlviii. 21 Kambitsis), *Hyps.* 1. 4. 33, S. *Ph.* 222, *OC* 572. Nor is there
any fault in the series τίς . . . πόθεν . . . ἐκ ποίας πάτρας; see *El.*
779–80 τίνες / πόθεν πορεύεσθ' ἔστε τ' (Musgrave: πορεύεσθέ τ' L)
ἐκ ποίας χθονός; *Rh.* 702 τίς ἦν; πόθεν; ποίας πάτρας; Two passages,
indeed, may be quoted from *Ion* in which the indirect interrogative
ὁποῖος is used in the connection in which I have said that the direct
interrogative ποῖος is not used: 573–4 ὅπως σύ τ', ὦ παῖ, μητέρ'
εὑρήσεις σέθεν, / ἐγώ θ' ὁποίας μοι γυναικὸς ἐξέφυς and 803 μητρὸς
δ' ὁποίας ἐστὶν οὐκ ἔχω φράσαι. But here it would be quite possible
to interpret the questions as meaning 'what sort of woman /
mother'.

286   See p. 51.

308 See p. 100.

323–30 See *PCPS* n.s. 20 (1974) 19 n. 1.

324   τάλαινά c᾽ ἡ τεκοῦc᾽ ἢ τίc ποτ᾽ ἦν ἄρα.

So L. The simplest correction is τάλαινά c᾽ ἡ τεκοῦca· τίc ποτ᾽ ἦν ἄρα; (R. P. Jodrell, *Illustrations of Euripides* 3 [1781] 258, and independently Hermann), accepted by Kirchhoff, Nauck, Wecklein, Murray, Wilamowitz, and Grégoire. But Creusa has already inquired about Ion's mother (308 cὐ δ᾽ εἶ τίc; ὥc cου τὴν τεκοῦcαν ὤλβιcα), and Ion has already told her that he does not know who she is (313 ὡc μὴ εἰδόθ᾽ ἥτιc μ᾽ ἔτεκεν ἐξ ὅτου τ᾽ ἔφυν). For Creusa to return with so bald and direct a question as τίc ποτ᾽ ἦν ἄρα; to an inquiry which has already been answered is most unwelcome.

The solution must (as Owen urges) lie either in τάλαινά c᾽ ἡ τεκοῦc᾽ ἄρ᾽, ἥτιc ἦν ποτε (Porson, *Adv.* 269) or in τάλαιν᾽ ἄρ᾽ ἡ τεκοῦcά c᾽, ἥτιc ἦν ποτε (Dobree, loc. cit. on 251, L. Dindorf). Both conjectures restore ἥτιc ἦν ποτε, which is 'almost a formula in pre-recognition scenes' (Bond on *Hyps.* 1. i. 5). Note above all *Hyps.* 1. i. 5 ὦ μακαρία cφῶιν ἡ τεκο[ῦc᾽, ἥ]τιc ποτ᾽ ἦν, where I see no cause to replace ὦ with ὡc, proposed by C. Austin, *CR* n.s. 16 (1966) 275. (For the exclamatory ὦ in this formula compare *Ion* 1354 ὦ μακαρία [Hermann: -ίων L] μοι φαcμάτων ἥδ᾽ ἡμέρα[1] and Petron. 94. 1 *o felicem . . . matrem tuam, quae te talem peperit.*) At 564 Ion says of his mother νῦν ποθῶ cε μᾶλλον ἢ πρίν, ἥτιc εἶ ποτ᾽, εἰcιδεῖν. Similarly ἥτιc εἶ ποτ᾽ 238, *IT* 483, ὅcτιc (ἥτιc) ποτ᾽ εἶ cύ *Alc.* 1062, *Tr.* 885, ὅcτιc ποθ᾽ οὗτόc ἐcθ᾽ *Hi.* 351. Two passages are worth quoting more fully because of verbal similarities with our line: *IT* 628 ὦ τάλαc, ὅcτιc ποτ᾽ εἶ, Men. *Epitr.* 310 (134 Koerte) τῆc μητρόc, ἥτιc ἦν ποτε.

Of these two conjectures it is Dobree's which editors have preferred (so Paley, Bayfield, Jerram, Verrall). But Porson's is the better conjecture, since not only does it entail one transposition instead of two but it also presents idiomatic word-order. The order (and the phraseology) c᾽ ἡ τεκοῦcα are found again at 671 and *El.* 264. Further instances of this order are given by Bruhn, *Anhang* 91. At

---

[1] Hermann's conjecture is confirmed by passages like Ar. *Equ.* 186 ὦ μακάριε τῆc τύχηc, *Vesp.* 1512 ὦ μακάριε τῆc εὐπαιδίαc, *Pax* 715 ὦ μακαρία βουλὴ cὐ τῆc θεωρίαc, *Au.* 1423 ὦ μακάριε τῆc τέχνηc.

Ion 308 ὧc cou τὴν τεκοῦcαν ὤλβιcα Blaydes (*Spicilegium tragicum* [1902] 146) proposed cε for cou; but the genitive is unexceptionable, whether we choose to explain it as objective genitive (cf. *Alc.* 167 αὐτῶν ἡ τεκοῦcα) or as causal genitive (cf. KG 1. 390d). The enclitic has migrated, as usual, towards the front of the sentence: see the literature cited in *CQ* n.s. 27 (1977) 236. For the position of ἄρα see Denniston, *GP* 41-2.

354-9 See *PCPS* n.s. 20 (1974) 16-19. On the elision εἶχ' ἄν in 354 (discussed ibid. p. 16 n. 5) see also *JHS* 95 (1975) 198, where I cast doubts on Daitz's report that six manuscripts have παρέcχ' ἄν at *Hec.* 1113. Professor Daitz has kindly confirmed my suspicion that they have in fact παρέcχεν ἄν. And Dr K. Matthiessen tells me that, according to his collations, 'there are twelve manuscripts which have παρέcχεν ἄν, the rest have παρέcχεν, *none* have παρέcχ' ἄν'. Another probable instance of this elision is *Or.* 502 ἔλαβ' ἄν ἀντὶ (Bergk: ἔλαβεν ἀντὶ uel ἔλαβεν ἄν τῆc codd.).

403-5   (*Ξο.*) μῶν χρόνιοc ἐλθών c' ἐξέπληξ' ὀρρωδίαι;
   Κρ.   οὐδέν γ'· ἀφίκου δ' ἐc μέριμναν. ἀλλά μοι
      λέξον κτλ.

'Did my long delay in arriving cause you to be frightened?' 'No.' The next words ἀφίκου δ' ἐc μέριμναν can have one meaning only, 'you reached a state of anxiety', 'you became anxious'. For the verb see *Ph.* 361 ἐc φόβον . . . ἀφικόμην, *Ba.* 610 εἰc ἀθυμίαν ἀφίκεcθ'. For the noun see two passages in this play: 244 τί ποτε μερίμνηc ἐc τόδ' ἦλθεc, ὦ γύναι; (a similar situation to this one: Ion asks why Creusa has been distressed by the sight of Apollo's temple) and 582-3 τί πρὸc γῆν ὄμμα còν βαλὼν ἔχειc / ἐc φροντίδαc τ' (Dindorf: δ' L) ἀπῆλθεc; (Xuthus asks Ion why he is troubled). But the train of thought is now destroyed. Badham's attempt to mend it by interpreting 'you have not frightened me, but (you fancy it because) you are anxious yourself' (1861 ed.) is (says Owen) 'unnecessarily complicated'. I should say, rather, that it is unnatural to the point of absurdity. Wilamowitz's note runs ' "Du kamst zu meinem Denken", zu der Zeit, die ich mir für deine Ankunft gedacht hatte, also ὡc προcεδόκων'. It would be correct to say ἀφίκου πρὸc προcδοκίαν, 'you arrived in accordance with my expectation' (cf. Thuc. 6. 63. 2 πρὸc . . . τὴν προcδοκίαν . . . οὐκ εὐθὺc ἐπέκειντο). But this does not justify the

assumption that ἀφίκου ἐς μέριμναν means 'you arrived in accordance
with my thought (that you would arrive)'. Equally, Owen's 'you
arrived when I was anxious', like Grégoire's 'tu fus l'objet de mon
inquiétude', defies analogy and perverts the natural meaning of the
words.

I see no escape but to accept Badham's ἀφίγμην for ἀφίκου (*Philologus*
7 [1852] 277 and 1853 ed.). This has, I think, never been put into the
text; Bayfield goes against the common opinion when he calls it
'very attractive'. The conjecture restores perfect coherence of thought.
The passage may be paraphrased in this way: 'Did my long delay in
arriving cause you to be frightened (for example, that I might have
met with an accident)?' 'No, not *frightened*; but I had become *con-
cerned.*' There is a double meaning. Apollo, as the audience knows,
is the cause of her concern; but she intends that Xuthus shall imagine
that he (or how he had fared in his consultation of Trophonios) is the
cause. 'But', she goes on, quickly turning all thoughts to this second
meaning, 'what news . . .?'

The corruption of ἀφίγμην to ἀφίκου is explained rather elaborately
by Badham: 'nempe ἀφίγμην in magis notum ἀφικόμην quasi sponte
sua transiit; quod deinde ab aliquo, qui uersui magis quam orationi
consulebat, in ἀφίκου mutatum est.' I should say that the change was
the work, conscious or accidental, of someone to whom Xuthus'
mention of his 'arrival' in 403 suggested that Xuthus must be the
subject of a verb meaning 'arrive' in the line which followed.

417–18 καλῶς· ἔχω δὴ πάνθ' ὅσων ἐχρῄζομεν.
             cτείχοιμ' ἂν εἴcω· καὶ γὰρ κτλ.

Badham's ἔχων for ἔχω is accepted by Bayfield, Wecklein, and
Wilamowitz (whose δέ for δή appears to be a slip). It should not be
impugned on Murray's subjective and disputable charge that 'amat
abrupte loqui haec persona' (a more elaborate form of this charge
is brought by Owen), but because customarily cτείχοιμ' ἄν is not
appended to a preceding clause but itself opens the abrupt announcement of an intention to depart: 668, 981,[1] *El.* 669, *Ba.* 515, 845, *Rh.*
201. There is one exception in tragedy: S. *Ant.* 1108 ὧδ' ὡc ἔχω
cτείχοιμ' ἄν. To plead that the transmitted asyndeton gives Xuthus
more grandiloquent style, as suits him, and that the removal of the

---

[1] But cτείχοιμ' ἄν here is odd, since everywhere else the words indicate an immediate intention to depart. Herwerden proposed cτείλαιμ' ἄν (loc. cit. [p. 85
above] 187–8), Nauck θέλοιμ' ἄν. We might also consider κτείνοιμ' ἄν.

asyndeton makes him speak more flatly, would also be to use a subjective argument, but in this case it would be a true one.

457 and 475–7 See *PCPS* n.s. 20 (1974) 19–21. To the instances quoted on p. 19 of the colon ∪∪–∪∪–∪–∪–– add *IT* 884. Murray's conjecture in 477 (p. 19) misuses ἐνί (see p. 46 above). On the possibility mentioned in p. 20 n. 1 see Kannicht, *Helena* i. 102 n. 17, with whom I should now side against Zuntz.

507 See p. 24.

537 Ιων cὸν γεγῶτ' ἢ δῶρον ἄλλων; Ξο. δῶρον, ὄντα δ' ἐξ ἐμοῦ.

ἄλλων Dobree: ἄλλως L

'δῶρον ἄλλως, just a gift' Bayfield and Owen, 'nil nisi donum' Matthiae, 'weiter nichts als ein Geschenk' Wilamowitz. No, because 'ἄλλως can only be used in the sense of *merely*, when an idea of *depreciation* or *disparagement* is conveyed' (Shilleto on Dem. *de falsa leg.* 24 [his 27]). Any such idea is false to the tone of this passage. Here are the instances of ἄλλως with a noun known to me from classical Greek: *Hi.* 197 μύθοις . . . ἄλλως, *Hec.* 489 δόξαν ἄλλως, 626–7 ἄλλως φροντίδων βουλεύματα / γλώccηc τε κόμποι (Murray's punctuation is astray here), *Tr.* 476 ἀριθμὸν ἄλλως, *Hel.* 755 ἄλλως δέλεαρ, 1421 ἄλλως πόνος, fr. 360. 27 (50. 27 Austin) cχήματ' ἄλλως, S. *Ph.* 947 εἴδωλον ἄλλως, Ar. *Nub.* 1203 πρόβατ' ἄλλως, vet. com. fr. 5. 8 Demianczuk κἄλλως ὄνειδος, Thuc. 8. 78 ἄλλως ὄνομα καὶ οὐκ ἔργον, Plat. *Rep.* 499 c ἄλλως εὐχαῖς ὅμοια, *Theaet.* 176 D γῆς ἄλλως ἄχθη, Dem. 19. 24 ὄχλος ἄλλως καὶ βαcκανία, 35. 25 ἄλλως ὕθλον καὶ φλυαρίαν, Call. *ep.* 18. 4 (1222 Gow–Page) ἄλλως οὔνομα. For examples from later prose see Blaydes on Ar. *Nub.* 1203.

With the line as a whole compare S. *OT* 1162–3.

638–9 θεῶν δ' ἐν εὐχαῖc ἢ λόγοιcιν ἢ βροτῶν
ὑπηρετῶν χαίρουcιν οὐ γοωμένοιc.

λόγοιcιν ἢ Musgrave: γόοιcιν ἢ L

Musgrave's conjecture is generally accepted, and rightly. γόοc is corrupted to λόγοc at *Su.* 111, 1142 (λόγουc P), *Ph.* 1309, 1335, *Or.* 1022, S. *El.* 379, *Ph.* 1401. Here the reverse corruption was caused by γοωμένοιc in the line below. Musgrave quotes a passage which is evidently derived from ours: Heliod. *Aeth.* 2. 27. 2 (the speaker is Apollo's acolyte) ἢ γὰρ πρὸς ἱεροῖς ἦν ἢ πρὸς θυσίαις ἐξηταζόμην . . . ἢ φιλοσοφοῦσι διελεγόμην. But I am not sure that the lines as emended have been rightly explained.

Commentators take ἦν with θεῶν ἐν εὐχαῖς and (ἐν) λόγοισιν βροτῶν. I transcribe Bayfield's note: ' "I was engaged in." For εἶναι ἐν cp. Hdt. 2. 82 οἱ ἐν ποιήσει γενόμενοι, Soph. *OT* 562 τότ' οὖν ὁ μάντις οὖτος ἦν ἐν τῆι τέχνηι; *Hipp.* 452 αὐτοί τ' εἰσὶν ἐν μούσαις ἀεί. ἐν φιλοσοφίαι εἶναι is common in Plato. So Hor. *S.* 19. 2 *totus in illis.*' For further illustration see Headlam on Hdas 8. 72. Passages like these show that Ion may appropriately say θεῶν ἐν εὐχαῖς ἦ, 'I was engaged in praying to the gods', for prayer is one of his professional activities. But they offer less good support for the expression ἐν λόγοισιν ἦ βροτῶν. One does not engage in conversation in the same way that one engages in poetry, soothsaying, philosophy, or religion.

Furthermore, if we translate 'I was engaged in praying to the gods and talking to men, serving the cheerful not the sad', the balance of the sentence is wrong. The primary message which it conveys is that Ion has spent his life praying to gods and talking to men. This, in its context, is not a very interesting or relevant remark. The secondary message, that those he served were cheerful, is more interesting in itself and more relevant to his argument, whose purpose is to contrast the friendliness of his present associates with the hostility of those who await him in Athens.

The balance is redressed if we take ἦ with ὑπηρετῶν: 'in praying to the gods and talking to men I served the cheerful not the sad.' For the combination of present participle and imperfect indicative see *Cycl.* 381 ἦτε πάσχοντες, *Herc.* 313 ἦν . . . ὑβρίζων, A. *Ch.* 852 ἦν . . . παρών, S. *Ai.* 1324 δρῶν . . . ἦν, *OT* 126 δοκοῦντα . . . ἦν, *Ph.* 412 ἦν . . . ζῶν. This periphrasis is discussed by G. Björck, *Ἦν Διδάσκων* (1940), J. Gonda, *Mnemos.* ser. iv 12 (1959) 97–112, W. J. Aerts, *Periphrastica* (1965). See also Bruhn, *Anhang* § 108 and (for Menandrean examples) Austin on Men. *Asp.* 181.

689 See p. 18.

692 See p. 115.

711–12 See *PCPS* n.s. 20 (1974) 21–2. Note also *Hi.* 1439 τοῦδε πλησίον κακοῦ, *Or.* 1159 πλησίον . . . κινδύνων.

731   ὃ μὴ γένοιτο δ', εἴ τι τυγχάνοι κακόν . . .[1]

ὃ Stephanus : ἃ L

Since Murray and Grégoire retain ἃ (and Stevens on *Andr.* 271
seems inclined to follow them), it is necessary to point out that the
evidence for ὃ in the deprecatory formula ὃ μὴ τύχοι, ὃ μὴ γένοιτο,
is overwhelming: *Hcld.* 714, *Ph.* 242, 571, fr. 525. 1, A. *ScT* 5, Ar.
Vesp. 535, *Lys.* 147, Men. *Misum.* 264 (66 Koerte), *Sam.* 728, Pap.
Didot 1. 28 (E. fr. 953. 28 N, Page, *GLP* no. 34, i. p. 144 Koerte, p. 329
Sandbach), [Dem.] 40. 56. There is one instance of ἃ: *Hcld.* 511–12
τῆϲδ', ἃ μὴ τύχοι ποτέ, / πόλεωϲ ἁλούϲηϲ. Here Lenting's ὃ has met
with less success than Stephanus' in *Ion* 731, and even editors who
print the latter (for example, Nauck, Kirchhoff, Paley, Wecklein)
ignore the former. I suspect that this inconsistency is connected less
with the merits of the individual conjectures than with the identity
of their proposers.

743–4   Κρ. βάκτρωι δ' ἐρείδου περιφερῆ ϲτίβον χθονός.
               Πρ. καὶ τοῦτο τυφλόν, ὅταν ἐγὼ βλέπω βραχύ.

'Prop with thy staff thy steps that stagger on the ground' (Owen).
The middle ἐρείδεϲθαι (and διερείδεϲθαι) is used, in tragedy, not with
an accusative object but intransitively: *Hec.* 66, *Tr.* 150, A. *Ag.* 64; cf.
Herc. 108–9. An apparent example of an accusative object is provided
by Ar. *Eccl.* 150 διερειϲαμένη τὸ ϲχῆμα τῆι βακτηρίαι, unless the accusa-
tive here is internal. For unequivocal instances one must turn to
'Simonides' 172 Bergk and the Hellenistic and later poets cited by
LSJ *s.u.* IV. 2, and in particular Meleag. *AP* 12. 84. 1–2 (4602–3
Gow–Page) ἐπὶ γαῖαν . . . ἴχνος ἐρειδόμενον, although the meaning there
is 'planting a foot on the ground'.

But even if ἐρείδου may take a direct object in the sense 'support',
ϲτίβον χθονός does not mean 'footstep(s)'. ϲτίβοϲ means either the
tread of a foot (footprint) or ground trodden under foot (path).
Whether ϲτίβοϲ ever means 'treading' ('as the "noun of action" for
ϲτείβειν', Fraenkel on *Ag.* 411), as is sometimes alleged, is doubtful.
At S. *Ph.* 206 (cited by Fraenkel) I see no reason (in spite of Jebb)
why it should not mean 'path', as it does at 48; and I doubt Jebb's
interpretation at 157 and 163. Jerram and Owen claim the sense
'footstep' at S. *Ph.* 29 καὶ ϲτίβου γ' (T: δ' GQRS: τ' cett.) οὐδεὶϲ

---

[1] With Stobaeus' misquotation of this line (4. 48. 22 εἰ δ' ἄρα ϲυμβαίνοι τι
δυϲχερέϲτερον) compare fr. 963 ἤν τι ϲυμβῆι δυϲχερέϲ.

κτύπος (LGᵞᵖQVZgZo : τύπος cett.), 'and of footsteps not a sound' (Jebb). But the use of καί . . . γε in such a negative clause is impossible. R. D. Dawe (Teubner ed. 1979) accepts Bergk's καὶ cτίβου γ' οὐδει τύπος. I prefer Mudge's καὶ cτίβου γ' οὐχ εἰc τύπος, 'yes, and there is more than one footprint'.

But suppose that ἐρείδου may take a direct object and that cτίβος may mean 'footstep'. What then is χθονός doing? Scaliger changed it to ποδός. What then is the meaning of περιφερῆ? LSJ says 'wavering', a sense unexampled and not very akin to the notion of circularity which, in various senses, this word expresses (it is used only once again in tragedy : Hel. 430 δῶμα περιφερὲς θριγκοῖς, 'encircled by'). Reiske proposed περιφερεῖ, unhappily attached to βάκτρωι, Jodrell (cited on 324) παράφορον, comparing Hec. 1050 παραφόρωι ποδί, Badham παραφόρου (with ποδός), Italie ἔπειγε (with ποδός). Conjectures which support anomalies should be treated coldly.

It *is* possible to extract a satisfactory meaning from περιφερῆ cτίβον χθονός : 'callem flexuosum, quales utique esse solent in locis cliuosis' (Musgrave). The Sacred Way, leading to Apollo's temple, can indeed be described as 'curving', and this use of the adjective, though not apparently attested, is at least compatible with attested uses. And there is point in using the adjective with such a meaning here : it helps to explain why the Old Man must watch his step (741) and why he mentions his poor eyesight as a cause of his hesitant progress (744). With Musgrave's interpretation we might in desperation write ἐρεύνα for ἐρείδου (G. F. Schoemann, Opusc. acad. 4 [1871] 147–8), comparing Ph. 92; although an easier change would be Badham's περιφερῆ cτείβων χθόνα or Herwerden's περιφερῆ cτείβων χθονός (constructed like Ph. 1486 ἁβρὰ παρηίδος; cf. S. Ant. 1209, 1265), which Wilamowitz hesitantly accepts. But crisper in style and preeminently corruptible is βάκτρωι δ' ἐρείδου· περιφερὴς cτίβος χθονός.

790–2   ὀτοτοτοῖ· τὸν ἐμὸν ἄτεκνον ἄτεκνον ἔλακ'
             ἆρα βίοτον, ἐρημίαι δ' ὀρφανοὺς
             δόμους οἰκήcω.

790 ὀτοτοτοῖ Hermann : ὀτοτοττοτοῖ Lᵃᶜ : ὀττ- Lᵖᶜ   τὸν Badham : τὸ δ' L   ἔλακ' post Murray (ἔλακεν) Conomis (Hermes 92 [1964] 33) : ἔλαβεν L : ἔλαβον Badham, ἔλαχον Herwerden, ἔλαχ' Wecklein

The arrangement printed above is the only one which I can devise which combines good metre with good style. In its support I observe :

(i) Scribes are prone to expand exclamations: see R. D. Dawe, *PCPS* n.s. 14 (1968) 16 and *Studies* iii. 128. I believe that something similar has happened at *Tr.* 1287 (= 1294) ὀτοτοτοτοῖ post Schroeder (ὀττ-) Diggle: ὀττοτοτοτοτοῖ VP. (ii) We do not want the δ'. (iii) The change of ἔλακ- to ἔλαβ- is found at *IT* 976 (λακὼν Scaliger: λαβὼν L) and S. *Ant.* 1094 (λαβεῖν for λακεῖν pars codd.).

Murray's text is less satisfactory: ὀττοτοττοτοῖ· τὸν δ' ἐμὸν ἄτεκνον ἄτεκνον ἔλακεν, a cretic and two dochmiacs. The dochmiacs do not divide very naturally. Resolution is divided in the last long of the first dochmiac, for which L. P. E. Parker, *CQ* n.s. 18 (1968) 267–8, cites only eight examples in Euripides. This is followed by divided resolution in the first long of the next dochmiac. This second incidence of divided resolution is common enough in itself; but in only one of the examples cited by Parker (*Ba.* 995 = 1015) does it follow divided resolution in a final long. Further, we still have the unwanted δ'. Wilamowitz restores two perfectly good dochmiacs: ὀττοτοτοῖ· τὸ δ' ἐμὸν ἄτεκνον ἄτεκνον ἔλαβ'. But, along with many of the restorations proposed in this line, it has a serious weakness, as I shall explain.

'τὸ ἐμόν, ganz gewöhnliche Periphrase', says Wilamowitz; 'τὸ δ' ἐμόν . . . , which almost = ἐγώ, is the subject of ἔλαβεν', Owen. But τὸ ἐμόν cannot be used promiscuously for ἐγώ. When used as the subject of a verb, it always expresses something of the speaker's condition or behaviour. Bayfield (though he finds no difficulty in τὸ δ' ἐμὸν here) puts the matter well in his note on 247: 'τὸ cόν, τὸ ἐμόν, and the like phrases, though commonly used by the tragedians as equivalents of cύ, ἐγώ, etc., are not absolute synonyms of these words. τὸ cόν, for instance, means *thou, in this or that relation, in such or such circumstances, behaving in this or that manner.* Thus τὸ cὸν λέγει would not be Greek for cὺ λέγεις, but τὸ cὸν οὐκ ἀπαιδεύτως ἔχει is a neat way of expressing, "thou, *by speaking thus,* showest feeling." ' Here are the Euripidean instances of τὸ ἐμόν used as the subject of a verb: *Hec.* 51 τοὐμὸν μὲν οὖν ὅσονπερ ἤθελον τυχεῖν / ἔσται ('my lot'), *Herc.* 165–6 ἔχει δὲ τοὐμὸν οὐκ ἀναίδειαν, γέρον, / ἀλλ' εὐλάβειαν ('my behaviour'), *Hel.* 892–3 τίς εἴc' ἀδελφῶι τόνδε cημανῶν ἐμῶι / παρόνθ', ὅπως ἂν τοὐμὸν ἀcφαλῶς ἔχηι; ('my position in the matter'), *Ph.* 995–6 τοὐμὸν δ' οὐχὶ cυγγνώμην ἔχει, / προδότην γενέcθαι πατρίδος ('my behaviour'), *Ba.* 844 ἔξεcτι· πάντηι τό γ' ἐμὸν εὐτρεπὲc πάρα ('my help'). I do not include *Ion* 709, to which Wilamowitz refers, since the text is lacunose and we do not know what is the role of τὸ ἐμόν. In the light of the passages quoted the expression 'τὸ δ' ἐμόν has gained a childless life' appears intolerable. Add to this that we do not want the δ', and Badham's τὸν ἐμόν becomes overwhelmingly attractive.

883   See *PCPS* n.s. 20 (1974) 22 n. 2.

889–90   See ibid. and above, p. 96.

898–9   See p. 97.

904–5   See *PCPS* n.s. 20 (1974) 24.

907–11   See ibid. 25 and above, p. 96.

912   See ibid. 23–4. It is not advisable to place ἰώ *extra metrum*. When single ἰώ is so placed it *begins* an anapaestic system. There is no secure instance in the middle of anapaests: at *Tr.* 173 the manuscripts are divided between ἰώ and ἰὼ ἰώ, and the latter is to be preferred; A. *ScT* 871 is spurious (cf. R. D. Dawe, *Dionysiaca* 90–2).

927–31   (Πρ.)   κακῶν γὰρ ἄρτι κῦμ' ὑπεξαντλῶν φρενί,
πρύμνηθεν αἴρει μ' ἄλλο cῶν λόγων ὕπο,
οὓc ἐκβαλοῦcα τῶν παρεcτώτων κακῶν
μετῆλθεc ἄλλων πημάτων κακὰc ὁδούc.   930
τί φήιc; τίνα λόγον Λοξίου κατηγορεῖc;

927 κακῶν Musurus: ¹ -ὸν L   928 ὕπο Lˢ¹: ὕπερ L   930 καινὰc Musgrave

The first pair of lines is unexceptionable. 'I was just now getting rid of a wave of troubles in my mind, and now another wave at the stern (i.e. which was yet behind) heaves me up in consequence of your words' (Paley's translation). With the anacoluthon ὑπεξαντλῶν . . . αἴρει με compare *Cycl.* 330–1, *Hi.* 23, *Hec.* 970–1, *Herc.* 185–6, *IT* 695–7, 947–8, 964–5, fr. 579, A. *Ag.* 1008–11, *Ch.* 520–1, *Eum.* 100–1, 477–8; see also KG 2. 105–7. But the second pair of lines has not yet received an acceptable explanation.

The old editors translated 'quae (uerba) profundens, a praesentibus

---

¹ This reading is ascribed by Wecklein, Murray, and Grégoire to the 'codex Riccardianus 32'. This manuscript is a sixteenth-century copy of an early printed edition: see Turyn, *The Byzantine Manuscript Tradition of the Tragedies of Euripides* (1957) 378. It should not be given credit for conjectures already found in the *editio princeps*.

malis transiisti ad malas uias aliorum malorum'. This is liable to two objections. (i) The construction κακῶν μετῆλθες, 'a malis transiisti', defies analogy. A separative genitive may be used with a noun indicating a place: for example 459–60 θαλάμων πταμένα, Med. 70 γῆς ἐλᾶν, Herc. 1050–1 εὐνᾶς ἐγείρετε (for further instances see KG 1. 394–5). But κακῶν can hardly be so used: in Od. 20. 53 κακῶν δ' ὑποδύσεαι (quoted by KG) the prefix ὑπο- makes all the difference. (ii) The expression τῶν παρεστώτων κακῶν is used oddly. It ought to refer to troubles *now present* (cf. Andr. 93–5 ἐμπέφυκε γὰρ / γυναιξὶ τέρψις τῶν παρεστώτων κακῶν / ἀνὰ στόμ' αἰεὶ καὶ διὰ γλώσσης ἔχειν, 1233–4 τοῖς παρεστῶσιν κακοῖς / μηδέν τι λίαν δυσφορεῖν, Su. 1042 φυλακὰς ἀνῆκα τοῖς παρεστῶσιν κακοῖς, S. fr. 409 P λαθέσθαι τῶν παρεστώτων κακῶν). 'Present troubles' may be contrasted with 'past troubles' (cf. Hel. 483–4 συμφορὰς γὰρ ἀθλίας / ἐκ τῶν πάροιθεν τὰς παρεστώσας κλύω). But it is strange to contrast 'present' with 'other' troubles, when the 'other' troubles follow the 'present' ones and, having already arisen, are no less present themselves. In short, τῶν παρεστώτων κακῶν is here required to mean τῶν πρὶν παρεστώτων κακῶν, 'past troubles'.

Other interpretations are even less acceptable. Badham (followed by Jerram) translates with some hesitation 'quae (uerba) transtulisti a praesentibus malis sc. ad alia et inaudita', an unheard-of use of the verb ἐκβάλλειν. Paley (followed by Bayfield) takes τῶν παρεστώτων κακῶν with οὓς (λόγους), 'words about your present misfortunes'. The construction of the genitive is then the same as in 385, Med. 541, El. 228, 347, 353, 937, IT 517, IA 842, A. PV 732–3, Men. Asp. 193; for further examples see KG 1. 335, Bruhn, Anhang 20–1. Paley translates '. . . in consequence of your words, which you had no sooner uttered concerning the grievances immediately before you, than you pursued an evil course of other woes'. This ruins the connection of thought. The first κῦμα designates Xuthus' treachery; and that is what the Old Man alludes to as τὰ παρεστῶτα κακά. The second κῦμα designates Creusa's rape by Apollo. The train of thought, as well as the language of 928, makes it plain that Creusa's λόγοι (her preceding monody) stirred up only the second wave; with the former wave, to which Paley makes them refer, they have nothing whatever to do.

Emendation has proved ineffectual. Musgrave proposed ὡς ἐκλαθοῦσα for οὓς ἐκβαλοῦσα, but the participle should have been middle. Kirchhoff's ὥς μ' ἐκκαλοῦσα uses the verb in an unexampled way.

Kayser's *ἐκβαλοῦς· ἐκ* gives the genitives a construction but leaves the line without a caesura (for the same proposal see F. W. Schmidt, *Krit. Stud. zu den griech. Dramatikern* 2 [1886] 303). Wecklein's *μετῆγες* serves no purpose at all. Beck's *οἷς* for *οὓς*, with *ἐκβαλοῦσα* taken as intransitive ('with which words moving from your present troubles...') is accepted by Wecklein, Grégoire, and Wilamowitz. But there is no justification for such an intransitive use of the verb *ἐκβάλλειν*: see Fraenkel on *Ag.* 1172, *Illinois Class. Stud.* 2 (1977) 119.

I owe to Sir Denys Page what I believe to be the right explanation of *τῶν παρεστώτων κακῶν*. I transcribe the note of Denniston and Page on A. *Ag.* 1053. '*τὰ λῶιστα τῶν παρεστώτων* here could mean "the best of the things that are at hand"; but *PV* 216 f., Ar. *Equ.* 30, where *τῶν παρεστώτων, τῶν παρόντων* occur with *κράτιστα without* the article, suggest that *τῶν παρ.* has become a stereotyped genitive absolute, "things being as they are".' So (as he suggested to me) we may translate our passage in this way: 'having uttered these words, our present evils being what they are [i.e. quite enough], you have gone on to other evil paths of pain.'

936-8   *Κρ.*   ἄκουε τοίνυν· οἶσθα Κεκροπίας πέτρας
πρόσβορρον ἄντρον, ἃς Μακρὰς κικλήσκομεν;
Πρ.   οἶδ', ἔνθα Πανὸς ἄδυτα καὶ βωμοὶ πέλας.

Line 937 was deleted by an anonymous writer in *Classical Journal* 2 (1810) 615 and independently by Badham. The deletion is accepted by Bayfield and Wecklein. The objections to 937 are (i) that the cave was not called 'the Long Rocks'; (ii) that ἃς has no antecedent; (iii) that the two lines 936-7 break the stichomythia. The line, if it is interpolated, will have been suggested to the interpolator by 11-13 ἔνθα προσβόρρους πέτρας | Παλλάδος ὑπ' ὄχθωι τῆς Ἀθηναίων χθονὸς | Μακρὰς καλοῦσι γῆς ἄνακτες Ἀτθίδος. If the line is omitted, the stichomythia will resemble 987-8 *Κρ.* ἄκουε τοίνυν· οἶσθα γηγενῆ μάχην; | *Πρ.* οἶδ', ἣν Φλέγραι Γίγαντες ἔστησαν θεοῖς.

The first two objections are unanswerable; the evasions offered by Wilamowitz and Owen add up to no answer at all, and I shall ignore them. The attempts which they make to show that the line is indispensable to its context are a little more persuasive but they are not conclusive. Wilamowitz claims that without 937 we have the comic picture of one Athenian asking another Athenian 'Do you know the Acropolis?' and receiving the answer 'Yes; it is near the shrine and

altar of Pan.' 'Der Fels des Kekrops ist natürlich der Burgfels.'
We might reply that what Creusa says is not 'der Fels' but 'die
Felsen'. For, if 937 is deleted, then Κεκροπίας πέτρας becomes accusa-
tive plural. 'The Cecropian *rock*' would undoubtedly signify the
Acropolis: compare 12 Παλλάδος ὑπ' ὄχθωι, *Hi.* 30 πέτραν . . .
Παλλάδος, *El.* 1289 ὄχθον (Valckenaer: οἶκον L) Κεκροπίας (on these
designations see p. 17). But 'the Cecropian *rocks*' would be an equally
fit designation for the Μακραὶ πέτραι.[1] Owen adds that 'the old man
could hardly have guessed that the grotto of Pan was meant by the
Cecropian rocks'. This argument had already been countered by
Badham: 'uerum quidem est Κεκροπίας πέτρας non idem esse ac
Panis sacellum; sed hoc maxime insignis in illis locus erat.' But
Badham's case is overstated, and it remains true that a question 'Do
you know the Cecropian rocks?' does not naturally invite the reply
'Yes; that is where the cave of Pan is.'

   The third objection, to the breaking of the stichomythia, is not at all
cogent. Some of the parallels adduced by Owen for such a break are
very doubtful and some are wrong. (*a*) *Herc.* 1111–12: the stichomythia has not yet begun, since these are Heracles' first words to Amphi-
tryon. (*b*) *Herc.* 1403–4: Wilamowitz placed a lacuna after 1403,
perhaps rightly. (*c*) *El.* 651–2: either a lacuna must be marked after
651 (Camper) or 651 must be deleted (Matthiae). (*d*) *El.* 965–6:
Nauck marked a lacuna after 966 (giving this line to Orestes);
Kirchhoff marked a lacuna after 965, in my view rightly (for the
distribution of speakers in the surrounding lines I follow Denniston
in his note on 959–66; a different view is taken by E.-R. Schwinge,
Die Verwendung der Stichomythie in den Dramen des Eur. [1968] 85–90).
(*e*) *IT* 735–6: Badham deleted 736, wrongly perhaps (cf. Schulze
[cited on p. 77] 61–2); but it takes two to make stichomythia, and
since Iphigenia has not yet started to speak in single lines the stichomythia has not yet begun. (*f*) *IT* 811–12: Monk deleted 811, but
it seems guaranteed by 822 (cf. Schulze 66–7). (*g*) *Hel.* 1197–8:
Hartung deleted 1197, perhaps rightly. But an exact parallel for a
two-line speech following immediately after the two initial one-line
exchanges, as we have here, is provided by a passage which Owen
does not mention, *IT* 69–70 (Badham's deletion of 70 is possible but

---

[1] Compare 1400, where Creusa says that she placed her child Κέκροπος ἐς
ἄντρα καὶ Μακρὰς πετρηρεφεῖς. Paley deletes the line because 'this can only mean
the cave of Aglauros, daughter of Cecrops'. No; as Barnes says, 'dicitur Cecropis
antrum, quia in Cecropia erat, hoc est sub acropoli.'

not probable; cf. Schulze 12–14). For other two-line interruptions, where deletion is not a possible cure, see *El.* 573–4, *Ba.* 1269–70, *IA* 1437–8; see also Denniston on *El.* 651–2, Kannicht on *Hel.* 780–1. If the two former objections cannot be answered, then 937 must be deleted. But one slight change will answer both objections: Κεκρο-πίων πετρῶν, which Sir Denys Page suggested to me. 'Do you know the northern cave belonging to the Cecropian rocks, which we call the Μακραί?' A scribe changed the genitive to the accusative (for I assume that he intended Κεκροπίας πέτρας as an accusative not as a genitive) under the influence of the preceding transitive verb οἶcθα.

959 See p. 51.

981 See p. 100 n. 1.

1035 See p. 18 n. 1.

1056–60 ∼ **1069–73** See *PCPS* n.s. 15 (1969) 48–9.

1074–7 ∼ **1090–3** See *PCPS* n.s. 20 (1974) 25–8. For Stinton's metrical analysis see also his *Euripides and the Judgement of Paris* (1965) 73 and *BICS* 22 (1975) 105 n. 1. On A. *PV* 117 see M. Griffith, *The Authenticity of 'Prometheus Bound'* (1977) 300 n. 10. The iambic scansion of 1077 ∼ 1093, which I now prefer, was adopted by Dale, *Metrical Analyses of Tragic Choruses* 1 (*BICS* Suppl. 21. 1, 1971) 93.

1131 See *PCPS* n.s. 15 (1969) 49–50.

1275–8 See *PCPS* n.s. 20 (1974) 28–30.

1314–19 See ibid. 30–1.

1343 See ibid. 31–6. Various addenda.

(i) To the 'eleven instances at 3²' (p. 32) add *Hec.* 958 φύρουcι δ' αὐτά (F² sicut coni. Hermann: αὖθ' οἱ uel sim. codd.) θεοί (cf. *JHS* 95 [1975] 198).

(ii) With Buecheler's conjecture at *Alc.* 1125 (p. 32) compare S. *Ai.* 278.

(iii) To the parallels (p. 32) for ληψόμεθα (*IT* 986) at that position in the line add *El.* 1272 (Clarke on *Il.* 4. 242 [1729], and again Wieseler, *Philologus* 7 [1852] 748, comparing Paus. 7. 25. 7),[1] *Herc.* 460 (Hirzel), *Alex.* 22 Page, A. *Pe.* 491, Sc*T* 1022, *Eum.* 107, S. *OC* 42, fr. 432. 3 P; similarly, with monosyllable followed by tribrach, *Med.* 505, *Or.* 244, 487, 671, *Ba.* 731, A. *Pe.* 332, S. *OT* 826.

(iv) To the parallels cited in support of the conjecture at *IA* 1034–5 (p. 33) add *Herc.* 347, *IT* 570, *IA* 394a; for ἐcθλῶν cf. A. *Ag.* 350, Bacchyl. 4. 20.

(v) To the examples of divided first-foot anapaest (p. 34) add *Cycl.* 183 περὶ τοῖν and *Antiope* 103 Page (fr. xlviii. 109 Kambitsis) ἴτε νυν.

(vi) On fr. 953 (p. 34 n. 2) see p. 104.

(vii) p. 36 n. 1: we may rule out Jackson's conjecture (*Marg. scaen.* 93) at S. *El.* 1403.

It is interesting that when Menander quotes A. (*Niobe*) fr. 156 N (273. 15–16 M) at *Asp.* 412–13 (70–1 Koerte) he introduces an instance of θεός at 2[2]: ὑπέρευγε. "θεὸς μὲν αἰτίαν φύει βροτοῖc κτλ." The suggestion of Gomme and Sandbach that 'probably it [θεός] was so scanned in *Niobe*' is almost certainly to be rejected.

1354–68   *Ιων* ὦ μακαρία μοι φαcμάτων ἤδ' ἡμέρα.
             Πρ. λαβών νυν αὐτὰ τὴν τεκοῦcαν ἐκπόνει.[2]   1355
                    πᾶcαν δ' ἐπελθὼν Ἀcιάδ' Εὐρώπης θ' ὅρους
                    γνώcηι τάδ' αὐτόc. τοῦ θεοῦ δ' ἕκατί cε
                    ἔθρεψά τ', ὦ παῖ, καὶ τάδ' ἀποδίδωμί cοι,
                    ἃ κεῖνος ἀκέλευcτόν μ' ἐβουλήθη λαβεῖν
                    †cῶcαί θ'· ὅτου δ' ἐβούλεθ' οὕνεκ' οὐκ ἔχω λέγειν†.
                    ἤιδει δὲ θνητῶν οὔτιc ἀνθρώπων τάδε   1361
                    ἔχονταc ἡμᾶc οὐδ' ἵν' ἦν κεκρυμμένα.
                    καὶ χαῖρ'· ἴcον γάρ c' ὡc τεκοῦc' ἀcπάζομαι.

---

[1] I draw attention to this conjecture because it has been neglected and because Seidler's condemnation of it ('numeris inconcinnis') needs to be exposed as fallacious. Defenders of the transmitted text may like to know of Metrodorus, *A.P.* 9. 360. 8 (undatable), where εὐcεβής has the passive sense 'venerable'.

[2] Euripides' use of the verb ἐκπονεῖν is discussed by J. M. Bremer, *CQ* n.s. 22 (1972) 236–40, with reference to *Herc.* 581. The nuance which Bremer wishes to read into the verb in that passage seems to me to be out of the question. The traditional rendering is fully defended by the use of ἐκμοχθεῖν at *Herc.* 309. 'The two verbs are indeed birds of a feather . . . the use of ἐκμοχθεῖν . . . is equally remarkable' (Bremer p. 238 n. 2). Exactly so. For the shift of meaning compare the uses of the verb ἐξομματοῦν at fr. 541 ('make blind') and at S. fr. 710 P ('give sight to').

[ἄρξαι δ' ὅθεν cὴν μητέρα ζητεῖν cε χρή·
πρῶτον μὲν εἴ τιc Δελφίδων τεκοῦcά cε   1365
ἐc τούcδε ναοὺc ἐξέθηκε παρθένοc,
ἔπειτα δ' εἴ τιc Ἑλλάc. ἐξ ἡμῶν δ' ἔχειc
ἅπαντα Φοίβου θ', ὃc μετέcχε τῆc τύχηc.]

1354 μακαρία Hermann: -ίων L¹ 1356 Ἀcιάδ' Scaliger: -ίαν L:
-ίδ' Nauck   1356–7 ⟨Ἰων⟩ πᾶcάν γ' ἐπελθών . . . ⟨Πρ.⟩ γνώcῃι Kirchhoff   1364–8 del. H. Hirzel apud W. Dindorf, *Philologus* 21 (1864) 148
1364 ζητεῖν cε Tr²: ζητεῖcθαι L

Hirzel's deletion of 1364–8 (proposed anew by Bayfield) is rightly
commended by M. D. Reeve, *GRBS* 14 (1973) 150–1. When Reeve
adds that '1364–68 are not the only interpolated lines in the passage,
but the others require a lengthier exposition', I do not know whether
his undivulged suspicions coincide with my own. The lines over which
I harbour doubts are 1357–62.

(i) In 1356–7 editors usually accept Kirchhoff's arrangement, on the
ground that 'it would be absurd for her [the Priestess] to advise him
to scour Europe and Asia, and then afterwards tell him to begin his
search at Delphi' (Owen). Reeve also commends Kirchhoff and
refers to Owen's note; but he has forgotten that once 1364–8 have
been deleted Owen's objection against these lines is removed. These
are indeed, in their transmitted form, very fumbling lines: 'and
having visited the whole of Asia and Europe you will discover this for
yourself.' What, we may ask, is 'this'? Unless we are to include 1356
in our suspicions, Kirchhoff's arrangement should be accepted. It
would not be absurd to suggest that the line is an interpolation,
modelled on *Tr.* 927; but, when it has been assigned to Ion, I find
nothing objectionable in the line, which is, as Owen says, 'a natural
enough remark to come from the impulsive boy'. Badham's objection
that 'quoniam *in his terris obeundis* matrem quaerere iubetur non
ἐπελθών sed ἐπιών dicendum erat' (*Mnem.* n.s. 2 [1874] 299) is hyper-
critical, and his own proposals Ἀcιάδ' ἐπέλθω πᾶcαν . . . ; and πῶc;
ἆρ' ἐπελθών . . . are not more appealing.

But in the next line γνώcῃι τάδ' αὐτόc ('I leave you to decide',
Owen) is a rather weak remark for the Priestess to make. And τάδ'
is odd. Elsewhere in the vicinity τάδε refers to the cradle and its
contents (1346, 1352, 1358, 1361), and so does the preceding αὐτά
in 1355. Contrast αὐτὸc γνώcῃι ('you must decide for yourself') at
Pl. *Gorg.* 505 c. L. Dindorf's τάχ' for τάδ' does not amend very much.

¹ See p. 99 n. 1.

(ii) Was the Priestess really ἀκέλευστος (1359)? See 1346–7 cὺ δ' ἐκ κελευσμῶν ἢ πόθεν cώιζεις τάδε; / : : ἐνθύμιόν μοι τότε τίθηcι Λοξίαc. 'There has been no direct command, only an ἐνθύμιον', says Jerram. But we may wonder whether she intends to make such a sharp distinction. The words are most naturally taken to mean that Apollo's wish or command *took the form of* an ἐνθύμιον, a thought implanted by him in her mind. And even if she were sharply distinguishing in 1346–7 between a direct order and an implanted thought, there is little point in her going out of her way to insist in 1359 that the god wished her to act without a direct order. Even less persuasive is Herwerden's explanation (*Mnem.* 31 [1903] 280) that 'Pythia quod nemo eam facere iusserat, tribuit uoluntati diuinae'.

(iii) It is hardly true that she did not know the god's purpose (1360). Lines 1352–3 show that she knew what the contents of the cradle were to be used for. But this unmetrical line is detachable and could be deleted without prejudice to the rest of the passage. The line remains unemended (see Reeve 150 n. 13). The suggestion of Broadhead (*Tragica* 163–4) to read ὅτωι for ὅτου and to delete οὕνεκ' (*del. Milton et incuria om. P*) does not help. The Priestess knew full well 'for whom' she was to keep the cradle; otherwise why did she give it to Ion?

(iv) θνητῶν . . . ἀνθρώπων (1361) is an epic combination, never found in tragedy. It occurs over fifty times in Homer, Hesiod, and the *Hymns*; also in Archil. 131 West, Theogn. 271, 327–8, 1011, 1171–2, *PMG* 913. θνητὸς ἀνήρ (*Alc.* 7, S. fr. 845 P) is different.

(v) The καί in καὶ χαῖρε should give us pause. When Euripides uses the phrase καὶ χαῖρε or καὶ χαίρετε he has always used an imperative immediately before, so that καί is the copula: *Alc.* 1149, *Hcld.* 600, *Hi.* 1437 (cοὶ παραινῶ . . . μὴ cτυγεῖν in 1435 is the equivalent of an imperative), *IT* 708, *Ion* 1604, *Hel.* 591, 1686, *Ph.* 1453, *Or.* 1068, fr. 362. 33 (53. 33 Austin), *Hyps.* fr. 64. ii. 67. Aeschylus uses καὶ χαῖρε without a preceding imperative at *Eum.* 775, but perhaps we should accept H. Voss's ὦ χαῖρε. In our line Wakefield's παῖ, χαῖρ' does not appeal.

Individually these oddities would give little ground for suspicion; their accumulation gives cause for alarm.

If lines 1357–62 are deleted, the scene with the Priestess ends like this:

Πρ. λαβών νυν αὐτὰ τὴν τεκοῦσαν ἐκπόνει.   1355
Ιων πᾶcάν γ' ἐπελθὼν Ἀcιάδ' Εὐρώπηc θ' ὅρουc.   1356
Πρ. καὶ χαῖρ'· ἴcον γάρ c' ὡc τεκοῦc' ἀcπάζομαι.   1363

The Priestess's part has become brisk and businesslike. After she has announced herself in four lines, the rest of her part consists of single-line exchanges with Ion, to which the lines deleted add nothing that needs saying. She came abruptly; abruptly she departs. χαῖρ', ὦ φίλη μοι μῆτερ, οὐ τεκοῦσά περ was Ion's greeting to her. καὶ χαῖρ'· ἴcον γάρ c' ὡc τεκοῦc' ἀcπάζομαι is her valediction to him.

1396 See p. 10.

1400 See p. 110 n. 1.

1410   παῦcαι πλέκουcα· λήψομαί c' ἐγὼ καλῶc.

c' Tyrwhitt: δ' L

'Stop weaving: I shall catch you nicely.' Commentators are not troubled that πλέκουcα is here uniquely used in a figurative sense without an object ('supply πλοκάc', Bayfield) or that καλῶc is rather curiously attached to λήψομαι (P. T. Stevens, *Colloquial Expressions in Eur.* [1976] 55, compares *Cycl.* 631, *El.* 965; 'a metaphor from the wrestling school . . . to get a good hold of the antagonist', Paley). The two separate oddities may be set right by a single change: παῦcαι πλέκουcα—λήψομαί c' ἐγώ—πλοκάc (Jacobs, *Animadu. in Eur. trag.* [1790] 179–80). For the expression see 826 κἄπλεκεν πλοκάc, *IA* 936 ἐμπλέκειν πλοκάc. For the verb with a different object see *Ion* 1279–80 τέχνην . . . ἔπλεξε, *Andr.* 66 μηχανὰc πλέκουcιν (so too A. fr. 373 N [726 M], Plat. *Symp.* 203 D), A. *Ch.* 220 δόλον . . . πλέκειc, Ar. *Vesp.* 644–5 πλέκειν . . . παλάμαc. Hence my conjecture at 692 πλέκει (ἔχει L) δόλον τέχναν (Schoemann [cited on 743–4] 146–7: τύχαν L) θ' ὁ παῖc (for the corruption of τέχνη to τύχη see A. *PV* 87 and S. *OT* 442 [Bentley], for the language see *Alc.* 33–4 δολίωι . . . τέχνηι, *IT* 1355 δόλια τεχνήματα). For the same metaphor in English see Shakespeare, *King Lear* I. i. 283 'plighted cunning'.[1]

The parenthesis went unrecognized, and πλοκάc found itself in a clause from which grammar precluded it, and so it was changed to a word which grammar permitted. Compare *Hi.* 402 κράτιcτον—οὐδεὶc ἀντερεῖ—βουλευμάτων, where most manuscripts have βουλεύμαcιν, because κράτιcτον was taken as the limit of the first clause. See

---

[1] 'Plighted' is the Folio reading; the reading of the Quarto is 'pleated'. The meaning is not affected (see *OED* s.v. 'plight').

also p. 46, and Jackson's remarks on the obliteration of parentheses, *Marg. scaen.* 128. Other examples of a parenthesis separating a verb or other governing word from its noun are *Cycl.* 121 *cπείρουcι δ'—ἢ τῶι ζῶcι;—Δήμητρος cτάχυν; Hi.* 936 *φεῦ τῆς βροτείας—ποῖ προβήcεται;—φρενός, Andr.* 691–2 *παύcαcθον ἤδη—λῶιcτα γὰρ μακρῶι τάδε— | λόγων ματαίων, Tr.* 299 *πιμπρᾶcιν—ἢ τί δρῶcι;—Τρωιάδες μυχούc; IT* 1072–3 *τίc ὑμῶν φηcιν ἢ τίc οὐ θέλειν* (Musgrave: *θέλει* L)*/—φθέγξαcθε—ταῦτα; Rh.* 565–6 *Διόμηδεc, οὐκ ἤκουcαc—ἢ κενὸc ψόφοc | cτάζει δι' ὤτων;—τευχέων τινὰ κτύπον;* A. *ScT* 200–1 *μέλει γὰρ ἀνδρί—μὴ γυνὴ βουλευέτω— | τἄξωθεν*, and probably S. *Ichn.* 198 (suppl. Wilamowitz). At *El.* 284 *νέα γάρ, οὐδὲν θαῦμ', ἀπεζεύχθηc νέου* editors speak of hyperbaton (Denniston calls it 'very harsh' and is troubled by it), but I should rather speak of parenthesis. Compare also *Andr.* 257, where the parenthetical *κοὐ τὸ cὸν προcκέψομαι* separates *προcοίcω* from a second object in 259 (Stevens misunderstands the point of Murray's punctuation).

1433–4   cτέφανον ἐλαίαc ἀμφέθηκά cοι τότε,
          ἣν πρῶτ' Ἀθάναc cκόπελον εἰcηνέγκατο.

Ἀθάνα Barnes   cκόπελοc ἐξηνέγκατο Stephanus (-οc) et Scaliger

Almost everyone accepts Barnes's Ἀθάνα for Ἀθάναc (attributing it to Matthiae). This gives the same construction as 841 *ἐcώικιc' οἴκουc* (sc. αὐτόν), *Hec.* 1148–9 *μ' εἰcάγει | δόμουc* (cf. *Alc.* 1112), *Su.* 875–6 *χρυcὸν . . . οὐκ εἰcεδέξατ' οἶκον, IT* 261 *βοῦc . . . πόντον εἰcεβάλλομεν, Hel.* 1566 *ταῦρον . . . εἰcέθεντο cέλματα, Ph.* 365–6 *μ' εἰcήγαγε | τείχη*. To this Badham (1853 ed.) objected with justice that 'Minerua oleam non terrae commisit, sed e terra cuspide tacta florescere fecit'. To reply that Euripides is 'fond of varying the ancient accounts both of persons and events' (Paley, similarly Owen) is an unpersuasive evasion. I suppose that Barnes's conjecture has won the day because editors have not realized how easily εἰc and ἐξ are confused (in L's script they are particularly alike). See *Alc.* 298 *ἐξέπραξεν* and *εἰcέπραξεν* codd.; *IT* 559 *ἐξεπράξατο* Elmsley: *εἰc-* L; S. *El.* 1128 *ἐξέπεμπον* and *εἰc-* codd.; *Tr.* 1167 *ἐξεγραψάμην* Elmsley: *εἰc-* codd. A further point in favour of *cκόπελοc ἐξηνέγκατο* is that it is more natural to refer to the Acropolis as 'the rock of Athena' than it is to refer to it simply as 'the rock': see 12 *Παλλάδοc ὑπ' ὄχθωι, Hi.* 30 *πέτραν . . . Παλλάδοc*, and p. 110.

1441–2   ... ὃν κατὰ γᾶς ἐνέρων

χθόνιον μετὰ Περσεφόνας τ' ἐδόκουν ναίειν.

χθονίων μέτα Heath

The word-order ἐνέρων ... μετὰ Περσεφόνας τ' is defended by G. Kiefner, *Die Versparung* (1964) 97 with reference to *IT* 298 λαγόνας ἐς πλευράς ⟨θ'⟩ ἱείς, *Ba.* 1008 ἦμαρ ἐς νύκτα τε, A. *ScT* 860 πάνδοκον εἰς ἀφανῆ τε χέρσον, *Ag.* 656 χειμῶνι τυφῶ σὺν ζάληι τ' ὀμβροκτύπωι. But the interposition of χθόνιον between ἐνέρων and μετὰ finds no parallel in these expressions and produces almost unbearable confusion. Heath's χθονίων μέτα should be accepted. Owen objects that κατὰ γᾶς ... χθόνιον is defended by *Alc.* 236–7 γυναῖκα μαραινομέναν νόcωι / κατὰ γᾶς χθόνιον παρ' Ἅιδαν. And Dale on that passage and Kannicht on *Hel.* 345 agree that χθόνιον goes with γυναῖκα. It goes with Ἅιδαν: see *Alc.* 743–4 χθόνιός θ' Ἑρμῆς / Ἅιδης τε (Ἅιδης / Ἑρμῆς τε V), *Andr.* 544 Ἅιδην χθόνιον. Otherwise we should have to write χθονίαν, since the masculine form of this adjective is used for the feminine form only where metre requires it (*Hi.* 1201, *Hel.* 345 [χρόνιον Orelli], S. *OC* 1726).

1472 See p. 20.

ADDENDA

Page xi. M. Sicherl, *Rh. Mus.* 118 (1975) 205–25, gives reasons for doubting that the Aldine editor was Musurus.

Page 3. Add *Med.* 422 ὑμνεῦcαι (*uel sim.*) ἀπιcτοcύναν codd.: ὑμνεῦc᾽ ἀπ- Tr.

Page 11. At *Andr.* 623 λαβεῖν is not imperatival infinitive (Stevens) but epexegetic.

Page 18 n. 1. The τι at Men. *Dysk.* 772 is confirmed by P. Oslo 168: see J. Lenaerts, *Pap. Brux.* 13 (1977) 25.

Pages 18–21. Other possible instances of resolution before syncopation: *Andr.* 1046 cκῆπτόc cτᾰλᾱc|cῶν Δᾰνᾱῐ|δᾱῐc φόνον (Δαναΐδαιc Campbell [*CR* 46 (1932) 196–7]: ἀίδα codd.: ⟨τὸν⟩ Ἄιδα Hermann: ⟨ὅδ᾽⟩ Wilamowitz, *Verskunst* 434 n. 3), fr. 152 τὸ δαῑμόνῐον | οὐχ ὁρᾱῐc (or τὸ δαῑμόνῐ|ον οὐχ ὁρᾱῐc).

There is a further observation which may be made about this phenomenon. When a cretic occurs in a colon (of whatever length) composed entirely of cretics, resolution of the final long of one cretic before another cretic is quite regular: *Hec.* 1100–1 ᾰμπτᾰμένοc | οὐρᾰνῐον | ὑψῐπέτεc | ἐc μέλᾰθρον, *Or.* 1423–4 πᾱῐδᾰ τᾱν | Τῡνδᾱρῐδ᾽ ὅ | μῆτρόφόν|τᾱc δρᾰκῶν, *Ba.* 160 λῶτόc ὅτᾱν | εὐκέλᾰδόc, 597–8 ⟨τόνδὲ⟩ Σέμέ|λᾱc ἱέρον | ᾰμφὶ τᾰφόν | ᾱν πότέ κέ|ραυνόβόλοc | ἐλῐπέ φλόγᾰ, *Hyps.* fr. 64. 92 ἔνέπ᾽ ἔνέπέ | μᾱτρὶ cᾱι, S. *El.* 1249 οὐδέ πότέ | λῆcόμένόν | ᾰμέτέρόν. Into this category fall, from my list on pp. 18–20, instances (ii), (v), (vi), (vii), (viii), (ix), (xv). Indeed, in the larger part of the instances listed, resolution is of the final long of one cretic before another cretic. It may be argued, as a consequence of this observation, that whereas, say, the sequence $- \cup \widehat{\cup\cup} \,|\, - \cup -$ (in whatever length of colon) is permissible, the sequence $\times - \cup \widehat{\cup\cup} \,|\, - \cup -$ is not. But I do not see what theoretical justification there could be for making such a distinction.

Page 21. Another instance of Ἀίδαc as a cretic is plausibly restored at *Hec.* 1033 θανάcιμον πρὸc Ἄιδαν· ὦ (T: ἰὼ cett.) τάλαc (so Porson: cf. N. C. Conomis, *Hermes* 92 [1964] 33).

Page 27. For the confusion of ἤ and καί see Wyse on Isae. 5. 5.

Page 37 (*El.* 568). To the instances of μή introducing a question add *Hec.* 1272 μορφῆc ἐπῳδὸν μή τι τῆc ἐμῆc ἐρεῖc; (μ[η] Pap. Oxy. 3. 877: ἤ codd.). ʿμ[ή] τι . . . would be a doubtful improvement' (edd. pr.). On the contrary, it is clearly the answer to this crux, though editors have not realized it.

Page 39 (*El.* 784–5). Add *Or.* 1091.

Page 42. Donald J. Mastronarde, *Contact and Discontinuity: Some Conventions of Speech and Action on the Greek Tragic Stage* (California Classical Studies, 21 [1979]) 30–1, has convinced me that Tournier's conjecture at *IT* 1307 should be removed from the list.

Page 44 (*El.* 1250–1). Add *Or.* 1656–7.

Page 46. Add A. *Pe.* 46 πολλοῖc ἅρμαcιν ἐξορμῶcιν.

Page 48. Mastronarde (op. cit. 46–8) has not allayed my doubts over *Hel.* 86–9.

Pages 50–2. In the conjecture of M. Cropp (*CQ* n.s. 29 [1979] 58–9) αἰδώc γ᾽ ἀποικεῖ τῆcδε γῆc θεὸc πρόcω, it will be imperative (though Cropp denies it) to accept αἰδώc; since θεὸc will otherwise be redundant. But the conjecture, attractive enough in itself, is not needed.

Page 56. At fr. 153. 3 νεύει βίοτοc, νεύει δὲ τύχα I am tempted to suggest βιοτά, since internal rhyme is so common in anapaestic dimeters. See *Med.* 131 (cited p. 56) and the passages cited in *CR* n.s. 18 (1968) 3–4 and *Phaeth.* 99 n.

Pages 65–6. Add *Or.* 826 ἰάχηcε, 1432 ἕλιccεν.

Page 66. Housman's punctuation of S. *OC* 981 is silently adopted by R. D. Dawe (Teubner 1979). To the illustrations of ἔχουcα . . . ἔχω add *Cycl.* 8 φέρ᾽ ἴδω, τοῦτ᾽ ἰδὼν ὄναρ λέγω;

Page 79 (*IT* 257). See the acute discussion of *IT* 252–7 by Mastronarde (op. cit. 66–7).

Page 93 (*IT* 1486). Wilamowitz (on *Herc.* 311) proposed χρὴ for χρεὼν in fr. 733. 3. To the instances of synizesis add *Alcm. Cor.* 2 Page Ἀλκμέωνι.

Page 96 (last para.). *Hec.* 164 is also followed by change of metre. On the text see *PCPS* n.s. 15 (1969) 44–5, ibid. 20 (1974) 6 n. 1.

Page 100 (*Ion* 354–9). I should add *Alc.* 125 ἦλθ᾽ ἂν (Monk: ἦλθεν codd.) and probably 362 ἔcχ᾽ ἂν (Lenting: ἔcχον codd.).

Page 102 (*Ion* 457). Another instance of this colon is *Hec.* 927~937.

Page 111 (*Ion* 1275-8). Mastronarde (op. cit. 110–12) defends the lines and the transmitted order, but he does not answer my objections to the language of 1276-7. For a more radical proposal see D. Bain, *CQ* n.s. 29 (1979) 263–7, who wrongly imputes to me the view that Ion does not see Creusa until 1279. The staging which I envisage is that envisaged by Mastronarde, and I believe that it disposes of Bain's objections to 1266–8.

Page 112 (iii). I suggest that there is another instance at *Hec.* 1008: read οὐκ οἶσθ' Ἀθάνας 'Ιλιά⟨δο⟩ς ἵνα στεγαί;

Page 112 (vii). And we may rule out Burges's θεοὺς for τοὺς at *Hec.* 791.

Page 117. For Ἅιδης χθόνιος see West on Hes. *Theog.* 767 and *Op.* 465.

INDEXES

SUBJECTS

GREEK WORDS

126 INDEXES

cκῆπτρον of persons 78–9
cμικρός and μικρός 50
cτέγω of verbal concealment 73–4
cτείχοιμ' ἄν abrupt announcement of
 intention to depart 101
cτίβος 104–5
cτόμα not synonym of λόγος 66
cτόμα ἔχειν 66
cυν-compounds combined with ὁμοῦ 39

ταύτηι 7
τί with word repeated in indignant or
 incredulous question (. . . τλάς. :: τί
 τλάς;) 51
τις ὅδε, τίς ὅδε 42–4
τίς (not ποῖος) πατήρ; 98
τί (enclitic and interrogative) cε, cέ τι,
 and cε τί 83–4
τὸ ἐμόν = ἐγώ 106

τῶν παρεcτώτων κακῶν genitive absolute 109

ὑπαείδειν 40

φαίνειν intransitive, 'shed radiance'
 41
φάλαρα 15–17
φεύγειν of stars 94–5
φῶς of persons 78–9

χαῖρε see καὶ χαῖρε
χθόνιος, masculine form used for
 feminine 117
— of Hades 117, 121

ὦ ἶτε 18
ὡς = ἴcθι ὡς 88
— for ὥcτε, with infinitive 8–9

PASSAGES

(This index does not list passages from the six plays of Euripides which are discussed in this book, since such passages are listed serially throughout the book.
An asterisk indicates that a new conjecture is proposed.)

Aeschylus
Ag. 1053   109
Ch. 130   22 n. 1
Eum. 775   114
 948   45
 993   46
Pe. 470   72 n. 3
 505   72 n. 3
PV 216–17   109
 902–3   12–13
 972*   51
ScT 827–8   45, 46
 867–8   45
 1068   46
Su. 622   9 n. 1
fr. 91 N (315 M)   45
 156 N (273. 15 M) 112
 309. 3 N (616. 3 M) 30

Aristophanes
Ach. 611   85
Eccl. 658   7
 1049–50   17 n. 2
Equ. 30   109
Lys. 727   43
 1035   85
Nub. 876   85

Plut. 660–1   91
Thes. 680   54

Demosthenes
18. 10   73

Euripides
Alc. 32–4   44
 81   46
 125   120
 236–7   117
 358   8
 362   120
 595∼604   72
 1126–7*   22
Andr. 242   56
 257   116
 289   66
 471   46
 589   22
 962   54
 1046   119
 1228   45
Ba. 68–9   47
Cycl. 647   8
 674*   38 n. 1
 707   37